"America's leading source of self-help legal
information"

—YAHOO!

LEGAL INFO ONLINE ANYTIME 24 hours a day

www.nolo.com

AT THE NOLO.COM SELF-HELP LAW CENTER, YOU'LL FIND

- Nolo's comprehensive Legal Encyclopedia filled with plain-English information on a variety of legal topics
- Nolo's Law Dictionary—legal terms **without** the legalese
- Auntie Nolo—if you'...
- The Law Store—over... Downloadable Softw...
- Legal and product upda...
- Frequently Asked Ques...
- NoloBriefs, our free...
- Legal Research Center,...
- Our ever-popular law...

Quality **LAW** **FOR...**

Nolo's user-friendly products a...

- A dozen in-house legal edito... ensure that our products ar...
- We continually update ever... to keep up with changes in...
- Our commitment to a mor...
- We appreciate & listen to y... return the card at the back o...

OUR "NO-HASSLE" GUARANTEE

Return anything you buy directly from Nolo for any reason and we'll cheerfully refund your purchase price. No ifs, ands or buts.

An Important Message to Our Readers

1st edition

Student & Tourist Visas

How to Come to the U.S.

by Attorneys Ilona Bray and Richard A. Boswell

NOLO

Keeping Up to Date

To keep its books up-to-date, Nolo issues new printings and new editions periodically. New printings reflect minor legal changes and technical corrections. New editions contain major legal changes, major text additions or major reorganizations. To find out if a later printing or edition of any Nolo book is available, call Nolo at 510-549-1976 or check our website at http://www.nolo.com.

To stay current, follow the "Update" service at our website at http://www.nolo.com/update. In another effort to help you use Nolo's latest materials, we offer a 35% discount off the purchase of the new edition of your Nolo book when you turn in the cover of an earlier edition. (See the "Special Upgrade Offer" in the back of the book.)

First Edition	SEPTEMBER 2001
Editor	JANET PORTMAN
Cover Design	TONI IHARA
Book Design	TERRI HEARSH
Index	THÉRÈSE SHERE
Proofreading	ROBERT WELLS
Printing	CONSOLIDATED PRINTERS, INC.

Bray, Ilona M., 1962-
    Student & tourist visas : how to come to the U.S. / by Ilona Bray and Richard A. Boswell.
        p. cm.
    Includes index.
    ISBN 0-87337-789-3
    1. Visas--United States--Popular works. 2. Student passports--United States--Popular works. I. Title: Student and tourist visas.   II. Boswell, Richard A. III. Title.

KF4827.Z9 B73 2001
342.73'082--dc21

                                        2001044675

For information on bulk purchases or corporate premium sales, please contact the Special Sales Department. For academic sales or textbook adoptions, ask for Academic Sales. Call 800-955-4775 or write to Nolo at 950 Parker Street, Berkeley, CA 94710.

Acknowledgments

Seeking an education is a daunting task for anyone. Coming to the United States to study can be a special challenge. I hope that this book can demystify the process a little bit. While I have long had the desire of making this information available beyond the corridors traveled by lawyers and judges, it could not have been accomplished without the inspiring example of the many immigration clients whom I have had the privilege of working with over the years. Getting this book to the public could only have been accomplished with the dedication of the staff at Nolo and especially the collaboration with Ilona Bray. That I could play my part in this effort is a source of great satisfaction. I could not have done my part without the constant support of my life partner, Karen Musalo, and my parents who gave me the confidence to persevere.

–Richard Boswell

A number of friends and colleagues have contributed to this book. In particular, thanks go to international student advisors Li-chen Chin at Bryn Mawr College, Ann Beaver at Heald College and Gina Burnett at Hastings College of the Law, who shared their experiences with helping students navigate the immigration laws. For their clear-minded organizing and editing, thank you to Nolo editors Mary Randolph and Janet Portman. For transforming the stacks of paper into print-worthy final form, thanks go to production staff Jaleh Doane and Terri Hearsh.

–Ilona Bray

Table of Contents

Glossary

Appendixes

Index

Deciding What You Want

In any one year, approximately ten million people will come to the United States as tourists, and another 500,000 will come to study in American schools and universities. With the right preparation and a little luck, you can be one of these people.

The key to getting a temporary visa as a tourist or student, however, is proper preparation. The numbers cited above hide the uncounted and large numbers of applicants who are refused entry as tourists and students every year. The U.S. government has become increasingly wary of people who use temporary visas to enter the U.S.—and then don't leave, or engage in criminal activity. To combat this problem, the government has set some high and often difficult standards for obtaining visitor and student visas.

This book will help you determine the likelihood that you'll be approved to come to the United States as a tourist or a student. If you're already here and want to continue your stay or change your visa status, we'll explain that process as well. We'll alert you to what the government officials looking at your case will be thinking and how you can overcome their suspicions or deal with visa denials. As we take you through the application process, we'll provide you with handy checklists to help you keep track of what you've accomplished and what still needs to be done. Finally, this book may be your companion for many months to come, since it also advises you on issues that come up after you've arrived in the United States—dealing with changed circumstances, extending your stay and more.

The visas we cover boil down to four. They are:

- the **Visa Waiver Program** (allowing tourists coming from certain countries for a short stay to enter without a visa)
- the **B-2 visitor visa** (for tourists and other visitors for pleasure)
- the **F-1 student visa** (for full-time study in an academic or degree program)
- the **M-1 vocational student visa** (for full-time study in a vocational program).

We'll help you determine which visa is best for you. Then we'll walk you through the application procedures. The procedures are different depending on whether you're coming from overseas or are already in the United States; we cover both paths in this book.

Relevant Visas Not Covered in This Book

There are a few visitor and student-related visas that are not covered in this book. These include the B-1 visa for visitors coming to do business in the United States, the H-3 visa for employees coming for brief training programs sponsored by their employer and the J visa for students coming on an exchange program. If you are interested in one of these visas, you should first talk to your employer, business partners or exchange program organizers about how to get a visa.

This book also doesn't cover using a fiancé visa to enter the United States in order to get married. If your plan is to come solely for the wedding and return home afterward, you could use either a fiancé visa or a tourist visa, the latter of which is covered in this book. However, some people prefer to use the fiancé visa—it avoids some suspicion at the border, where the officials may assume you're actually planning to stay in the U.S. permanently with your new spouse. Border patrol officials don't look kindly on people who enter on tourist visas with no intention of leaving, but this is not an issue with a fiancé visa, where you always have the option to stay permanently. To read more about this issue, and for full instructions on applying for fiancé and marriage-based visas, see *Fiancé and Marriage Visas: A Couple's Guide to U.S. Immigration*, by Ilona Bray (Nolo).

What if your real plan is to stay in the United States permanently? For example, many people who are engaged or married to U.S. citizens take a look at how long it will take to get a fiancé or a marriage-based visa to come to the United States, and they get frustrated. These applications can take anywhere between six months and a year or more to get approved, whereas a person might get a tourist visa in as little as a day. So, people figure, why not enter the United States on a tourist visa and finish the green card application here? The answer is that this constitutes visa fraud. Pretending that your visit is temporary when your plan is to stay permanently is a violation of the immigration laws that will make you inadmissible—thereby preventing you from receiving any type of visa or green card.

 If you happen to fit the example above and are engaged or married to a U.S. citizen or permanent resident, your rights and the procedures for applying for a fiancé or marriage visa or green card are covered in depth in *Fiancé and Marriage Visas: A Couple's Guide to U.S. Immigration*, by Ilona Bray (Nolo).

 If your goal is to work in the United States, find another visa. Tourists are not allowed to work at all. Students can work only incidentally to their study and are required to pay for their studies without relying on U.S. work. For information on visas allowing you to work in the United States, see *U.S. Immigration Made Easy*, by Laurence A. Canter and Martha S. Siegel (Nolo).

How Will the U.S.'s Struggle with Terrorism Affect Your Visa Application?

Some of the terrorists responsible for the horrific September 11, 2001 attacks on the World Trade Center and Pentagon may have entered the U.S. using student and tourist visas. Needless to say, this is causing the U.S. government to reexamine every aspect of visa eligibility and procedures. There was talk of imposing a six-month moratorium on student visas, but this was dropped.

As this book went to print, Congress was coming to realize that the existing standards and procedures for granting visas include plenty of security protections—but that the systems and technology that back these up need more attention. The government is now working to improve identity checks, criminal record-gathering and international communication. You're unlikely to see many changes to the standards and procedures described in this book—but expect delays in visa decisions, careful scrutiny of your request to enter the U.S., and close monitoring by your school if you're a student. As always, check for changes in the Legal Updates section of Nolo's website at http://www.nolo.com.

Icons Used in This Book

To aid you in using this book, we use the following icons:

 The caution icon warns you of potential problems.

 This icon indicates that the information is a useful tip.

 This icon refers you to helpful books or other resources.

 This icon indicates when you should consider consulting an attorney or other expert.

 This icon tells you that the form or checklist shown is available in tear-out form in the Appendix.

 This icon refers you to a further discussion of the topic somewhere else in this book.

This icon tells you where to go in the book once you've completed the steps just described.

This icon tells you when you can skip to a later discussion in the book.

A. What Are Your Plans?

The visa that is most appropriate for you depends on your current situation and your plans. For example, where are you now—overseas or in the United States? How long do you want to stay in the United States? Is there a chance that your reasons for coming may change once you're in the United States and you'll want to apply to stay longer? If you plan to study, what degree or subject will it be? Have you chosen a school, or will you need to enter as a tourist to look at schools first?

To help you figure out what type of visa will best match your needs, take a look at the "road map" below and read the discussion that follows the two or three scenarios closest to yours. These discussions will refer you to chapters that will guide you through the application process.

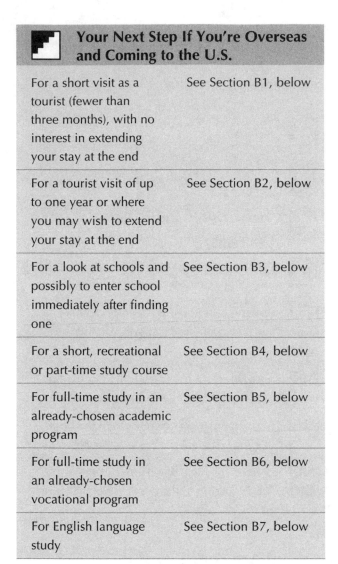

⚠️ If you're in the U.S. illegally, this book may not help you. No one is permitted to switch from an illegal stay to a temporary stay while in the United States—even if their last visa expired only a few days before. In most cases, as long as you haven't already stayed in the United States illegally for more than six months, you can return to your home country and apply for a visa from there. See Chapter 2 for a discussion on the penalties for staying in the United States illegally for six months or more.

The Government Offices You'll Be Dealing With

Immigration to the United States is governed by two separate government agencies: the State Department, which is in charge of overseas consulates; and the Immigration and Naturalization Service (INS), which is in charge of the borders and internal immigration matters. You won't need to understand much more about them to apply for your visa or other benefits. This book will tell you which application goes to which office.

B. Applicants Coming From Overseas

The following subsections explore the visitor and student visa options, and point you toward the appropriate procedures, if you're currently living outside the United States.

1. Coming for a Short Visit

Although most people wanting to come to the United States as a tourist will first have to go to a U.S. consulate and apply for a visa, you may be able to avoid this if you are:

- from a country on the list below
- have not violated the terms of any past nonimmigrant visa (for example, have not stayed in

the U.S. beyond the time your previous stays expired, and

- want to visit the United States for three months or less.

If all these things are true of you, you have an option that others don't. You may enter the United States without a visa, under the Visa Waiver Program. This may sound like just the ticket—why go through a lot of application procedures if you don't have to? However, after weighing the advantages and disadvantages of the Visa Waiver Program, you may opt to apply for a tourist visa after all (see Section B2, below, for discussion of the tourist visa). The fact that you're from a Visa Waiver country does not prevent you from applying for a tourist visa.

Countries Participating in the Visa Waiver Program

The countries whose citizens do not need a visa to enter the United States include the following, plus Canada (under its NAFTA agreement with the United States). More may be added in the future; check for changes on the U.S. State Department's website at http://travel.state.gov/vwp.html, or ask your local U.S. consulate for information. The countries are chosen based on how many of their applicants are refused U.S. visitor visas annually— the lower the refusal rate, the more the U.S can presume the country's applicants really intend to comply with the terms of their visa or entry. See I.N.A. §217; 8 U.S.C. §1187.

Andorra	Iceland	Portugal
Argentina	Ireland	San Marino
Austria	Italy	Singapore
Australia	Japan	Slovenia
Belgium	Liechtenstein	Spain
Brunei	Luxembourg	Sweden
Denmark	Monaco	Switzerland
Finland	The Netherlands	The United
France	New Zealand	Kingdom
Germany	Norway	Uruguay

The countries on the Visa Waiver list have agreements with the United States allowing easy travel back and forth. If you're from a Visa Waiver country or from Canada, you can pack your bags, grab your passport and get on a plane, bus or other carrier. Unless you're coming in your own car, however, you will need to have a return ticket in hand when you arrive. Before using the Visa Waiver option, give careful thought to two issues:

- are you likely to be turned back at the U.S. border, and
- are you willing to give up most of the rights that immigrants with "real" visas receive?

We'll explain these issues below.

a. Will You Be Turned Back at the U.S. Border?

The U.S. borders are carefully guarded. No one, not even someone from a Visa Waiver country, is allowed to walk in without an examination to see if he or she poses a health, security or other risk. Before you arrive from a Visa Waiver country, the airline or other carrier will give you a form to fill out (I-94W) to determine whether you should be excluded. When you arrive, the border patrol officer will review this form and also check your name against an electronic database to see whether you've overstayed any past visas or have a criminal history.

The border patrol officers have the power to deny any person entry and insist that they return home immediately—no hearing, no second opinion. People who enter on tourist visas run this same risk, but at least they've given their application for entry a "test run" past a U.S. consular official, who would probably deny their visa on the spot and save them a plane trip.

As a Visa Waiver entrant, you would, after being denied entry, be allowed to try to return to the United States anytime (unlike people who enter on visas, who may have to wait five years if they're refused entry). However, you would still have to leave the United States first.

The main reasons that you could be refused entry are called the Grounds of Inadmissibility. They are listed in Chapter 2 of this book. If you see that you fall into one of the grounds of inadmissibility—for example, you have a communicable disease such as HIV or tuberculosis, don't have sufficient funds to get you through your trip or are a known criminal or spy—don't waste your plane fare trying to come on a Visa Waiver. The most likely reason for being refused entry is that the border patrol officer believes you intend to stay in the U.S. permanently—for example, if your luggage includes letters from potential employers or a wedding dress and all your summer and winter clothes.

b.   What Procedural Rights Will You Give Up?

People who take the time to get themselves a visa before they enter the United States can count on a few things that tourists without visas don't have. One of these is that if the U.S. government wants to deport them (send them home), they will be permitted a hearing first, in front of an Immigration Judge (see subsection i, below). Another is that if they want to extend their visit or apply for a different non-immigrant (temporary) visa, they can submit their application and get an approval without having to leave the United States first (see subsection ii, below).

If you enter the United States using the Visa Waiver Program, you don't get these basic rights. Your deal with the U.S. government is short and sweet: It will let you in with a very little fuss, so long as you promise to leave with very little fuss. There are only a few exceptions, discussed in subsection iii, below.

i.   No Right to a Hearing

If you stay past your 90-day limit or the INS decides to deport you for some other reason, you won't have an opportunity to complain. It won't matter how sympathetic your situation might be. For example, even if you've received a job offer, lived in the United States for the last ten years or your two children were born here, no one will listen. You won't be able to see an Immigration Judge to plead your case, and you'll have to return home as soon as the INS orders you to (unless you fall into one of the exceptions in

section iii). By contrast, people who enter on visas may request a hearing, and might be able to resist deportation based on the examples above or certain other legal bases.

ii.   No Right to Extend or Change Your Status

Your stay in the United States after entering on a Visa Waiver may feel too short—but you'll have to leave when your 90 days are up, no extensions allowed. Even if you break your foot and spend your whole 90 days in bed, the U.S. government will insist that you return home at the end. If you had obtained a tourist visa, however, your permitted stay would more likely have been six months or, in rare cases, one year. What's more, a broken foot or far less drastic circumstances would allow you to apply for an extension of your stay, up to another six months.

Similarly, only people on tourist visas can apply to change to another temporary or permanent immigration status in the United States (except as described in subsection iii, below). For example, if you enter on the Visa Waiver Program and find a school that wants to admit you and classes start tomorrow, you will have to leave the United States and submit your student visa application from overseas. Similarly, if you receive a job offer and your new U.S. employer is willing to sponsor you for an employment visa or green card, your Visa Waiver status will not allow you to apply for it without first leaving the United States. People who enter on actual visas, however, have the right to submit an application for a Change of Status to an INS office in the United States.

iii.   Exceptions

There are a couple of exceptions to the rules above. If you're having a true medical or other emergency, the INS might give you a little more time (up to 30 days)—pulling you out of a hospital bed doesn't look very good on the evening news. Also, if you fear persecution in your home country, you will be allowed a hearing to apply for political asylum. And if you happen to marry a U.S. citizen or are the Immediate Relative of a U.S. citizen (his or her minor unmarried child or parent) you will be able to apply for a green card while you're in the United States. (But if staying permanently was your plan when you entered the United States, you will have committed visa fraud and could be denied the green card for that reason. Such misuses of temporary visas are normally forgiven in cases of political asylum seekers, but forgiveness in family-based cases is rare.) If any of these exceptional situations apply to you, see a lawyer. Chapter 14 has tips on finding a good one.

If you're sure a Visa Waiver is what you want to use, you can stop reading this chapter now. Because entering under the Visa Waiver Program involves no applications, this book does not go into more detail regarding obtaining a Visa Waiver. Just remember your passport and return ticket, and don't say or do anything at the border that makes it look like you plan to stay permanently. Read Chapter 9 for general information on meeting with U.S. border patrol officials.

ing part in amateur (unpaid) arts and entertainment events or contests, accompanying relatives on other temporary visas, attending short classes and receiving medical treatment.

When you enter the United States, the border patrol will give you a card called an "I-94" that shows how long you can stay on that particular visit—usually six months, but the legal maximum is one year. Once in the United States, you'll be free to travel wherever you like, without needing to follow any preset itinerary or check in with any government officials. If you run out of time, you can apply for an extension of your stay, up to six months at a time. Or, you can take advantage of your visa's "in and out" privileges. With any luck, you will have been granted a visa that allows more than one entry into the United States. Such "multiple entry" visas allow you to leave one day and return the next, up until the visa expires or the border patrol decides you're spending too much time here. We'll talk more about the rights and

2. Coming for a Longer Tourist Visit

If you're coming from overseas and the Visa Waiver option described in Section B1, above won't work for you, you may need to apply for a tourist visa. The more technical term for this is a "B-2 visa" for "visitors for pleasure."

Don't confuse the B-2 visa with the B-1 visa. There are two kinds of visitor visas to the United States: visitors for business (code name "B-1") and visitors for pleasure (code name "B-2"). This book covers only visas for visitors coming as tourists.

A tourist visa is appropriate for you if you're coming to the United States for purposes encompassed by the word "pleasure." Luckily, the "pleasure" allowed under the B-2 visa includes more than just traveling around the United States with a camera hanging from your neck. Many types of activities qualify, such as participating in conferences (though for some business-related conferences it's advisable to use a B-1 visa instead), visiting friends and family, looking into potential colleges or other schools, tak-

Golden Gate Bridge
San Francisco, California

responsibilities that come with a tourist visa later in this book.

If you're sure that a tourist visa is what you want, see Chapter 3 to see whether you're eligible for one. To find out how to apply for a tourist visa from overseas, go to Chapter 5.

3. Coming to Look at Schools

If you know you'd like to come to the United States to study but don't feel comfortable choosing a school from overseas, a special combination of visas has been designed for you. You can come to the U.S. as a tourist (but with a special notation in your visa) and, if you wish, apply directly to the U.S. INS to stay on as a student once you've been admitted to a school.

Taking a look at schools before committing to one is a good idea, particularly if you're applying to a long program such as four years of college. Seeing the campus and meeting professors and students could make a huge difference in your final choice. It's hard to get an idea of what your day-to-day life will be like by looking at the school's literature— some schools advertise themselves as aggressively as any other business.

The school may also be interested in meeting you. Some schools require an on-campus admissions interview or entrance exam (though other schools may be able to arrange for these to be held in your home country). Most schools will also be happy to give you a tour and to let you sit in on a class.

Applying for a B-2 visitor visa is a simple process, done in person at a U.S. embassy or consulate in your country. You'll get full instructions within this book. The consulate will want to see that you have written up a travel itinerary (a detailed plan of where you'll be going and what you'll be doing) and have made some thoughtful choices about which schools you'll be visiting. Once your visa is approved, you'll need to make sure that the consulate makes a notation in your visa stating "Prospective Student." Sometimes this will be followed by additional explanation, such as "school not selected" or "school

entrance examination." The visa itself will eventually expire some years into the future, but you won't find out until you get to the U.S. border how long you can stay on that particular visit. The maximum is usually six months. If you're planning to start school without going home first, you'll have to find a school and start classes within that time.

It is particularly important to get the Prospective Student notation in your visa if you hope to find a program to admit you immediately and start classes without leaving the United States. Starting school without going home first will be impossible if you came on a regular tourist visa, without the Prospective Student notation. That's because, with a regular tourist visa, you'll have to apply to the INS to change your status to student—but if they see that you entered as an ordinary tourist, they will suspect you of having lied about your plans to leave when you entered. That will probably lead them to deny your application to change status, and you'll have to return home and try again at a U.S. consulate.

If you do find a school to admit you, the school will give you a form called an I-20 that you can use for the next stage in your application process: applying for a "Change of Status" to become a student. This simply means asking to continue your stay in the United States under a different category of eligibility. One important thing to notice is that you will not, technically, be applying for a student "visa." A visa is only an entry document to get you into the United States, and can only be gotten from an overseas U.S. consulate. You won't need a visa until the first time you leave the United States, at which time it's a simple matter to go to a U.S. consulate and apply for a student visa with which to return.

If you're sure that this combination of visas and status is right for you, see Chapter 3 to see whether you're eligible for a tourist visa. To apply for a tourist visa, see Chapter 5. To see what you'll need to prove to be eligible for a student visa, see Chapter 3. If you do find a school, and wish to start school without leaving the United States, see Chapter 8 for application instructions. If you find a school but need or want to return home before starting school, see Chapter 7 for how to apply from overseas.

4. Coming for a Short, Recreational or Part-Time Study Course

Most people coming to the United States to study at a college or university will apply for a student visa. The criteria for student visas are rather strict—you must be coming for full-time study in an INS-approved academic or vocational program. But what if your plans are for more casual or fun study—for example, a few weeks of cooking, yoga or art classes? Or perhaps you just want to take a short or part-time academic course and spend the rest of your time traveling in the United States. For these purposes, a tourist visa may be sufficient. If it is sufficient, it is also preferable to applying for a student visa. The application process will be shorter and simpler.

The immigration laws and regulations don't give any clear-cut rules on which type of programs will require you to get a full-fledged student visa and which ones won't. In fact, the State Department recognizes that the consular officers themselves may have trouble making this distinction, and advises them to contact INS officials in the United States when in doubt. The best way to figure out whether a tourist visa will be enough to allow you entry into the United States is to talk to the school or program you'll be attending and then to your local U.S. consulate. Hopefully you'll get consistent advice that's based on the past experience of your school and the INS.

If you decide to enter as a tourist, you'll need to fit the normal eligibility criteria for a tourist visa. When you apply for your visa, you'll have to show that your trip is for the purpose of pleasure and that you don't plan to stay in the United States permanently. The maximum stay you will be allowed is usually six months, but if your course lasts longer, you may be allowed up to a year.

When you get your tourist visa, the consulate should put a special notation in it regarding your study plans: "Study incidental to visit: I-20 not required." Examine your visa when you get it, and request such a notation if it's not there. This notation will avoid confusion at the border and in the United States, and shows that you aren't misusing a visa meant primarily for tourists. (The "I-20" is simply a form that academic and vocational students must receive from their school before applying for their visa.) If the consulate doesn't put this notation in your visa, it shouldn't stop you from entering the United States—but when you get to the border, be very sure to state that the main purpose of your trip is to be a tourist. You can mention the classes later, but if you start out by saying, "I'm here to study," the border patrol officials will quiz you on why you didn't get a student visa.

If you're sure a tourist visa is what you want, see Chapter 3 to see whether you're eligible. To apply for a tourist visa, see Chapter 5.

5. Coming for Full-Time Academic Study

The classic "student" is someone attending a degree or diploma program at a school (any level), college or university. If this describes you and you have been admitted or believe you will be admitted to a program in the United States, an F-1 or student visa is the one for you. There are no limits on the number of students who can receive F-1 visas.

An F-1 visa allows you to come to the United States along with your family members, pursue academic studies for as long as it reasonably takes you to finish them (plus 60 days to leave the United States), travel freely in and out of the United States during your studies and work on the school campus and, in some limited circumstances, off campus. You may switch programs within your school or even transfer schools on the same visa.

If you're looking to spend a long time grounding yourself in the language and culture of the United States, an F-1 student visa is ideal. Most academic programs take a relatively long time to complete, but your visa will cover the entire program. College degrees, for example, take four years to obtain in the United States, certain graduate programs take between two and six years and a Ph.D. program can last as long as it takes you to write your dissertation —for some students, it feels like forever.

On the other hand, the F-1 visa can also be used for certain short-term programs, such as a six-week

English course. If you're looking to take a short course, also read Section B4, above.

An F-1 visa may also allow you to extend your stay in the United States as you pursue higher education. In theory, with an F-1 visa and multiple extensions, you could come to the United States in your high school years, advance to an undergraduate college program and move on to a graduate degree, spending 15 years in the United States. In reality, it can be difficult to get approval of these repeated visas, but it is not unheard of. It's even easier to stay this length of time if you don't switch schools. You can finish one program, such as a B.A. (Bachelor of Arts or college degree), and advance directly to another within that school, such as an M.A. (Master of Arts), without having to get a new visa. The INS asks only that your school advise them so that they can update their records regarding your expected completion date and make sure you still qualify for the visa.

Because the F-1 visa allows you to get a valuable academic degree and in some cases allows you to work while you're in school, it may make you attractive to U.S. and international employers and lead to you qualifying for a U.S. labor-based visa or green card. However, getting a student visa will not lead to a green card in any direct way and there are no guarantees that you will find a job or other means of qualifying to immigrate permanently. Remember that if finding a way to stay in the United States permanently is your motive in applying, you will not be granted the student visa.

A final warning before you launch into the F-1 application process: Academic programs can be very challenging to keep up with. You will have to carry a full-time study load—the school may authorize certain reductions in your schedule if you're struggling academically, but you don't want to rely on this in advance. You must also have ample financial resources. The law requires that, before you are given student status, you prove that you will be able to support yourself and any spouse or children who live with you for your entire program of study. Trusting that luck will help you pay the bills when the time comes could lead to disaster. If you are not ready for either the academic or the financial require-

ments, you could fall out of student status. This could result in your being deported and could jeopardize your ability to get future U.S. visas.

To learn how to become eligible for an F-1 student visa, see Chapter 3. For instructions on how to apply for a student visa, see Chapter 7.

6. Coming for Full-Time Vocational Study

College students aren't the only ones eligible for student visas. The U.S. offers a separate "M-1 visa" for "vocational study," meaning training in a technical, mechanical or other field—usually one that involves working with your hands. An M-1 visa would be appropriate if you want to attend a technical or business school or program, a vocational high school or a specialized course of study in a more traditional school or college. There are no limits on the number of students who can receive M-1 visas.

An M-1 visa allows you to complete a program of vocational training that lasts up to one year. You can apply for one extension, and you'll always be given an extra 30 days at the end of your stay to prepare to leave the United States. You may freely travel in and out of the United States for as long as your visa is valid (meaning that it hasn't expired and you haven't violated its terms). Although you cannot work while you are in school, you can spend up to six months doing paid practical training in your field after completing your studies.

The M-1 visa has certain disadvantages when compared with the F-1 visa. If you are in a field of study where an F-1 visa (for academic study) might also be an option (such as for certain types of computer training) you're better off finding a study program that qualifies you for the F-1 visa. With an F-1 visa, you can stay in the United States until your studies are completed, which may add up to several years. But with an M-1 visa, the maximum time you can spend completing your vocational program (even after a visa extension) is two-and-a-half years (two years' study plus six months' practical training). Also, unlike academic or F-1 visa students, M-1 visa students have no right to be employed in the United

States except during the limited period of practical training at the end of their study. They cannot work at on-campus or off-campus jobs. Your ability to transfer schools on an M-1 visa is also quite limited and you absolutely cannot change study programs within your school.

The M-1 visa may allow you training that makes you attractive to U.S. and international employers, which may in turn allow you to qualify for a U.S. labor-based visa or green card. However, the M-1 student visa will not lead to a green card in any direct way, and there are no guarantees that you will find a job or other means of qualifying to immigrate permanently. Remember that if finding a way to stay in the United States permanently is your motive in applying, you will not be granted the M-1 student visa.

If you are sure an M-1 student visa is what you want, see Chapter 3 for how to become eligible. For information on how to apply for a student visa, see Chapter 7.

7. Coming to Learn English

Some students come to the United States for the sole purpose of learning English. If you plan on a full-time course or one that is longer than one year, you'll need to apply for an F-1 student visa—learning English is not considered vocational, so an M-1 student visa will not work. Read Section B5, above, regarding the F-1 student visa. If, however, you're just looking at a short, part-time course, a B-2 tourist visa may be sufficient. See Section 2, above, for further information.

C. Applicants Already in the U.S. on Another Visa

The following subsections explore the visitor and student visa options, and point you toward the appropriate procedures, if you're currently living in the United States on another visa.

This section assumes that since you are in the United States already, you would like to switch to visitor or student status without having to leave the United States first. The procedure for doing this is called a "Change of Status." Applying for a Change of Status simply means asking to continue your stay in the United States under a different category of eligibility (in this book, tourist or student). To see whether you're eligible to change your status in the United States, see Section 1, below—not everyone will be allowed to use this procedure. To determine whether you want to use this option, see Section 2, below.

1. Who Is Allowed to Submit a Change of Status Application?

There are limits on who can apply for a change of status. You are completely prohibited from applying if you are here on a C (transit), D (crewmember), K (fiancé(e)) or S (witness in a criminal investigation) visa. You cannot apply if you are in transit without a visa (changing planes at a U.S. airport, for example) or if you entered as a tourist without a visa under the Visa Waiver Program. People on J (exchange student) visas are allowed to change their status only if they are foreign medical school graduates and meet additional criteria (see an attorney if you are on a J visa).

Even if your visa allows you to apply for a change of status, your inquiry isn't over. You must also make sure that your visa is still valid when you apply to change your status. This means that your permitted stay in the United States has not expired and that you haven't violated the terms of the visa (such as by working when you weren't allowed to) or been ordered by the INS to leave.

2. Tactical Advantages to Leaving the U.S.

There may be a reason for you to go home and apply for a visa through a consulate, even if you can apply for a Change of Status in the United States. The INS is skeptical of requests for Changes of Status, particularly when the switch is from tourist to student status. Remember, tourist visas are meant to be used only by people whose true intention is to turn around and go right home after their stay, unless the visitor made clear that looking at schools was part of the plan, as explained above in Section B3. If the INS suspects that your unstated intention was to switch to student status, they will deny your Change of Status application. By going home and applying for a student visa from abroad, you avoid this risk.

3. Practical Advantages to Leaving the U.S.

Another reason to return home to apply for a visa (rather than changing your status while you're in the United States) is that it will simplify your first trip out of (and back into) the United States. This is especially relevant for students, who may make several trips back and forth before their studies are over.

Here's how it works: Changing status within the United States will not give you a visa stamp, which you (and every noncitizen) will need to get back into the United States once you leave. If you change status in the United States and go home for the holidays during a school vacation, for example, you'll need to allow extra time on your trip so that you can go to the consulate and get a visa stamp. Once you show the consulate that you've been approved—changed status—for student status and haven't violated your status, getting the student visa for reentry shouldn't be a problem. Those who, at the outset, get a student visa by applying at a consulate won't have to go through this extra step.

4. Staying on to Be a Tourist

If you've been living in the United States on another temporary visa, perhaps as a student, temporary worker or government official, you may want to finish your stay with a little vacation. In most cases, you can do this by applying for a "Change of Status" to tourist, or visitor status.

Tourist (or more technically, "visitor") status is appropriate if you're staying in the United States for

purposes encompassed by the word "pleasure." Luckily, the allowable "pleasure" includes more than just traveling around the United States with a camera hanging from your neck. Many types of activities qualify, such as participating in conferences, visiting friends and family, looking into potential colleges or other schools, taking part in amateur (unpaid) arts and entertainment events or contests, attending short classes and receiving medical treatment.

Most tourist stays last six months, although the legal maximum is one year. You'll be free to travel wherever you like, without needing to follow any preset itinerary or check in with any government officials. If you run out of time, you can apply for extensions of up to six months at a time. We'll talk more about the rights and responsibilities that come with being a tourist later in this book.

If you're sure that tourist status is what you want, see Chapter 3 to make sure you're eligible. For instructions on how to apply for a change to tourist status, go to Chapter 6.

5. Staying on for a Short, Recreational or Part-Time Study Course

Most people planning to stay in the United States to study at a college or university will apply for student status. However, the criteria for student status are rather strict. You must be planning full-time study in an INS-approved academic or vocational program. But what if your plans are for more casual instruction —for example, a few weeks of cooking, yoga or art classes? Or perhaps you just want to take a short or part-time academic course and spend the rest of your time traveling in the United States. For these purposes, a change to tourist (B-2) status may be sufficient. If B-2 status fits your plans, it is also preferable to applying for student status because the application process is shorter and simpler.

The immigration laws and regulations don't include any clear rules on which type of programs will require you to get full-fledged student status and which ones won't. The best way to figure out whether tourist status will be enough is to talk to the school or program you'll be attending or to an attorney.

Read more about tourist status in Section C4, above. You'll need to fit the normal eligibility criteria for a tourist visa, including that your trip is for the purpose of pleasure, and that you'll return home when your permitted stay expires. The maximum stay you will be allowed is usually six months, but if your course lasts longer, you may be given up to one year.

If you're sure that tourist status is what you want, see Chapter 3 for whether you're eligible. To apply for a change to tourist status, see Chapter 6.

6. Study in a Full-Time Academic Program

The classic "student" is someone attending a degree program at a school, college or university. If this describes you, and you have been admitted or believe you will be admitted to a program in the United States, F-1 student status is the one for you to pursue. There are no limits on the number of students who can receive F-1 status or visas.

F-1 status allows you to stay in the United States along with your family members, pursue academic studies for as long as it reasonably takes you to finish them (plus 60 days to leave the United States) and travel freely in and out of the United States during your studies (although you'll need to stop at a U.S. consulate on your first trip out and pick up an F-1 visa with which to return, as explained above in Section B3). You may be permitted to work on the school campus and, in some limited circumstances, off campus. If you wish, you may switch programs within your school or even transfer schools with a minimum of added paperwork.

If you're looking to spend a long time grounding yourself in the language and culture of the United States, F-1 student status is ideal. Most academic programs take a relatively long time to complete, and your status will cover the entire program. College degrees, for example, take four years to obtain in the United States, certain graduate programs take between two and six years and a Ph.D. program can

last as long as it takes you to write your dissertation —for some students, it feels like forever.

On the other hand, F status can also be used for certain short-term programs, such as a six-week English course. If you're looking to take a short course, also read Section C5, above.

F-1 status may also allow you to extend your stay in the United States as you pursue higher education. In theory, with F-1 status and multiple extensions, you could come to the United States in your high school years, advance to an undergraduate college program and move on to a graduate degree, spending 15 years in the United States. In reality, it can be difficult to get approval of these repeated status changes, but it is not unheard of. It's even easier to stay this length of time if you don't switch schools. You can finish one program, such as a B.A. (Bachelor of Arts or college degree), and advance directly to another program at the same school, such as an M.A. (Master of Arts), without having to get a new status or visa. The INS asks only that your school advise them so that they can update their records regarding your expected completion date and make sure you still qualify as a student.

Because F-1 status allows you to get a valuable academic degree and in some cases allows you to work while you're in school, it may make you attractive to U.S. and international employers and lead to you qualifying for a U.S. labor-based visa or green card. However, getting student status will not lead to a green card in any direct way and there are no guarantees that you will find a job or other means of qualifying to immigrate permanently. Remember that if finding a way to stay in the United States permanently is your motive in applying, you will not be granted student status.

A final warning before you launch into the F-1 application process: Academic programs can be very challenging to keep up with. You will have to carry a full-time study load—the school may authorize certain reductions in your schedule if you're struggling academically, but you don't want to rely on this in advance. You must also have ample financial resources. The law requires that, before you are given student status, you prove that you will be able to support yourself and any spouse or children who live with you for your entire program of study. Trusting that luck will help you pay the bills when the time comes could lead to disaster. If you are not ready for either the academic or the financial requirements, you could fall out of student status. This could result in your being deported and would jeopardize your ability to get future U.S. visas.

If you're sure that F-1 student status is what you want, see Chapter 3 for how to become eligible. For instructions on how to apply for a change to student status, see Chapter 8.

7. Study in a Full-Time Vocational Program

College students aren't the only ones eligible to study in the United States. There is a separate "M-1" status for "vocational study," meaning training in a technical, mechanical or other field—usually one that involves working with your hands. An M-1 visa is appropriate if you want to attend a technical or business school or program, a vocational high school or a specialized vocational program at a more traditional school or college. There are no limits on the number of students who can receive M-1 status or visas.

M-1 status allows you to complete a program of vocational training that lasts up to one year. You can apply for one extension, and you'll always be given an extra 30 days at the end of your stay to prepare to leave the United States. You may freely travel in and out of the United States for as long as your status is valid (meaning that it hasn't expired, and you haven't violated its terms)—but the first time you leave, you'll have to stop by a U.S. consulate and obtain an M-1 student visa in order to return, as explained above in Section B3. Although you cannot work while in school, you can spend up to six months in paid practical training in your field after completing your studies.

M-1 status has certain disadvantages when compared with F-1 status. If you are in a field of study where F-1 status (for academic study) might also be

an option (such as for certain types of computer training) you're better off finding a study program that qualifies you for F-1 status. With F-1 status, you can stay in the United States until your studies are completed, which may add up to several years. But with M-1 status, the maximum time you can spend completing your vocational program (even after a visa extension) is two-and-a-half years (two years' study plus six months' practical training). Also, unlike academic or F-1 visa students, M-1 students have no right to be employed in the United States except during the limited period of practical training at the end of their study. They cannot work at on-campus or off-campus jobs. Your ability to transfer schools on M-1 status is also quite limited and you absolutely cannot change study programs within your school.

M-1 status may give you training that makes you attractive to U.S. and international employers and in turn allow you to qualify for a U.S. labor-based visa or green card. However, M-1 student status will not lead to a green card in any direct way, and there are no guarantees that you will find a job or other means of qualifying to immigrate permanently. Remember that if finding a way to stay in the United States permanently is your motive in applying, you will not be granted M-1 student status.

If you're sure that M-1 student status is what you want, see Chapter 3 for how to become eligible. For information on how to apply for a change to student status, see Chapter 8.

8. Study of the English Language

Some students come to the United States for the sole purpose of learning English. If you plan on a full-time course or one that is longer than one year, you'll need to apply for F-1 student status—learning English is not considered vocational, so M-1 student status will not work. Read Section C6, above, regarding F-1 student status. If, however, you're just looking at a short, part-time course a B-2 tourist visa may be sufficient. See Section C5, above, for further information. ■

Can You Enter the U.S. at All?

Whether you're coming to the United States for a short visit or to stay forever, the U.S. government has the power to tell you "no." Many people are shocked to realize that even though they've chosen an appropriate visa or status and filled out all the paperwork, they still are not guaranteed an approval. Every applicant to come to or stay in the United States must also clear a set of hurdles known as the "grounds of inadmissibility." To be "inadmissible" means, in legal terms, that you present a risk so great that no matter what visa or status you apply for, you will not be allowed to cross the border into, or remain in, the United States.

A. What Are the Grounds of Inadmissibility?

The law makes people inadmissible if they have histories of health, criminal, security and other problems. Some of the grounds make obvious sense— few would argue about refusing entry to an international terrorist, for example. Other grounds are the topic of more controversy, such as excluding people who are infected with HIV or have committed certain immigration violations.

A list of the main grounds of inadmissibility is provided in "What Makes You Inadmissible?" below. If you're in doubt about whether you're inadmissible, you'll need to do further research or consult an attorney. Sometimes you can apply for exceptions or waivers (a waiver is legalese for forgiveness), but these waivers are not covered here. You'll need an attorney's help if you determine that you must apply for a waiver.

You can read the law concerning inadmissibility yourself. The grounds of inadmissibility are in the Immigration and Nationality Act at I.N.A. § 212(a); 8 U.S.C.§1182. You will find this Act at your local law library; at Nolo's Legal Research Center at http://www.nolo.com, or excerpted on the U.S. State Department's website at http://www.travel.state.gov/visa;ineligible.html. For more information on inadmissibility in plain English, see *U.S. Immigration Made Easy*, by Laurence A. Canter & Martha S. Siegel (Nolo).

What Makes You Inadmissible?

The United States will not allow you to enter or remain here if you:

- have a communicable disease such as tuberculosis or HIV
- have a physical or mental disorder that makes you harmful to others
- are likely to become a public charge (dependent on welfare)
- are a drug abuser ("tried it more than once" in the last three years is enough for the INS)
- have committed or been convicted of a crime of "moral turpitude," (a crime considered morally wrong or done with a bad intention)
- have been convicted of multiple crimes
- have been convicted of certain specified crimes such as prostitution or drug trafficking
- are the immediate family member of a drug trafficker and have knowingly benefited from their illicit money within the last five years
- have committed espionage or sabotage
- are a member of a totalitarian party (particularly the Communist Party)
- are a Nazi or have participated in genocide
- have violated the immigration laws or committed immigration fraud
- have falsely claimed to be a U.S. citizen
- are unlawfully present in the United States or haven't obtained proper documentation to enter the United States
- were previously removed or deported from the United States
- are a polygamist (have married more than one person at the same time)
- have committed international child abduction
- are or were on a J-1 or J-2 exchange visitor visa and are subject to the two-year foreign residence requirement.

The ordinary person shouldn't fall into any of the grounds of inadmissibility. But one of the grounds most likely to cause you trouble is the one concerning past violations of the U.S. immigration laws. If you have visited the United States before and violated your visa status or stayed too long, read the section immediately below.

Immigrants From Overseas Must Also Pass U.S. Customs

When you come to the United States, you'll not only have to think about whether you'll be admitted, but whether the contents of your luggage will be allowed in with you. The U.S. Customs Service regulates the goods and currency that all travelers bring to the United States. After you pass Immigration, you will meet with a Customs officer who will question you and may search your luggage. Certain items are completely prohibited (such as drugs and weapons); others can be brought in only in limited amounts (such as alcohol and tobacco) and others are subject to more specific restrictions or taxes.

Customs officers are also trained to look for things that might indicate that you might not be admissible under the visa that you were given, such as bank statements and resumes that might be in your language or a book that talks about how you can become a permanent resident—and they can refer you back to the INS for further inspection. For more information, see the Customs Service's website at http://www.customs.gov/travel/travel.htm, or ask your local U.S. consulate for Customs information.

B. Dealing With Unlawful Time in the United States

In the late 1990s, Congress decided to punish people who spend time in the United States unlawfully (without INS permission). It created a penalty that prevents these people from coming or returning to the United States for three years or ten years, depending on how long they previously stayed in the country unlawfully. These penalties are usually referred to as the Three- and Ten-Year Bars or the Time Bars. If you have spent time in the United States unlawfully at any time after April 1997, you must read this section.

There is another bar called the Permanent Bar. It applies to people who lived in the United States illegally for more than a year and then left or were deported, but who are returning, have returned or are caught trying to return to the United States illegally. Such people will never be allowed to enter the United States. The Permanent Bar is still a muddy area of the law, so it's not appropriate to discuss it at length in a self-help book like this. However, if you have been to the United States more than once, spent more than a year here unlawfully or been deported, and one of your entries was illegal, you should absolutely see a lawyer before going any further.

If you've never been in the United States, or never spent time here without permission, you don't have to worry about the Time Bars or the Permanent Bar for now—but should read this section after you have gotten your visa or status, to understand what will happen if you misuse it.

"Unlawful" is a difficult legal term. If you know that you were here without INS permission, it's safe to say that your stay was unlawful. But the boundaries are less clear if, for example, you were waiting for the INS to approve or deny an application you'd filed, were in removal (immigration court) proceedings or had a visa but violated its rules. For situations such as these, you'll need to consult a lawyer.

1. The Three- and Ten-Year Time Bars

The first thing to understand about the Time Bars is that they are only imposed on people who are overseas and trying to return to the United States, not people who are already here and have the right to apply for a Change of Status here. Unfortunately, a number of people have no choice but to apply for their tourist or immigrant visa through an overseas U.S. consulate, either because they are already overseas, or because they are in the United States but have stayed past the permitted expiration of their stay and must leave. If you are one of these people, the Time Bars could delay your coming to the United States as follows:

- **Three Years.** If you've spent more than 180 days (approximately six months) in the United States unlawfully, you could be barred from coming back for three years.
- **Ten Years.** If you've spent more than one year in the United States unlawfully, you could be barred from coming back for ten years.

2. Loopholes in the Time Bar Law

Not everyone who has ever lived in the United States unlawfully will have a Time Bar problem. The law contains a few loopholes, including the following:

- Since the law didn't go into effect until April 1, 1997, no unlawful time before that date counts.
- None of your unlawful time when you were under the age of 18 counts.
- The law only punishes "continuous" time, so a few months here and there don't count, as long as one illegal stay was not 180 days or more.

Using these loopholes and some basic math, you might find that people who look as though they have a Time Bar problem are safe after all. Here are some examples:

- Rosalie was a student in the United States from 1990 to 1995. She continued to live here unlawfully until April 1, 1997. She is not subject to the Time Bars because unlawful time doesn't start to count until April 1, 1997.
- Rosalie just checked her calendar and realized she stayed until July 1, 1997. But she still isn't subject to the Time Bars because her stay was for less than 180 continuous days after April 1, 1997.
- Juan crossed the Mexican border illegally six times in 2000 and stayed in the United States

for time periods of two months each, for a total of 12 months. Now Juan wants to enter legally. The Time Bars will not apply to him because he did not stay for more than 180 continuous days.

- Soraya entered the United States as a visitor on June 1, 2000, and her visa expired three months later. She stayed in the United States until June 6, 2001. Soraya turned 18 on February 1, 2001. The Time Bars will not apply to her because only about four months of her unlawful time—less than 180 days—was while she was over the age of 18.

3. What to Do If You Face the Time Bars

If you think you have stayed in the United States unlawfully for long enough to face a Three- or Ten-year Time Bar, consult with an attorney. The attorney can confirm whether or not the Time Bars apply in your situation and advise you on whether any new options have become available. If nothing else works, you may have to wait out the three or ten years before applying for your tourist or student visa.

EXAMPLE: Graham, a British citizen, drove into the United States from Canada in June of 1997 and lived here until June of 2001—a total of over one year's illegal time. He returned to England for awhile and applied for a tourist visa to come to the United States. Because he had spent more than one year here unlawfully, he was denied the visa. He won't be able to return to the United States until June of 2011.

4. Make Sure Your U.S. Stay Doesn't Turn Unlawful

The Three- and Ten-Year Time Bars may be an issue for you to consider even after you've received your visa. Like a wasp, they can sting many times. Every time you enter the United States—for example, after you've gotten a student visa and are returning from your summer vacation overseas—the consular or border patrol officer can check to see whether you've spent unlawful time in the United States. If you've violated the terms of your visa or status (for example, by quitting school and staying more than six months or a year, without permission), you could be barred for three or ten years.

It's not unusual to spend time in the United States waiting for an INS decision on certain applications (including applications to extend your stay or change to a new immigration status). Even though your visa or status may be expired, this waiting time doesn't count toward the Time Bars, up to a maximum of 120 days. But you lose this benefit if you didn't really qualify for the change or extension, but only filed a fake or frivolous application to try and gain time. In that case, all of the time after your permitted stay had ended would be considered unlawful.

EXAMPLE 1: Gedeminas is in the United States on a six-month tourist stay. During the sixth month (September), he is invited to take part in an international folk dancing event in Chicago in December. He applies for an extension of his stay. The INS doesn't approve his extension until late November. However, because it was a valid application, his stay between September and November is considered lawful.

EXAMPLE 2: Ramute is in the United States as a vocational (M-1) student. Although she will finish her program within the one year allowed on her visa, she doesn't want to leave yet. At her boyfriend's urging, she submits an application for an extension of her stay, falsely claiming that the school wouldn't let her register for all the classes she needed. Six months after her visa expires, the INS finally responds, denying her extension request. All of those six months are unlawful. Not even the first 120 days are considered lawful, because this application was frivolous. Ramute will face a three-year bar on reentering the United States.

C. How Would They Find Out You're Inadmissible?

After looking at the list of inadmissibility grounds, you might be wondering "how would they know?" The first answer is that they will ask. As you'll see later in this book, the forms that you will have to fill out ask you about all the grounds of inadmissibility. Assuming that you answer honestly, the consulate or INS will know you're inadmissible as soon as they review your application (and this is not a section that they are likely to skip over).

Skyline
Chicago, Illinois

You may be tempted to answer dishonestly, especially if the issue is something that happened a long time ago and doesn't seem important anymore. But hiding the truth is a huge risk. Although you might not get caught in a lie, if you are caught, this lie will take on a weighty new name: "visa fraud." Visa fraud is a ground of inadmissibility. Once it is on your record, you can count on this and possibly every U.S. immigration-related application being denied.

The second way that the consulate or INS might find out that you are inadmissible is to order further information. This probably won't happen unless they get suspicious, but suspicions are high these days. For example, they could ask for a medical exam, a police report or other follow-up documentation. Or, if a government official suspects that you have spent time in the United States unlawfully, she could demand that you prove otherwise.

If the government suspects that you might have lived in the United States unlawfully, providing further information becomes your problem. You will have to prove to the U.S. government that you *didn't* live here unlawfully, not the other way around. People in this situation must come up with copies of their plane tickets, rent receipts, credit card statements, pay stubs, medical records, school transcripts and more, all to prove that they were in the United States until a certain date and then left.

EXAMPLE 1: Chariya came to the United States from Thailand on a six-month tourist stay in March 2000, but didn't leave until January of 2001—a four-month overstay. She was then accepted to a graduate program in the U.S. When she went to the U.S. consulate in Bangkok for the interview to get her F-1 student visa, Chariya explained the four-month overstay. She knew that this wasn't long enough to subject her to any penalty, not even the three-year Time Bar. But the consulate demanded proof that she hadn't been in the United States for longer than four months past the expiration of her tourist stay.

Chariya had lived with her parents after she returned home and had thrown out her plane tickets. She had no paperwork with her to prove when she had returned to Thailand. Luckily, the consulate gave her more time and she eventually came up with a copy of her frequent flier statement showing the date of her travel, as well as a prescription that she got in February 2001 in Bangkok. The visa was granted.

If you have spent any time in the United States since 1997, make sure you are prepared to prove that you returned home on time. Begin gathering all relevant documents now, such as rent receipts, plane tickets, credit card statements and more.

D. When Would They Tell You You're Inadmissible?

Normally, you would find out about your inadmissibility at your visa or INS interview. At that point, the officer reviewing your application would tell which ground of inadmissibility you fit into. He would either conclude that he can't possibly approve your application or offer you an opportunity to submit a waiver request (for which you'll need an attorney's help).

If you're coming from overseas, there is a second occasion on which you might be found inadmissible —your entry to the United States. Regardless of the fact that you convinced the U.S. consulate to grant you a visa, the border patrol officer has the power to reexamine your application. He may deny your entry and order you to return home if he believes that you lied to get the visa or don't really plan to return home after your stay. This power is called "expedited removal." We cover it in more detail, and give tips on handling your entry at the U.S. border, in Chapter 9. ■

Are You Eligible for the Visa or Status You Want?

Before you start filling out application forms or packing your suitcase, let's make sure that you qualify for the visa or status that you want. Establishing your legal eligibility is very important—the government officers who are deciding your case will strictly follow the rules that govern who gets to come to the United States—and who doesn't. Unless they find that you clearly meet the legal criteria, they cannot and will not approve you. Tourist visa eligibility is discussed in Section B, and student visa eligibility is discussed in Section C.

For ease of reference, we will refer only to your eligibility for a "visa" from this point forward—even though applicants who are already in the United States will not be applying for a "visa," but for a Change of Status. The eligibility criteria are, however, the same.

A. Convincing Skeptical Government Officials

As part of applying for a tourist or student visa, you will have to convince a skeptical officer at a U.S. consulate that you meet all of the eligibility criteria for these visas described in Sections B and C, below.

This is no easy task. New security concerns mean that every aspect of your application will be carefully examined. Also, unfair as it seems, U.S. consular officers are legally required to assume that your real plan is to stay permanently in the United States. See I.N.A. §214(b), 8 U.S.C. § 1184(b). For this reason, your word alone (even your most solemn promise that you'll stay in the United States only as long as you're allowed and then go home) will not be enough. You must come up with hard evidence to support your promise to return—without it, the consular officer will deny your application. The way to overcome this official suspicion is to present believable and compelling documents, which we'll cover in the chapters concerning the application process.

You may be tempted to lie during this process—perhaps to make your income look greater or to conceal the presence of family members with U.S. citizenship. We strongly recommend against lying, and not for moral reasons alone. U.S. government officials are pretty good at catching people at lies, and are continually finding more ways to detect lies. Once you're caught, not only will your application be denied, but a notation will be made on your record that you made a fraudulent statement. Fraud can disqualify you on future applications for visas or other U.S. immigration benefits (in fact, it's a stated ground of inadmissibility, as described in Chapter 2, Section A).

On the other hand, being honest doesn't mean that you have to offer every detail about your life. If an officer doesn't ask you about an aspect of your life or your plans, you don't have to give them the information. And since the officials will be interpreting the law strictly, so can you. For example, your "intention" can still be to return to your home country even if, in the back of your mind, you think it wouldn't be all bad if, during your student days, you fell in love with an American citizen and decided to get married. That's not information that the consular, border or INS officer needs to hear.

Alamo
San Antonio, Texas

Harsh Visa Decisions by U.S. Consulate

The U.S. consulate in China has attracted criticism for refusing visas to thousands of Chinese who hoped to study or travel in the United States. Chinese applicants complain that the interviewers spend only a few minutes with them—then inform them that they've failed to present adequate proof of their ultimate intent to return to China. In one sample period, 41% of Chinese student visa applications were denied. Applicants are turning to Internet chat rooms as they try to learn more about the personalities, preferences and whims of individual visa officers. ("Tough U.S. Visa Policy Angers Chinese Scholars," by Elisabeth Rosenthal, *The New York Times*, September 10, 2001.)

B. Are You Eligible for a B-2 Tourist Visa?

Qualifying for a B-2 tourist visa depends primarily on what you plan to do during your visit and whether you'll really return home afterward. The INS or consular officer will want to see that you:

- are coming to the United States solely for pleasure or for medical treatment, and not for other reasons (such as to work or to stay permanently), as discussed in subsection 1, below
- plan to stay for a limited, specific period of time, as explained in subsection 2, below
- have a residence (a place to call home) outside the United States as well as other binding ties which will assure your return home after your visit, as discussed in subsection 3, below
- have permission to enter a foreign country (probably your own) at the end of your stay, as explained in subsection 4, below, and
- are able to pay for your visit to and departure from the United States. as explained in subsection 5, below.

1. Your Visit Must Be for Pleasure Purposes

What does it mean to be coming to the United States for pleasure? Here is how the U.S. State Department's regulations describe it:

> *Legitimate activities of a recreational character, including tourism, amusement, visits with friends or relatives, rest, medical treatment and activities of a fraternal, social or service nature. 22 C.F.R. § 41.31(b)(2).*

This definition allows for a range of activities, from sightseeing to taking classes to attending conferences. It does not, however, allow visits for the purpose of working for pay or conducting other business activities, such as attending trade conventions, giving consultations, selling international products or even serving as a minister or missionary. A separate visa (the B-1) exists for certain business activities (business visas are not covered in this book). Pleasure also cannot include working as a member of the foreign press or information media, since there is a separate visa for this (the I visa). An intent to commit a crime doesn't qualify someone for a tourist visa either, no matter how pleasurable the rest of their planned visit.

> **EXAMPLE:** Rajiv is a classical musician. He has always dreamed of hearing all the major U.S. symphonies play and puts together an itinerary where he can hear a succession of their performances in their home symphony halls. Rajiv's visa is granted. His friend, Ramesh, is also a musician. Rajiv invites Ramesh to come along. Ramesh, however, makes the mistake of telling the consular officer that he will fund his trip by playing his violin on U.S. streetcorners. This transforms Ramesh's trip into a money-making venture, not just a pleasure trip. Ramesh's visa is denied and Rajiv will have to make the trip alone.

There are some reasons for visiting the United States that don't sound like pure pleasure to most people, but are recognized by the State Department as sufficient to qualify for a B-2 visa. Medical treatment—which not many people would consider pleasurable—is specifically covered by this visa. Also, someone accompanying a visitor for business (B-1) or certain other temporary visa holders will usually be given a B-2 visa. Similarly, family or household members of someone coming on another temporary visa (such as students, diplomats or temporary workers) who don't qualify for what's called "derivative status" and an automatic visa of their own as that person's spouse or children can be given a B-2. Derivative visas are not covered in this book—many U.S. visas allow spouses and children to come as derivatives, but not all do, so the B-2 visa can be used to avoid family separation in such instances. Being able to come to the United States as a B-2 visa holder also prevents separation of domestic partners, homosexual partners, elderly parents and others (see sidebar, "Special Advice for Those Accompanying Another Visa Holder.")

> **EXAMPLE:** Samuel has been granted an F-1 visa to study in a special private high school for advanced training in math and science. Though he's a genius, he is certainly not ready to live on his own. His mother is granted a B-2 visa to accompany him.

> **EXAMPLE:** Antonia has been granted an H-1B visa to work as a medical engineer in Boston. Her female partner of 11 years, Jana, would like to accompany her. Jana is given a B-2 visa.

Someone wanting to get married in the United States but not planning to stay and apply for a green card could also use a B-2 visa. A student looking into potential schools or colleges could also use a B-2 visa whether or not she plans to return home before enrolling (but should make her intentions clear, so that she isn't accused of visa fraud if she decides to enter school immediately, without leaving the United States). And people who have served in the U.S. military and become eligible for U.S. citizenship as a result can use a B-2 visa to come and submit their citizenship application.

Special Advice for Those Accompanying Another Visa Holder

In most cases, people who get visas to the United States can bring their spouses and children along almost automatically, on what are called "derivative visas." (For example, K-1 fiancé visa holders can bring their children as K-2 visa holders.) However, there are exceptions, depending on the visa obtained by the primary traveler—not every visa has its own derivative. If someone close to you is traveling to the U.S. on a temporary visa and the rules covering that visa don't allow you to accompany him or her, the consulate may grant you a B-2 visa instead. You will have to meet all the eligibility criteria of the B-2 visa, but will not need to show any "pleasure" other than accompanying the primary visa holder. (No need to plan a year's worth of trips to Disneyland, in other words.)

Unmarried partners of the same or opposite sex who want to come to the U.S. with their partner have historically had trouble obtaining visas. They are not allowed derivative status without a marriage certificate. Yet not all U.S. consulates have been forthcoming in granting them B-2 visas. This situation should improve soon, however. In July of 2001, the U.S. State Department sent a special cable reminding consulates that the B-2 option applies not only to spouses, but to unmarried partners of the same or opposite sex.

The State Department also advised the border posts to give incoming B-2 visa holders a full one year's stay, if necessary to avoid separation with the primary visa holder, instead of the more standard six months. However, if you are given a one-year B-2 stay but your visa-holding friend or partner will be staying in the United States for more than a year, you can apply for an extension of your stay (see Chapter 10 for instructions).

2. You Must Plan to Stay for a Limited Time

When you apply for your visa, you'll have to show the consular officer that your plan to visit the United States is coupled with a plan to leave again, and to leave fairly soon. By means of maps and schedules, you'll want to show that your length of stay is based on something real, like a planned event or itinerary, and not just on a desire to stay for as long you can. The *Foreign Affairs Manual* (FAM), a government document followed by the officials who will decide whether to give you a visa, specifically cautions that "the applicant's intentions must not be expressed in terms of remaining in the United State for the maximum period allowable by U.S. authorities." See FAM § 41.31 N2.5 to 22 C.F.R. Part 41. Before your trip, think about what you want to see or accomplish while you are in the United States and allot the right amount of time to cover this.

> **EXAMPLE:** Matteo plans to make a road trip across the United States. When he applies for his visa, he shows the consular officer his route, his calculations of miles he can cover per day and his list of what he will see at each stopping place. Because of his careful plans, he knows his exact departure date. His visa is granted.

> **EXAMPLE:** Thaddeus also plans a road trip across the United States. He however tells the consular officer that "whatever road calls me, I will follow." He sees his trip as a spiritual journey, but assures the officer that the spirits will guide him back to an appropriate airport at the right time. The visa is denied.

If you're starting to wonder how anyone has the time to plan a trip to the United States, here's a word of comfort. You probably won't have to do this much work for future trips. If you succeed in getting this visa, and you return on time, the next time you apply for a tourist visa you may be granted one that's good for more than one trip—called a "multiple entry" visa. (First-time visa applicants usually receive only single entry visas.) With a multiple entry visa, you won't have to show the consulate proof of your travel itinerary or other eligibility criteria before you leave for the United States—although you will still have to answer some fairly specific questions when you show up at the U.S. border, as we'll discuss in Chapter 9.

3. You Must Have a Residence and Other Ties to Your Country

The toughest requirement for most applicants is not the need to prove your well-planned trip *to* the United States—it's the requirement that you have a residence and other reasons compelling you to *return* to your home country at the end of your visit. The forces pulling you home might include a house, a family or a stable job. It's especially tough because the person reviewing your application presumes that you really want to stay in the United States permanently even before he has met you. It will be entirely up to you to disprove this presumption (for more on this issue, see Section A, above).

Young applicants in particular—the ones who, ironically, may have the most free time to travel—are the least likely to have a stable residence or other convincing ties. Luckily, the rules do not specify exactly what types of ties to your home country you must show. In fact, even your "residence" does not need to be your own house or apartment—living in someone else's household is fine, as is returning to a different residence than the one you'll leave behind. You may need to get creative, looking at your involvement in community organizations, hobbies, educational plans or other activities that will pull you back when your U.S. visit is over.

> **EXAMPLE:** Malasha is 19 years old and lives with her parents, with whom she doesn't get along. She has finished high school, but didn't get into a college she wanted to attend. She tells the officer that she'll return home because of her parents, but can't help rolling her eyes and looking pained when she talks about them. The visa is denied.

EXAMPLE: Li-feng is 18 years old and has just finished high school. Although she didn't get into college on the first try, she enrolled in a demanding college preparatory course and paid the entry fee. The course starts after Li-feng returns from the United States. By showing the officer proof of her course registration and payment and talking with the officer about how important it is for her to find a college that allows her to live with her parents, she convinces him to grant her the visa.

4. You Must Have Permission to Enter or Reenter a Foreign Country After You Leave

The United States doesn't want to be stuck with anyone who comes as a tourist and then has no place to return. If you're coming from your home country and returning home afterwards, your country will presumably let you back in, except in highly unusual political circumstances.

If, however, you will be travelling to a third country after visiting the United States, be prepared to show that you have a visa or other permission to enter that country.

EXAMPLE: Primo, who lives in Italy, has purchased a plane ticket that allows him around-the-world travel. He'll be coming first to the United States and continuing on to China. He will need to obtain a visa to China before he applies for his U.S. visa. That way he can show the U.S. consular officer the visa to China as proof that he not only has a plane ticket to depart the United States, but will be permitted to go on to his next destination.

5. You Must Be Able to Pay for Your Visit and Departure

Every day that you spend in the United States is going to cost money. Your hotel stay, rental car, food, tickets and other items will add up fast, and the U.S. government knows it. You will have to show that you have the savings to cover your trip, or that someone else is willing to be responsible for supporting you. If your trip is going to be difficult on your budget, do some research to find out exactly how much you are likely to spend and how you will afford it. The U.S. consulate itself may have a library that can help you learn this sort of information, or you can check a reputable and up-to-date travel

Diamond Head
Honolulu, Hawaii

guide such as those by Lonely Planet, Fodor's or Baedeker.

The more people in your traveling party, the more expensive your stay will be. For example, a person coming to the U.S. to visit Disneyland and other sights with their spouse and three children for three weeks will have to show that they have enough money to pay for hotel, food and other expenses for five people. Too many folks to feed and entertain and you might not get a visa at all—the consul will want to see that all of the expenses for all of travelers will be covered (though you can combine the family members' incomes and resources). But leaving family members at home may not be the answer. If you are the principal wage earner for your spouse and children and they are not traveling with you, you will have to show that they will be provided for while you are away—particularly if you're planning a long trip. If it looks like your family will be going hungry while you're traveling, the official deciding your case may assume that there's more to your trip than meets the eye—perhaps that you are hoping to find employment in the United States.

C. Are You Eligible for a Student Visa?

Knowing that you want to study in the United States, or even gaining admission to a school is not enough by itself to qualify you for a student visa. Regardless of whether you're interested in an academic (F-1) or vocational (M-1) visa, you'll also need to satisfy the U.S. consulate or INS that you are:

- admitted to a U.S. school that has been approved by the INS (as discussed in subsection 1, below)
- a "bona fide" student (see subsection 2, below)
- qualified and ready for your planned course of study (see subsection 3, below)
- planning only a temporary stay in the United States (see subsection 4, below), and
- able to pay for your studies (see subsection 5, below).

Where Do International Students Come From?

The United States hosts international students from virtually every country on the globe. An impressive majority of them, however, come from Asia. China, Japan, Korea, India and Taiwan top the list. Most of these students study in and around Los Angeles, New York and other major U.S. cities. For details, see http://www.opendoorsweb.org/Lead%20Stories/international_studs.htm, and http://www.opendoorsweb.org/Lead%20Stories/counties.htm.

1. You Have Been Admitted to an Established, INS-Approved School or Program

You can't get a student visa unless your intended school or program has already been approved by the INS to receive foreign students. Most established schools have such approval—the school itself should be able to confirm this for you.

If you plan to come on an F-1 visa, the school must be a college, university, seminary, conservatory, academic high school or other academic institution or a language training program.

If you plan to come on an M-1 visa, you must attend a community or junior college that provides vocational training and gives out associate degrees. Or, you must enroll in a vocational high school or other approved program. M-1 students can't come to the United States for the sole purpose of studying English—but if your program will include some English-language training that will help you "understand the vocational or technical course of study," that won't be a hindrance to getting your visa. See 8 C.F.R. § 214.3(a)(2)(iv).

You Can't Use a Student Visa to Attend a Free Public School

In the 1990s, Congress decided that the United States should not pay to educate people from other countries. It amended the immigration laws to provide that no student visa will be issued to a person wishing to attend a public elementary school (kindergarten through 8th grade) or a publicly funded adult education program. The rules are slightly different for high schools. You can attend a maximum of one year of public high school (9th through 12th grade), but you will have to pay the local school district for the entire cost of your education for that year.

The cost of a year in a U.S. high school depends on the local school district—you'll have to contact the district directly. The average cost is between $3,400 and $10,000. Some school districts are not able to calculate their costs. If you plan to attend school in one of these districts, you won't be allowed a visa.

There's nothing to stop you from attending a private elementary or high school—except maybe the tuition, which can be as high as U.S. college tuition. You should also know that some immigrants are allowed to attend public schools, such as those accompanying their parents on another visa, as well as undocumented children (whose rights are protected by the Supreme Court's decision in *Plyler v. Doe*, 457 U.S. 202 (1982)). However, the point of the legislation described above is to prevent children who have the option of attending school in their home country from taking advantage of the U.S. school system.

2. You Are a Bona Fide Student, and Nothing Else

Since students stay longer and learn more skills than people on many other types of visas, the U.S. government's suspicion that you want to stay permanently is particularly high. You'll have to convince the government that you are a bona fide (real) student, whose intention in coming to the United States is not to get a job, find a spouse, or even just enjoy the scenery. You won't be given a visa unless you can show that you're ready and able to "hit the books" and study.

EXAMPLE: Ananya applies for a student visa in order to pursue a degree in women's studies at a small eastern women's college. She was a top student at her high school and won a performance-based scholarship. Ananya is already married and her husband will be staying in India during her studies. The visa is granted.

EXAMPLE: Parnika applies for a visa to an American military academy. She has been out of school for a few years, but her grades were not impressive. Since school, she's been working as a journalist and is known for her articles advocating pacifism. The consular officer believes Parnika is actually planning to write an exposé on U.S. military training rather than complete a study program, and denies the visa.

3. You Are Qualified to Pursue a Full Course of Study

The requirement that you are "qualified" to study is loaded with meaning. You must have the appropriate background, including study, training or experience, for the program that you will be entering. Also, you must be sufficiently proficient in English to complete your studies (unless you plan to come on an F-1 visa for the sole purpose of studying English).

a. Showing Your English Proficiency

You'll have to prove your proficiency in English twice. First, you'll have to prove it to the school that admits you. They may require you to take an English test in your home country, such as the "TOEFL" (Test of English as a Foreign Language). Second, you'll have to prove it to the U.S. government officer who decides whether to grant you the F-1 or M-1 visa. The government knows that the school has tested your English already, but seems to want to double-check it—perhaps because the consulate or INS has a chance to meet you personally, whereas the school might not.

If your English is not quite good enough for American classroom study, there are alternatives. You may qualify for a visa by showing that English classes will be part of your curriculum—and that the classes will enable you to catch up quickly. Some schools offer special programs to get you up to speed, for example in the summer before the start of formal classes. If, however, it looks like you're going to be spending so much time learning English that you can't maintain the rest of your studies, your visa is likely to be denied.

b. Definition of a "Full Course of Study" for F-1 Students

For F-1 students, a "full course of study" means that you can't be a part-time student. Your study must "lead to the attainment of a specific educational or professional objective." This objective can be a degree, such as a Bachelor's, Master's, Ph.D. or other certification. However, you don't actually have to complete that degree in the United States. You could come to the United States to take a semester of college courses as your "objective," so long as your study is full time during that one semester. The following types of study are acceptable:

- Postgraduate or postdoctoral study at a college, university, conservatory or religious seminary.
- Undergraduate study at a college or university; at least 12 credit hours per term (for schools on the semester or quarter system), except during the last term if fewer hours are needed to finish.
- Study at a post-high school institution (such as a community college) that awards "associate" or comparable degrees.
- Study in a language, liberal arts, fine arts or other nonvocational training program; at least

18 actual hours of attendance per week, 22 hours if most of the study time is spent in a laboratory.

- Study at a high school (9th through 12th grade) or elementary school (first through 8th grade); at least the number of classroom hours per week that the school requires for normal progress toward graduation; but see the sidebar in Section C1, above, "You Can't Use a Student Visa to Attend a Free Public School." (See 8 C.F.R. § 214.2(f)(6).)

As discussed in Chapter 11 on the need to maintain your status as a student, you will be allowed some breaks in your study regimen. These include time for school vacations, illness and exam preparation periods, but not for personally scheduled vacations that take you out of class. Also, the rules covering minimum hours at school can be changed if your school authorizes you to take fewer study hours for academic or medical reasons (including pregnancy).

c. Definition of a "Full Course of Study" for M-1 Students

A "full course of study" for vocational (M-1) students must "lead to the attainment of a specific educational or vocational objective." 8 C.F.R. § 214.2(m)(9). This objective can be a degree, a certificate or the completion of a program. On the way to that objective, you must spend your time studying in or at one of the following: (See 8 C.F.R. § 214.2(m)(9).)

- A community college or junior college of at least 12 semester or quarter hours of instruction per academic term, except during the last term if you need fewer hours to finish the program.
- A post-secondary vocational or other business school (not language training) of at least 12 hours weekly (or its equivalent), at a school that gives associate or other degrees (or gives credits that are accepted unconditionally by at least three institutions of higher learning).
- A vocational or other nonacademic curriculum (not language training) consisting of at least 18 hours of classroom attendance per week or

22 hours per week if the dominant part of the course is shop or laboratory work.

- A vocational or other nonacademic high school curriculum, for the minimum number of hours the school requires for normal progress toward graduation.

As discussed in Chapter 11 on maintaining your status, you will be allowed some breaks in your study regimen, such as for school vacations, illness and exam preparation periods. Also, your school can authorize fewer study hours if appropriate for academic or medical reasons (including pregnancy).

4. Your Stay Will Be Only Temporary

The toughest part of getting a student visa is persuading a consular or INS officer that you plan to return home when your temporary stay is over. It's especially tough because the law forces the person reviewing your application to presume that you want to stay in the United States even before he has met you. It will be entirely up to you to convince

the official otherwise (for more on this issue, see Section A, above).

You will have to show evidence that your true, long-term residence is in a foreign country, and that you have ties to that country that will naturally pull you home when your studies are completed. These ties could include your family, a home, a job or any other personal situation or obligation. We cover how to provide documents proving such ties in the chapters covering application procedures, further on in this book.

EXAMPLE: Cheikh applies for a student visa to attend a six-month cooking course in New York. Cheikh is employed as a chef in a premier restaurant in his native African nation, and can show that he plans to return to that job when the course is over. His visa is granted.

EXAMPLE: Taye applies for a student visa to an American law school. His native country doesn't follow the American legal system. Taye owns no property and is unmarried. The visa officer believes that Taye plans to stay in the United States and look for a job as a lawyer, and denies his visa.

EPCOT Center (Disney World)
Orlando, Florida

You don't need to show that you can't get the same education in your home country. Don't worry if your home country has perfectly good schools offering the same courses of study as your target school in the United States. The consular and INS officers will not consider this in approving your student visa.

5. You Are Able to Pay for Your Studies

You must show that your education will be fully financed and all your day-to-day living expenses (including the expenses of your spouse or children if they plan to come with you) will be paid without your having to work in the United States. (If your family will not be coming with you, and you normally support them, you may also be asked how they'll be supported while you're gone.) Although some students will be permitted to work during their student years, you cannot rely on this work to prove your visa eligibility. In fact, you probably won't know until you get to the United States what type of work you'll be able to get. The permitted work will probably be low-paying or a small part of your study program in any case.

Your financing can come from your own resources or from family, friends or scholarships. We'll talk about how to prove that these are actual, reliable resources in the chapters covering application procedures later in this book.

How Are You Going to Pay for This?

Tuition in the United States can be high, ranging from about $5,000 a year at state schools to $25,000 a year at prestigious private colleges or universities. Graduate and professional schools—even public ones—can be even more expensive. You will probably want to look for sources of aid, such as scholarships, fellowships or loans. International students cannot receive financial aid from sources supported by the U.S. government. That means that most schools, having few non-federal alternatives, cannot offer much financial aid directly to international students. Your school may, however, be able to help you locate other sources of aid.

You can do some advance research of your own at http://www.nafsa.org/students/funding.html (the National Association of Foreign Student Advisors), http://www.isoa.org (the International Student Organization) or www.iie.org (the Institute for International Education).

Beware of services that offer to research scholarships for you at a cost. Many of them go to the same resources that are available to you for free—and some commit outright criminal frauds. For more information on the scams, see the U.S. Federal Trade Commission's website at http://www.ftc.gov.

⚠ Find out how much money you can take out of your country. Some countries place a limit on the amount of money that you can take outside the country. The U.S. government is aware of these restrictions and will not grant you a visa if they don't think you'll be able to transfer sufficient funds to pay for your education. Talk to other foreign students or a lawyer in your home country to see whether there is a way to legally get around this.

D. Is There Another Visa That Might Suit You Better?

If you don't quite fit the eligibility criteria for a tourist or student visa, there might be another visa that would be appropriate. There are special visas for religious workers, temporary workers, exchange program participants and others. Unfortunately this book cannot cover all the possibilities, but there are other resources to help you.

EXAMPLE: Atahualpa and his Peruvian wind instrument group are invited to participate in a cultural-exchange program with the United States. At first Atahualpa assumes that a tourist visa will be appropriate. However, because the group will be performing, and will receive some compensation for their performances, a tourist visa will not work. Atahualpa does a little research and discovers that the Q-1 visa has been designed specifically for cultural exchange visitors. He successfully applies for visas for his group.

To begin your research regarding other types of U.S. visas or immigration benefits, see the list below. For more information, see *U.S. Immigration Made Easy*, by Laurence A. Canter & Martha S. Siegel (Nolo), or the INS website at http://www.ins.gov.

Immigrant Visas (for Permanent Resident Status)

Type of Visa or Benefit	Basis for Eligibility
Family Based	
Immediate Relative	Minor unmarried children or spouses of a U.S. citizen; parent of an over-21-year-old U.S. citizen.
First Preference	Unmarried adult child of a U.S. citizen.
Second Preference: 2A	Spouses and unmarried sons and daughters of lawful permanent residents.
Second Preference: 2B	Unmarried sons and daughters, over the age of 21, of lawful permanent residents.
Third Preference	Married sons and daughters of U.S. citizens.
Fourth Preference	Brothers and sisters of U.S. citizens.
Employment Based	
First Preference	Priority workers who have "extraordinary ability" or are "outstanding professors and researchers" in their field. Also certain multinational executives and managers.
Second Preference	"Members of the professions holding advanced degrees" or "aliens of exceptional ability" in their field.
Third Preference	Skilled workers (two years' training or experience), professionals, and "other workers" (capable of performing unskilled, but not temporary or seasonal labor).
Fourth Preference	Special immigrants including ministers, religious workers, former U.S. government employees and others.
Fifth Preference	Investors in job-creating enterprises in the U.S. ($500,000 to $3 million).
Other Benefits or Remedies	
Refugees and Political Asylees	People who fear persecution in their home country based on their race, religion, nationality, political opinion or membership in a particular social group. Refugees are processed overseas, asylees within the United States.

Immigrant Visas (for Permanent Resident Status) (continued)

Type of Visa or Benefit	Basis for Eligibility

Other Benefits or Remedies (continued)

"NACARA" for Nicaraguans and Cubans	An amnesty-like program for Nicaraguans and Cubans who entered the United States before December 1, 1995.
"NACARA" Suspension of Deportation	For Salvadorans, Guatemalans and nationals of several former Soviet and Eastern European countries who entered the United States before 1990 (exact date varies by country) and who applied for asylum, "ABC" or Temporary Protected Status by certain dates; they can apply for "suspension of deportation," described below.
Suspension of Deportation	A remedy normally only available to persons placed in deportation proceedings before April 1, 1997. If the person can prove that they have lived in the United States for seven continuous years, had good moral character and that the person's deportation would cause extreme hardship to themselves or their spouse, parent or children who are U.S. citizens or permanent residents, a judge can grant them permanent residency.
Cancellation of Removal	A remedy only available to persons in removal proceedings. If the person can prove that they have lived in the United States for ten continuous years, have good moral character, haven't been convicted of certain crimes and that their deportation would cause exceptional and extreme hardship to their lawful permanent resident or U.S. citizen spouse, child or parent, then a judge may approve them for permanent residency.
"VAWA" Cancellation of Removal	For spouses and children of U.S. citizens and permanent residents who have been battered or been victims of extreme cruelty. If such persons can prove that they not only fall into this category but have lived continuously in the United States for three years, have been of good moral character and not committed certain crimes and that their removal would cause extreme hardship to them, their child or (if the applicant is a child), their parent, a judge may approve them for permanent residency.
Registry	People who have lived in the United States continuously since January 1, 1972, can apply to adjust status to permanent residence.
Temporary Protected Status	People from certain Congressionally designated countries experiencing war or civil strife; they may apply for a temporary right to stay in the United States until conditions in their home country have improved.

Nonimmigrant Visas

Type of Visa or Benefit	Basis for Eligibility
A-1	Diplomatic employees
A-2	Officials or employees of foreign governments
B-1	Business visitors
B-2	Tourists
C-1 "Transit visa"	For passing through at a U.S. airport or seaport
D-1 "Crewmember"	For people serving on a ship or plane, landing or docking temporarily
E-1	Treaty traders
E-2	Treaty investors
F-1	Students; academic, including at colleges, universities, seminaries, conservatories, academic high schools, other academic institutions, and in language training
G-1	Employees of International Organizations who are representing foreign governments
H-1B	Temporary professionals (for specialty occupations such as doctors, engineers, physical therapists, computer professionals; must have at least a bachelor's degree)
H-2A	Temporary agricultural workers
H-2B	Temporary and seasonal workers
H-3	Trainees
I	Representatives of international media
J-1	Exchange visitors
K-1	Fiancées and fiancés of U.S. citizens.
K-3	After implementation of December 2000 "LIFE" amendments, spouses of U.S. citizens awaiting approval of their visa petition and a green card
L-1	Intracompany transferees
M-1	Vocational students
O-1	People with extraordinary ability in sciences, arts, business, athletics or education, and their support staff
P-1	Entertainers, performers and athletes and their support staff
P-2	Cultural exchange entertainers
P-3	Artists and entertainers presenting culturally unique programs
Q-1	Exchange visitors
R-1	Religious workers
S-1	Witnesses in a criminal investigation
T	Women and children who are in the United States because they are victims of human trafficking
U	Victims of criminal abuse in the United States who are assisting law enforcement authorities
V	Spouses and unmarried sons and daughters (2A) of U.S. lawful permanent residents who have already waited three years for approval of their visa petition or the availability of a green card, and whose visa petition was on file by December 21, 2000

The Right Way to Prepare, Collect and Manage the Paperwork

As you've probably figured out by now, you're going to have to collect and keep track of a lot of paperwork. This chapter will give you instructions on how to keep the paperwork organized and how to make sure that all documents are of a type and quality that the INS and consulates will accept (Sections A and B). We also tell you how to locate and translate some of the documents that you'll need to support certain applications (Section C). And finally, Section D explains how to protect your application from INS losses before you mail it. (If you're currently overseas, you don't have to worry about this section yet—but will want to return to it if, during your visit to the United States, you need to apply for an extension or other benefit.)

A. Getting Organized

Start by setting up a good system to keep track of all the forms and documents that you'll need during your application process. This will minimize the chance that you'll find yourself in front of an impatient government official, desperately going through piles of stuff looking for a vital slip of paper he's asked to see. Take our word for it, in order to bring order to the many documents that will constitute your application, you'll need a lot more than one jumbo file folder.

We suggest using manila file folders and putting them in a box or drawer (or use a series of large envelopes or an accordion file). Label these according to what they contain. For example, you might have one file for the INS or consular forms that you've prepared, another for proof of your reasons to return to your home country and another for proof of financial capacity. If you're applying for a student visa or status, you'll also want folders for your proof of academic credentials and all correspondence or materials from your school.

You should also keep a separate file for correspondence from the INS or consulate. Include in this file your handwritten notes on any phone conversations you've had with INS or consular personnel. Don't forget to write the date on your notes, so you can refer to them later in further correspondence.

How Nightmarish Can It Get?

Maybe you'll turn in your application and everything will go like clockwork: INS and consular files all in order, approval received on time. Educating yourself about the process and preparing everything carefully certainly improves your chances. But we wouldn't be doing our job if we didn't warn you about how the government bureaucracy can chew up and spit out even the best-prepared application.

Every immigration lawyer has his or her favorite horror stories. For instance, consider the client whose visa petitions were lost by the INS—after many months, the lawyer filed new petitions and cancelled the checks that went with the lost ones. But the INS then tried to cash the "lost" checks and to collect from the client for the bank charges when the checks bounced.

We've also heard about the woman who waited over six months for the INS to approve her work permit—only to receive a work permit with someone else's name and photo. By the time the mistake got straightened out, the work permit had expired and the INS forced her to apply—and pay again—for a new one.

And let's not forget the woman who was almost denied entry because the INS refused to renew her Refugee Travel Document—on the grounds that she hadn't provided a valid address in the application. She had provided the address—the same one that the INS had been using to correspond with her for years.

What can you do about such absurd and Orwellian horrors? Mostly just know in advance that they may happen to you, leave time to deal with them and keep copies of everything.

Finally, make a folder for old drafts and copies. Instead of throwing anything out, move unneeded paperwork to this folder until the process is over.

As you're preparing your forms and documents, attach our Checklists to the outside of each folder or envelope and check the boxes off as the items have been completed and put inside. When you're finished filling a folder or envelope, take out some of the old drafts or items you've decided not to use and move them to the Old Drafts/Copies folder, so as not to clutter up the materials you'll take to your interview. Carefully write "final copy, mailed xx/xx/20xx" (you fill in the date) on the top of the copy of any application or petition you turn in to the INS or consulate.

If you are mailing a large collection of forms and documents to the INS or consulate, a cover letter stating what application you're filing and listing everything included—or a simple list of the documents attached to the top of the stack—can be helpful. Our checklists will help you organize this cover letter or list. If you really want to impress the person at the other end, number the items on your list and attach corresponding number tabs to the different documents.

⚠️ Watch for changes in rules and fees. Immigration laws, policies, and procedures change regularly. In particular, the INS is expected to raise many of its application fees in January of 2002. Before you submit anything, check the INS website at http://www.ins.gov and the Legal Updates section of Nolo's website at http://www.nolo.com.

B. How to Prepare INS and Consular Forms

Now, let's do our best to make sure the government doesn't return your forms for technical reasons. Follow these instructions for printing and filling out the forms.

1. How to Print the Forms

There's not an INS or consular application that doesn't involve forms, and usually a combination of several of them. Most of the forms you'll need are provided as tear-outs in the Appendix to this book. When photocopying them or downloading additional copies from government websites, here are some things to keep in mind.

a. Color and Orientation

Certain of the forms are traditionally printed on colored paper, and sometimes there's a different color for multiple copies of the same form. For forms that are two-sided, the backs are usually meant to be printed upside down. The INS and consulates keep these forms in file folders clipped at the top, and they like to be able to lift the page from the bottom and have the back of it look right-side-up (a form like this is said to run "head to foot"). Try this yourself and it will make sense. A few forms might need to be printed "head to head," the more traditional way one sees things printed (as in this book).

b. Easing of Printing Restrictions

The INS and consulates used to be very choosy about how they wanted their forms printed out or copied. If you didn't use a form provided directly by the government, you were expected to reproduce it on paper the exact color as the original, with the same orientation from front to back. If you printed the form out wrong, the INS or consulate would send it back to you.

Recently, however, the government said that it will ease up on these printing requirements, recognizing the difficulty it causes people who download forms from the government's websites. In theory, now you don't have to worry about what color paper to use, or the front-to-back orientation of two-sided forms. Unfortunately, some government bureaucrats still reject forms that don't match their idea of the correct way to print them. Also, since they're accustomed to the colored forms, they have an easier time working with files in which they can locate certain forms by color. For these reasons, our instructions for each form advise you how to print it as closely as possible to the original forms.

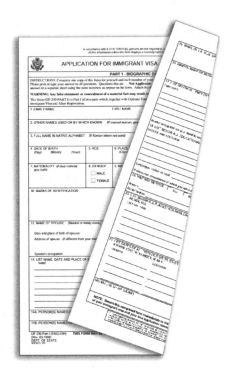

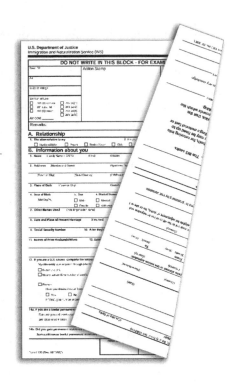

Example of a Head to Head Form

Example of a Head to Foot Form

c. Getting Forms Straight From the Source

If printing the forms yourself seems like too much trouble and you want to get the INS forms directly from them, the telephone order number is 800-870-3676. It usually takes a few weeks for the forms to arrive by mail. To download INS forms from their website, go to http://www.ins.gov. Consular forms can be obtained directly from the particular consulate only. Some consulates are starting to put their forms online—check the consulate's website via the State Department's website at http://www.state.gov (under Travel and Living Abroad, click on More, then under Other Information click on U.S. Embassy and Consulate Websites).

2. Form Names, Numbers and Revision Dates

The government tends not to refer to its forms by their name or title, but instead by the tiny numbers in the lower left or right corner. For example, if you look at the first form in Appendix D, you'll see "Optional Form 156" at the bottom left. Because the INS and consulates use these numbers, we usually do, too.

The government also puts the date of the form's last revision at the bottom of the first page. Again, look at Form OF-156—you'll see "10-2000" just below "Optional Form 156." The forms provided in this book were up-to-date when the book went to print, but you should check for subsequent form revisions—when a form is revised, the INS and State Department sometimes refuse to accept the old versions.

In most cases, you can check for revisions by going to the INS website at http://www.ins.gov. Click on the link for "INS Forms, Fees and Fingerprints," then the link for "Forms and Fees." Scroll down until you find the "Forms, Fees and Filing Locations Chart." Click on the number of the relevant form. The instructions may tell you whether the form has been revised and whether or for how long the old version is being accepted. If not, click on the link to the form's pdf file, which will show you a picture of the actual form. Look at the bottom for the revision date. If it's more recent than the one in this book, print it out yourself or call the INS forms line for a copy: 800-870-3676.

For non-INS forms, your best bet is to get the most recent form directly from your local U.S. consulate. Some, but not many forms can be accessed through the State Department's site at http://www.travel.state.gov.

3. Instructions That Come With the Forms

The government usually provides instructions with each form. Save yourself a little postage and don't send the instruction pages back to them if you're mailing an application. They want only the part of the form you fill in. Sadly, the instructions are often hard to understand (that's why we wrote this book) and at times they even contain information that is wrong or misleading (which we point out whenever possible).

4. Filing Fees

Many of the immigration forms require you to pay a fee in order to file them. (No, you can't get your money back if your application is not approved.) Don't go by the fees listed on the form instructions; they're often out of date. The current fees are supplied in this book. You must, however, double-check that these have not changed—the INS implements fee increases with alarming regularity. Visit the INS website at http://www.ins.gov or call their information line at 800-375-5283. If you're already at the stage of working with an overseas consulate, contact the consulate directly regarding fee issues.

5. Typing or Ink?

This isn't the time to express your individuality with purple ink. Fill in all immigration forms using a typewriter or, if you must prepare them by hand, use black ink.

6. Inapplicable Questions

If a question just doesn't fit your situation, write "N/A" (not applicable) rather than leaving the space blank. But if you're not sure how or whether to answer a question, seek skilled legal help.

7. Tell the Truth

It may seem so easy to lie on a written form—to hide a ground of inadmissibility or avoid questions about previous visits to the United States, for example. But lying to the government can get you in bigger trouble than the problem you are lying about. And you've never seen anyone angrier than an INS or State Department official who discovers that you've lied to them.

If you feel you just can't complete the form without hiding a certain piece of information—or you really don't know how to answer or explain a key question—see a lawyer. The lawyer may be able to show you how to be truthful in a way that doesn't risk having your application denied.

8. What's Your Name?

The easiest thing on a form should be filling out your name, right? Not in this bureaucratic morass. The INS will want not only your current name, but on certain of its forms, "other names used." Here are some important things to get straight before you start writing your name(s) in the forms:

- **Married name.** If you're married and have changed your last name as part of your marriage, use your married name even if the marriage recently took place.
- **Current name.** When your current name is requested, it is best to insert the name you currently use for legal purposes. This will normally be the name on your bank account, driver's license or passport. If you've always gone by a nickname (for example, your name is Richard but you always use the common nickname "Dick"), it's okay to fill in the appli-

cation as "Dick" as long as you list "Richard" where the form asks for other names used. This will avoid confusion when the INS compares your application form with the accompanying documents (your employer, for example, will probably write a letter saying "Dick worked here . . ."). But there's no way to avoid a little confusion, since your birth certificate will still say Richard.

- **Legal name changes.** If you've done a court-sanctioned name change, include a copy of the court order, to help dispel some of the inevitable confusion. If you have changed your name without a court order (by simply beginning to use a different name and using it consistently, which is legal in many states) and you use your changed name for all legal purposes, list it as your current name.
- **Other names.** The category for "other names used" could include nicknames. The INS will want to know about nicknames that might have made their way onto your various legal documents (or criminal record). You should also include names by which you have been commonly known, especially as an adult. However, "pet" names, (like being called "Little One" by your parents) need not be included. Nor should unwanted childhood nicknames.
- **Previous married names.** If you have been married previously, don't forget to list your name from that marriage in any boxes requesting other names used.

9. Be Consistent

As you might have guessed from the previous section, it's important not to cause confusion when filling out the forms. At worst, not getting your facts straight can cause the person reviewing your application to think you cannot be believed. If, for example, you live with your parents but sometimes use a friend's address to receive mail, make up your mind which address to use and then stick to it.

C. How to Obtain Needed Documents

It would be nice if forms were the only paperwork you had to worry about—but no, there are documents, too. At a minimum, you are going to need an unexpired passport from your own country (either to travel to the United States or to hold a stamp showing your change of status). If you will be bringing a spouse and children along, you will need your marriage and birth certificates to show the family relationship.

Records should be obtained from official, government sources wherever possible. The sources that the INS and State Department consider acceptable are listed in the State Department's *Foreign Affairs Manual* (FAM), accessible at http://www.foia.state.gov/fam/fam.asp. U.S. law libraries may also be able to locate copies of the FAM for you. Volume 9, Appendix C, of the FAM tells you where to go to get the documents you'll need—for example, the place to obtain vital documents in Lithuania is called the Marriage Palace. If you are overseas and do not have Web access, talk to your local U.S. consulate about what form of record will be acceptable, particularly if you need to document a marriage, birth or other event for which your government can or will not issue you a certificate.

1. Translate Non-English Documents

If the documents you are submitting are in a language other than English, you will need to submit both a copy of the original document and a certified, word-for-word translation (summaries are not acceptable). Translation is always necessary if you're submitting the document to a U.S. INS office. Consulates can often deal with documents that are in the language of that country (their instructions will usually tell you if they can't).

There is no need to spend big bucks to obtain certified translations. Any trustworthy friend who is fluent in English and the language of the document can do the certified translation. The translator should simply type out the translated text, then add at the bottom:

I certify that I am competent to translate from _[the language of the document]_ to English and that the above is a correct and true translation to the best of my knowledge and belief.

Signed, _____ _[translator's full name]_ _____

Date: _____

If you prefer, you can hire a professional translator, who should also add the same certification at the bottom of the translation.

2. Substitutions for Unavailable Documents

If you cannot obtain a needed document, the INS may accept another type of evidence. They are more likely to accept a substitute where you can show that the original is unavailable because of something beyond your control, such the takeover of your native country by a hostile power that won't allow you access rather than your inability to locate the appropriate vital records office. For example, if your child's birth certificate was destroyed in a fire and you need to prove that you are his parent, the INS may accept school records kept by school officials. If you substitute a new form of evidence for a missing document, you should also, if possible, include a statement from the civil authorities ex-plaining why the original document is unavailable.

3. Homemade Documents

One form of substitute document that you may need to use is a sworn declaration. For example, you might need to ask a friend or family member to prepare one affirming your child's date and place of birth. If so, emphasize to the person that when it comes to convincing an immigration official to accept his or her word in place of an official document, fancy legal language is not as important as detailed facts.

For example, someone could write, "I swear that Francois was born in Paris in 1962 to Mr. and Mrs. Marti." But it would be much more compelling for him

to write, "I swear that I am Francois's older brother. I remember the morning that my mother brought him home from the hospital in 1962 (I was then ten years old). We grew up together in our parents' home (Mr. and Mrs. Xavier Marti) in Paris."

The full declaration should be longer and contain more details than the example above. The more details that are offered, the more likely the INS or consulate is to accept the declaration as the truth. To start the declaration, the writer should state his or her complete name, address and country of citizenship. At the bottom of the declaration, the person should write:

I swear, under penalty of perjury, that the foregoing is true and correct to the best of my knowledge.

Signed, _____

Date: _____

If preparing sworn declarations seems like too much to accomplish, you could hire a lawyer for this task only. Below is a sample of a full sworn declaration, written to prove that an applicant is actually married. Remember, when writing your own declaration, tailor it to your situation—don't follow the wording of the sample too closely.

Don't confuse a declaration with an affidavit. An affidavit is very similar—a written statement that the author dates and signs—but it has one additional feature. Affidavits are notarized, which means that they are signed in front of someone who is autho-rized by the government to attest to, or certify, the authenticity of signatures. When you bring a decla-ration to a notary, that person will ask for identifica-tion, such as your passport or driver's license, to make sure that you are the person whose signature is called for on the declaration. You sign the declaration in the presence of the notary, who makes a note of this in his or her notary book. The notary also places a stamp, or seal, on your document. As you can see, affidavits are more formal and more trouble than simple declarations. An affidavit is not required for substitute documents like the ones we're describ-ing now—but if you want to make the document look more official and you know where to find a notary, you might want to take the extra trouble. If an immigration process described in this book requires an affidavit, we'll alert you.

Sample Sworn Declaration

Affidavit in Support of Application of Guofeng Zheng

I, Shaoling Liu, hereby say and declare as follows:

1. I am a U.S. permanent resident, residing at 222 Rhododendron Drive, Seattle, WA 98111. My telephone number is 206-555-1212. I have been living in the United States since January 2, 1997.

2. I am originally from Mainland China, where I grew up in the same town (called Dahuo, in Suzhou province) as Guofeng Zheng.

3. I knew Guofeng's first wife, Meihua. I attended their wedding, and had dinner at their home several times. I also remember when Meihua fell ill with cancer. She was sick for many months before passing away on October 31, 1996.

4. I received the news of Meihua's death a few days later, in early November of 1996. I knew the doctor who had treated her, and he was very sad that his treatments had failed. I also attended Meihua's funeral on November 7th. Her ashes are buried in the local cemetery.

5. I am also aware that the municipal records office, where all deaths are recorded, burnt down in the year 2000. I myself had difficulty with this, when I tried to get a copy of my mother's birth certificate last year.

I swear, under penalty of perjury, that the foregoing is true and correct to the best of my knowledge.

Signed: *Shaoling Liu*

Date: _____

---

4. Make Sure All Documents Have Your Name on Them

Documents seem to have a way of flying out of people's immigration files. Look at every document that you send in and ask yourself, "If this were found on the floor of a crowded INS warehouse, would they know whose file to return it to?" At a minimum, everything you send in should have your name on it. If it's not already in the text of the document, write or type in one corner "Application of *[your name]*." If adding this to the front of the document is not appropriate, write it on the back. It's also very helpful to add your date of birth and any identification numbers assigned to you by the INS—an A-number or student admission number, for example.

D. Before You Submit the Application

The INS is reported to have lost a total of 80,000 applications in the year 1998, so it's best not to trust to luck when you turn your precious application over to them. There are four rules to remember before you submit anything to an INS, consulate or other government office:

1. Make copies.
2. If mailing your applications, use a traceable method.
3. If submitting applications in person, get receipts or date stamps.
4. Don't give them anything that you can't replace.

We'll explain the reasons for these maxims—and how to follow them.

1. Make Complete Copies

When you've at last finished preparing an immigration application, your first instinct will be to seal it in an envelope, pop it in the mail and forget about it for a while. If you don't make a copy of the application first, you could waste all of your hard work.

Find a photocopy machine and make copies of every page of every application, as well as the photos, documents, checks and money orders. This will help you recreate these pages and items if they're lost in the mail or in the overstuffed files of some government office. It may also help convince the INS or consulate to take another look for the lost items.

Always make photocopies on one-sided, 8½- by 11-inch paper. Some applicants have been known to try to create exact copies of small documents by making the copy on 8½- by 11-inch paper but then cutting the image out—creating, for example, a tiny photocopied identity card. The government doesn't appreciate these mini-copies, which it will have to recopy onto a full-size sheet of paper. By the same token, 8½- by 14-inch paper (or larger) doesn't fit well into the government's files—use a photocopy machine that will reduce your document image to 8½ by 11, if possible.

2. Mail by a Traceable Method

In any government agency, things get lost. It's not uncommon for applications to be misplaced when they first arrive in the INS mail rooms. If this happens to your application, you'll need to prove that you mailed it in the first place.

If you are mailing from within the United States, it's best to go to the Post Office and use certified mail with a return receipt for all your applications or correspondence with the INS or consulates. When you request a return receipt, you will prepare a little postcard that is attached to your envelope and will be signed by the person at the INS or consulate who physically receives your envelope. The postcard will be mailed to you, which will be your proof that the envelope was received. You can use this postcard to convince the INS or consulate to look for the application if it gets misplaced.

If you're mailing something from overseas, you'll have to find out the most reliable method. Unfortunately, courier services often don't work because they can't deliver to a post office box, and many INS addresses (in particular those of the Service Centers)

are at post office boxes. You'll have to use regular mail if mailing to a P.O. box.

3. Get Proof When You Submit in Person

A few applications can be turned in personally to the INS or consulate. If you'll be going home again afterwards to await their decision, make sure you can prove you filed the application in the first place, in case it's lost.

If you pay a filing fee, you'll normally be given a fee receipt. This is excellent proof that you filed, so don't just stuff it into the bottom of your bag with the grocery receipts. If you aren't paying any fees, bring your personal copy of your application along and ask the person who accepts the original to "date stamp" your copy. Most offices have these stamps, which show the name of their office and the date. If the office you're dealing with doesn't have a date stamp, write down the name of the person to whom you handed the document, or better yet, get her to hand-write her name and the date on your copy.

Las Vegas
Nevada

4. If You Want It Back, Don't Send It

Many INS forms require that certain documents be attached (paper-clipping them to the form is fine). Whatever you do, *don't send originals* to the INS or consulate (with the occasional exception of your I-94 card, discussed below).

You may come across INS forms that say that you are required to send original documents such as birth or marriage certificates. This information is often wrong or out-of-date. People who send originals run a serious risk of losing them. Instead, simply photocopy any document (as long as the original is the official version), and send the copy to the INS or consulate. The INS or consular officer will have a chance to view the originals when you bring them to your interview. (Of course, if they make a special request that you mail them the original, you'll want to comply—but make copies for yourself first!) It's best to add the following text, right on the front of the copy, if there's room:

Copies of documents submitted are exact photocopies of unaltered original documents and I understand that I may be required to submit original documents to an Immigration or Consular official at a later date.

Signature: _____

Typed or Printed Name: _____

Date: _____

The one partial exception to the never-send-originals rule is your I-94 card (the little white card you'll get at the U.S. border showing how long you can stay). If you apply for an extension of your stay or for certain other benefits, the INS will tell you to send an original I-94. They don't always need the original—our instructions try to give you the latest word on whether you really need to part with it. On the other hand, you probably won't need the original yourself—so if you want to make sure your application goes quickly and smoothly, you're better off sending it. Then again, if you send a copy and that's not enough for the INS, they can always send a follow-up request for the original. ■

Applying for a Tourist Visa From Overseas

The process of applying for a B-2 or tourist visa is fairly straightforward. You fill out a single form, assemble some supporting documents, present it and your passport to the U.S. government and receive your answer. Your local U.S. consulate can usually make the decision the day you present your application. If you are approved, the consulate will stamp your passport with a U.S. visa, and you will be on your way.

Don't let the simplicity of the application process fool you, however. Unless you have carefully thought out how you will prepare and present your application, your visa could be denied faster than you can say "official discretion." And it's worth getting it right the first time—once you have your visa, it's likely to be good for many entries to the United States over a period of years (a "multiple entry" visa).

Below, we give you line-by-line instructions on filling out the application form, as well as detailed information on what documents might be most convincing for you to show. At the end of this chapter is a Checklist covering all the forms and documents. Use the Checklist to help you organize and complete the application process.

A. Contact Your Local U.S. Consulate

You will be applying for your tourist visa at a U.S. embassy or consulate. Start by finding out where the nearest one is. Even if you live in a country other than your country of citizenship, look for a consulate in the country where you live. There is probably an embassy in your country's capital city and maybe smaller consulates in other major cities. You can locate consulates by checking the U.S. State Department website, http://www.state.gov, or by calling the State Department in Washington, D.C., at 202-663-1225. If the country where you live has no U.S. consulate, there will most likely be a consulate in an adjoining country that has been chosen by the State Department to handle visa requests from your country.

Although you can, in theory, apply for your tourist visa at any consulate in the world, in reality consulates are reluctant to accept applications from stray travelers. If you are in this predicament, go ahead and try to apply to the consulate in the country where you are. Be prepared for questions about why you could not go to your home country's U.S. consulate. You will not be hurt by the fact that you were turned down for a visa if the only reason for the refusal was that you went to the wrong consulate.

Ask the consulate about their requirements and procedures for the visa application. For example, you'll want to know whether you need an appointment or can just walk your application in to the consulate. Find out how soon you will get an answer (it's often within one day, but don't count on this). The State Department warns that the consulates tend to be especially busy with visa applications during the months of June, July and August. The consulate may also have made some minor additions to the application procedures that we describe in this chapter. Some consulates have websites containing a good deal of information, which you can access via the State Department's Web page at http://travel.state.gov/links.html.

B. The Application Form

Only one government form is required for your tourist visa application, called State Department Form OF-156, pictured below. The consulate uses Form OF-156 to gather basic biographical information about you, find out why you're traveling and investigate reasons that you might not follow through on your promises to return home afterward.

The standard version of Form OF-156 is provided as a tear-out in the Appendix to this book. To be safe, use the version that you get from the consulate—it may be slightly different. Our instructions should be usable on any version you obtain from the consulate, but refer to the OF-156 version in this book to make sure the consulate hasn't renumbered the questions.

When you've got a copy of Form OF-156 in hand, follow these line-by-line instructions for filling it out.

Questions 1 through 3: Mostly self-explanatory. In question 3, "maiden" name means the name a woman uses before she is married (if she changed it after marriage).

Questions 4 through 7: Self-explanatory.

Question 8: Mostly self-explanatory, but note that the date that your passport expires must be six months beyond the date when your visa is approved.

Questions 9 through 13: Self-explanatory.

Question 14: For this question, you enter only the names of close family members such as your spouse and children who will be traveling with you. However, as the form indicates, your family members must prepare their own tourist visa applications. All of you will be interviewed at the same time.

Question 15: This question asks first whether you have ever applied for a U.S. nonimmigrant visa. Nonimmigrant visas include not only tourist visas, but any other visas for temporary stays in the United States, such as student, transit or temporary work visas. You must tell the truth here. If you have previously applied for a visa, the consulate will check your files. It will look to see whether you lied or used fraud in that previous application and if you got a visa, whether there is a record of your violating its terms. If you have any record of fraud or other violations, this will naturally make the consulate less likely to approve this present tourist visa application.

Question 15 goes on to ask whether you have previously applied for any immigrant visa (an immigrant visa is otherwise known as permanent residence or a green card). For example, if you had married a U.S. citizen or received a job offer from a U.S. employer and then applied for a green card, you would need to say yes to this question. (If your family member or employer has simply filed a visa petition on your behalf, but you haven't yet taken the next step and applied for a visa, you don't have to answer yes—but be prepared for the consular officer to ask you about this possibility in your interview.) The cautions in the previous paragraph apply here too. If you are still waiting for an immigrant visa (U.S. permanent residence), your tourist visa may be denied. That is because the consulate will assume that your real reason in requesting a tourist visa is not to be a tourist, but

to complete the green card application process while living in the United States. You will have to work extra hard to convince the consulate that you will return home after your visit to continue your wait.

Question 16: This asks whether you have ever had a visa cancelled. The INS or State Department cancels a visa when they discover that the holder has violated the terms of the visa, such as by staying in the United States too long or working when they are not allowed to. If you have had a visa cancelled, you will have a tough time getting a tourist visa (or any other visa) approved.

Question 17: You must answer no to this question about whether you plan to work in the United States. If your answer is yes, you do not meet the basic requirements for a visa—tourists are not allowed to come to the United States with plans to work.

Question 18: If you plan to study in the United States, the class will need to be shorter than the maximum one year that a tourist visa can provide. Also, talk to the class organizers and the U.S. consulate in advance to make sure that it's not the type of class that requires you to obtain a student visa. See Chapter 1 for more on using a tourist visa for short or recreational study courses.

Question 19: Your "present occupation" means your job or other primary daily activity. Even if you don't have a regular 9:00 to 5:00 job, try to list something here (like "house husband," "self-employed contractor" or "business owner")—this will help show that you have some activity that will pull you back home when your visit to the United States is over.

Question 20: This asks for the name of the person who has agreed to support you financially while you're in the United States. If someone has agreed to support you, their name should also be on separate documents that you'll include with your application, as covered in Section C, below. If you're self-supporting, you can enter "N/A" here.

Question 21: The address at which you will stay in the United States does not have to cover your entire trip. It can be a hotel, if you will be staying at one.

Question 22: The "purpose of your trip" can be simply "pleasure trip," but it may help to state something more specific, such as "backpack in the Catskill mountains," "attend cousin's wedding" or "take my children to Disneyland." This will help show your intent to stay for a limited time.

Questions 23 through 24: Self-explanatory. Remember, however, that you are probably not likely to be allowed to stay for more than six months without a specific and convincing reason for needing this much time.

Question 25: If you answer yes here, indicating that you have been in the United States before, the consulate will look to see whether you left on time. If you did, this will actually improve your chances, since it shows that you honored the requirement to return home. However, if the consulate sees that you didn't leave when you were supposed to at the end of a prior trip, you may have difficulty getting a visa now. Similarly, if the consulate sees that you have been stringing together visas in order to spend much or all of your time in the United States, it may doubt your plans to stay temporarily and deny the visa. The consulate may also check the records to see whether you committed any violations of the rules covering your past visas.

Question 26: If your answer is "yes" to any of these questions, the consulate will conclude that you want to immigrate to the United States and will be less likely to approve your tourist visa. Be prepared with a good reason for why you are no longer interested in immigrating to the United States—and back your reason up with documentary evidence of any change in circumstances that you claim.

Question 27: All of the people on this list are relatives who could file a visa petition sponsoring you for U.S. permanent residence, provided they themselves are U.S. citizens or lawful permanent residents. If you have any of the types of relatives on this list living in the United States, the consulate will take a hard look to see whether you're hoping to immigrate through one of them. Don't worry—having such relatives doesn't mean the consulate will automatically deny your tourist visa. After all,

it makes sense that you would want to visit close family members in the United States. But showing that you have specific plans to return to your country after your visit will be particularly important in this set of circumstances.

Question 28: The consulate may use this information on countries where you have lived to conduct a security check on you. They can ask the governments of these countries to check whether you have a police record, although it's not clear that they always do.

Question 29: These questions reflect the grounds of inadmissibility (discussed in Chapter 2). Checking a "yes" box will guarantee that you do not receive a tourist visa. In a few cases, however, waivers (legal forgiveness) or other cures may be available. Consult an experienced immigration lawyer if you need to ask for a waiver.

C. Documents You'll Need

Anyone can fill out a form—but what will set you apart from the thousands of other people applying for tourist visas is the quality of your supporting documentary evidence. Along with the form itself, you'll need to provide copies of your official and personal papers, which will give the consulate a clear, strong idea of who you are, what your plans are and why they can trust you with a visa into the United States.

In general, use the most official-sounding documents or letters that you can find. Letters you gather from family and friends can be helpful in combination with other documents, but consular officers know that your family and friends are on your side. Therefore, the officer will be more impressed by records that were not created by your supporters just to get you a visa. Medical or school records and letters from people with a professional reputation, like doctors, employers and teachers, will be the most convincing. Unless the consulate specifically tells you that it will review non-English documents, don't forget to obtain translations, word-for-word, of any documents that are not in English.

You'll need to assemble the following:

Form OF-156, Nonimmigrant Visa Application—Page 1

PLEASE TYPE OR PRINT YOUR ANSWERS IN THE SPACE PROVIDED BELOW EACH ITEM.

1. SURNAMES OR FAMILY NAMES (Exactly as in Passport)

2. FIRST NAME AND MIDDLE NAME (Exactly as in Passport)

3. OTHER NAMES (Maiden, Religious, Professional, Aliases)

4. DATE OF BIRTH (mm-dd-yyyy)

8. PASSPORT NUMBER

5. PLACE OF BIRTH
City, Province   Country

DATE PASSPORT ISSUED
(mm-dd-yyyy)

6. NATIONALITY

7. SEX
[ ] MALE
[ ] FEMALE

DATE PASSPORT EXPIRES
(mm-dd-yyyy)

9. HOME ADDRESS (Include apartment no., street, city, province, and postal zone)

10. NAME AND STREET ADDRESS OF PRESENT EMPLOYER OR SCHOOL
(Postal box number unacceptable)

11. HOME TELEPHONE NO.

12. BUSINESS TELEPHONE NO.

13. MARITAL STATUS
[ ] Married [ ] Single [ ] Widowed [ ] Divorced [ ] Separated
If married, give name and nationality of spouse

14. NAMES AND RELATIONSHIPS OF PERSONS TRAVELING WITH YOU
(NOTE: A separate application must be made for a visa for each traveler, regardless of age.)

15. HAVE YOU EVER APPLIED FOR A U.S. NONIMMIGRANT VISA?
[ ] NO [ ] YES
HAVE YOU EVER APPLIED FOR A U.S. IMMIGRANT VISA?
[ ] NO [ ] YES
WHERE? _____
WHEN? _____
VISA WAS ISSUED [ ]   VISA WAS REFUSED [ ]

16. HAS YOUR U.S. VISA EVER BEEN CANCELED?
[ ] NO [ ] YES
WHERE? _____
WHEN? _____
BY WHOM? _____

17. Bearers of visitor visas may generally not work or study in the U.S.
DO YOU INTEND TO WORK IN THE U.S.?   [ ] NO [ ] YES
If YES, explain.

18. DO YOU INTEND TO STUDY IN THE U.S.?   [ ] NO [ ] YES
If YES, write name and address of school as it appears on Form I-20.

DO NOT WRITE IN THIS SPACE

B-1/B-2 MAX   B-1 MAX   B-2 MAX

OTHER_____ MAX
Visa Classification

MULT OR _____
Number Applications

MONTHS_____
Validity

L.O. CHECKED

ON_____ BY _____

ISSUED/REFUSED

ON_____ BY _____

UNDER SEC.   214(b)   221(g)

OTHER: _____ INA

REFUSAL REVIEWED BY _____

19. PRESENT OCCUPATION (If retired, state past occupation)

20. WHO WILL FURNISH FINANCIAL SUPPORT, INCLUDING TICKETS?

21. AT WHAT ADDRESS WILL YOU STAY IN THE U.S.A.?

22. WHAT IS THE PURPOSE OF YOUR TRIP?

23. WHEN DO YOU INTEND TO ARRIVE IN THE U.S.A.?

24. HOW LONG DO YOU PLAN TO STAY IN THE U.S.A.?

25. HAVE YOU EVER BEEN IN THE U.S.A.?
[ ] NO [ ] YES
WHEN? _____
FOR HOW LONG? _____

NONIMMIGRANT VISA APPLICATION

COMPLETE ALL QUESTI...
REVERSE OF F...

OPTIONAL FORM 156   PAGE 1   50156-108   NS...
10-2000   PREVIOUS EDITIONS OBSOLETE
U.S. Department of State

Additional pages not shown.

- a passport valid for travel to the United States, with an expiration date at least six months beyond the date you plan to enter the United States
- two photographs, 1½ inches square (37 x 37 mm), showing your full face, without head covering, against a light background
- application fee (currently $45)
- documents showing the purpose of your trip (see subsection 1 below)
- documents showing your plan to remain in the United States for a limited time period (see subsection 2 below)
- documents showing that you have a residence in your home country and other binding ties that will draw you back (see subsection 3 below)
- documentation showing that you will be able to support yourself financially while you are in the United States (see subsection 4 below).

After you've reviewed the individual subsections on providing these documents, move on to subsection 5, where we explain how to pull all the documents together. There are examples and a sample worksheet that you can copy for your use.

1. Showing Your Purpose in Traveling

You'll need to assemble documents that will answer the question "Why do you want to visit the United States?" You might have a specific purpose, such as a conference or event, or you might simply wish to see the sights. A combination of purposes is fine, too—such as going to a wedding and then traveling to other cities afterward. No matter what your plans, gather documents to demonstrate that they are serious ones, not just empty talk intended to get you a visa. You'll also need to show that the purpose of your trip matches the type of visa—in other words, your plans must be entirely for pleasure (or medical treatment), not for business or an effort to stay in the United States permanently. Examples of documents to show your purpose might include:

- an invitation to an event, such as a printed wedding invitation

- a detailed travel itinerary, showing where you'll visit, what hotels you'll stay in and how you'll get around, such as the kind prepared by a travel agent
- an appointment with a doctor, evidenced by an appointment slip or letter
- registration for a conference, as shown by your ticket to the event or your cancelled check, or
- a whirlwind tour of the United States, as evidenced by your "See the U.S." bus ticket that will take you anywhere during a limited time.

2. Showing Your Plans to Stay for a Limited Time

Think of this category as answering the question, "How much time will you need to accomplish the purpose of your visit?" Every well-thought-out plan should have an ending, and you'll need to demonstrate that yours does too. One of the best forms of evidence is a two-way plane or other ticket to and from the United States—in fact some consulates specifically request that you show this.

You could also include items showing that you need or plan to return home by a specific time, such as a letter from your employer saying, "We approve your one month vacation and expect to see you back on June 21, 200x."

If you have made past trips to the United States using a tourist or any other visa and can show that you left the U.S. on time, this will help your application. Check your passport to see if the stamps show the day you left and returned, or look for other evidence of the specific dates, such as copies of plane tickets.

3. Showing Your Residence in and Ties to Your Home Country

Think about finding documents that will answer the question, "Why would you want to return home after your trip?" This question may sound patronizing to you—but the U.S. government makes no secret of believing that this is the best country in the world and that everyone is angling for a way to cross our borders and never leave.

Your home, family and employment situations will probably be the best sources of proof that you have a reason to return. Possible documents might include:

- a copy of your home title or rental agreement showing that you have a stable place to live
- a letter from your employer on company stationery like the "Sample Overseas Employer Letter," below, indicating that you have a job to return to, or, if you're self-employed, a business license or other proof that the business is ongoing
- copies of your most recent pay stubs
- birth or marriage certificates showing your ties to family who live in your home country, or
- letters from family in your home country confirming that they live there and explaining any special reasons that you are likely to return to them.

Sample Overseas Employer Letter

TIVOLI PRODUCTIONS, INC.
TIVOLI ALLE 100
2000 COPENHAGEN

July 11, 200x

To Whom It May Concern:

We have authorized our employee, Dag Moller, three weeks paid vacation leave for this coming August. Mr. Moller is the head of events planning at our office and a valued employee. He is currently in the middle of several important projects that he initiated, including planning an anniversary celebration for this December. We expect him back at work on August 28th, 200x.

Very truly yours,

Karl Follerup

Karl Follerup
Director

⚠ Consulates sometimes call the employer to see if you truly have a job there. Plan ahead for this—warn your employer to expect such a call.

4. Showing Your Ability to Pay for Your Trip

If you have the funds to pay for your trip, this will be the easiest category to document: a copy of your bank statement will be sufficient. If your trip will be funded by some other source, include documentary proof that the money has been promised—and, better, already paid. For example, if you received a scholarship to attend a conference, include copies of the award letter. If you don't have your own source of funds, you'll need to show that someone else is able and willing to support you. See subsection a, below, on how your friends and family can help.

a. How Your Friends and Family Can Help

If they're willing to help, offers of financial support from your friends or family in the United States or abroad can make all the difference in getting you a tourist visa. There are two ways in which friends or family members can support your application: one, by writing a letter describing your visit and/or their financial support for you (see subsection b, below); and two, by signing a form promising financial support (see subsection c, below).

⚠ Having family in the United States may also hurt your chances for a tourist visa. Because close family members in the United States could apply for a green card for you, the consulate may think that your secret plan is to take advantage of this and never leave. This doesn't mean that you should hide your family's existence—just be especially careful in documenting the reasons that you would choose to return. For more information on which family relationships allow for sponsorship, see the Immigration and Green Cards section of Nolo's legal encyclopedia at http://www.nolo.com.

Your U.S. relatives or sponsors may wonder how far their obligation will go after they sign a support letter or Form I-134. If you take a tumble in the Grand Canyon and are in the hospital for six weeks, will they get stuck with the hospital bill? Unfortunately, we can't give you any clear guidance on this. On the one hand, you can reassure your sponsors that their obligation will be more moral than legal—no immigration attorney we know has heard of the INS going after a sponsor for support money. In the unlikely event that your sponsor were to be asked to support you (or, more likely, reimburse the U.S. government for anything it paid out on your behalf), it's probable the INS wouldn't succeed. Most lawyers think that Form I-134 is a flawed legal contract and wouldn't hold up in court. On the other hand, there's no guarantee that the INS would never try to pressure the family of a foreign visitor or take them to court. And, of course, a hospital or other service provider would still have a right to demand that you find a way to pay for services you've used. They couldn't demand that your sponsor pay, but the practical reality is that you might look to your sponsor for help. Since accidents or other medical issues are the most likely source of out-of-control expenses, you might want to look into traveler's insurance to cover this risk.

b. The Support Letter

The easiest way for your friends or family to demonstrate their willingness to fund your trip is to write a letter that says so. (If your family or friends prefer to use a form, they may do so—see subsection c, below.) The letter should discuss the purpose of your planned visit, how long you will be staying with them or where you will stay and how much of your expenses, if any, they plan to cover. If they will be covering expenses, it will be helpful if they attach copies of their most recent tax returns, bank statements and a letter from their employer confirming their income.

A sample of a family support letter is shown below. Of course, this is just a sample—you don't need to match the facts described. Note how the personal details supplied by the writer are much more convincing than fancy legal language.

Sample Family Support Letter

555 Sunnyside Way
Palo Alto, CA 9xxxx
May 1, 200x

Re: Application of Gundars Mann for B-2
    visitor visa

To Whom It May Concern:

We are U.S. permanent residents living at the above address. We would like to help our nephew, Gundars, celebrate having finished high school. We've invited him to visit us in the United States.

Our plan is that Gundars will spend the first three weeks of his six-week stay with us in California. During this time, we will be responsible for his food, lodging, transportation and all other daily expenses. We plan to take him on various car trips in the California area.

After those three weeks, Gundars will leave us to travel with a friend. It is our understanding that he and his parents will be responsible for supporting him financially during this time. However, we are helping him plan and budget this part of his trip. Also, if he has any problems, we will be available to help out financially and in other ways. In fact, he is free to stay in our house for as much of his time in the U.S. as he likes.

To prove our capacity to provide support to Gundars, we are enclosing a copy of our last year's tax return and a bank statement.

Thank you for your consideration of Gundars' application. We look forward to visiting with him.

Very truly yours,
Eric Mann
Eric Mann

Karen Blakely-Mann
Karen Blakely-Mann
Encl.

c. Affidavit of Support on Form I-134

If your friends and family would rather sign a form instead of write a letter as described just above, use the official INS form for this purpose, Form I-134, pictured below. (You may not have a choice—some consulates require the form.) Form I-134 was originally designed for people applying for green cards (permanent U.S. residence). Although the form covers the basic information that you will need to show the consulate, it is really not meant for temporary visas. For that reason, a letter is probably an easier and clearer way of presenting the information to the consulate. However, if your family or friends are more comfortable presenting the information on a form (or if you must use it), use the Form I-134 in this book. Our line-by-line instructions are next.

 You'll find a tear-out version of this form in Appendix D.

If you choose to download this form from the INS site, print the instructions to Form I-134 as a separate page. The rest is traditionally printed out double-sided, head to foot. (See Chapter 4, Section B, for information on printing and filling out INS forms.)

Paragraph 1: The financial sponsor fills in his or her name and address.

Question 1: The financial sponsor fills in his or her date and place of birth. If the sponsor lives outside the United States, he or she is probably not a citizen or permanent resident of the United States. That's fine; the sponsor can simply ignore parts a, b, c and d of this question.

Question 2: Self-explanatory for U.S. citizens or residents. If the sponsor is not a resident of the United States, he or she can simply enter "N/A" for the second half of this question.

Question 3: This is for information about you, the foreign visitor. The questions are self-explanatory. Enter only the names of any spouse and children who will actually be accompanying you to the United States.

Items 4 through 6: There is nothing to fill in here, but this is where you'll notice that the form is primarily used for permanent immigrants, not for

tourists. The language about posting a bond and holding the sponsor responsible for three years is meant to prevent immigrants from becoming "public charges" (going on welfare) in the United States. It is highly unlikely that your sponsor will be asked to post a bond.

Question 7: The sponsor must enter information about his or her place of employment. For "type of business," it is appropriate to put one's position (such as "secretary" or "accountant") or a more generic description, such as "medicine" or "sales."

On the next set of lines, the sponsor enters information about his or her income and assets. The question about the amount **"on deposit in savings banks in the United States"** is a little misleading—it's okay to include amounts in savings *or* checking accounts, as well as amounts in the sponsor's home country. For **"personal property,"** the sponsor does not need to be completely scientific, and can enter an approximate total value for cars, jewelry, appliances (stereo, television, refrigerator), automobiles, cameras and other equipment. The sponsor should also supply proof of ownership, such as a deed or sales receipt.

Question 8: A sponsor living in the United States will list the people who were named as dependents on the sponsor's income tax forms. If the sponsor lives outside the United States and that country has a tax system comparable to the United States, in which a taxpayer lists dependents on tax returns, the names of these dependent persons should be entered here.

Question 9: This question attempts to find out whether the sponsor would be overextending himself by supporting you. If he or she has filled out this form, or a Form I-864 (another version of the Affidavit of Support, used only in applications of people seeking permanent residence) for any other U.S. immigrant, these lines should be filled in. If not, the sponsor can enter "N/A" here.

Question 10: This question applies only to a sponsor who is a U.S. citizen or permanent resident (green card holder). It attempts to find out whether the sponsor is planning to sponsor anyone else, having submitted a visa petition on that person's behalf. Non-U.S. citizen or non-U.S. permanent resident sponsors can enter "N/A."

Form I-134, Affidavit of Support—Page 1

OMB No. 1115-0062

U.S. Department of Justice
Immigration and Naturalization Service

Affidavit of Support

(Answer All Items: Fill in with Typewriter or Print in Block Letters in Ink.)

I, _____ residing at _____
(Name)   (Street and Number)

_____
(City)   (State)   (Zip Code if in U.S.)   (Country)

BEING DULY SWORN DEPOSE AND SAY:

1. I was born on _____ at _____
(Date)   (City)   (Country)

    If you are **not** a native born United States citizen, answer the following as appropriate:
    a. If a United States citizen through naturalization, give certificate of naturalization number _____
    b. If a United States citizen through parent(s) or marriage, give citizenship certificate number _____
    c. If United States citizenship was derived by some other method, attach a statement of explanation.
    d. If a lawfully admitted permanent resident of the United States, give "A" number _____

2. That I am _____ years of age and have resided in the United States since (date) _____
3. That this affidavit is executed in behalf of the following person:

Name		Gender	Age
Citizen of (Country)	Marital Status	Relationship to Sponsor	
Presently resides at (Street and Number)	(City)	(State)	(Country)

Name of spouse and children accompanying or following to join person:

Spouse	Gender	Age	Child	Gender	Age
Child	Gender	Age	Child	Gender	Age
Child	Gender	Age	Child	Gender	Age

4. That this affidavit is made by me for the purpose of assuring the United States Government that the person(s) named in item 3 will not become a public charge in the United States.

5. That I am willing and able to receive, maintain and support the person(s) named in item 3. That I am ready and willing to deposit a bond, if necessary, to guarantee that such person(s) will not become a public charge during his or her stay in the United States, or to guarantee that the above named person(s) will maintain his or her nonimmigrant status, if admitted temporarily and will depart prior to the expiration of his or her authorized stay in the United States.

6. That I understand this affidavit will be binding upon me for a period of three (3) years after entry of the person(s) named in item 3 and that the information and documentation provided by me may be made available to the Secretary of Health and Human Services and the Secretary of Agriculture, who may make it available to a public assistance agency.

7. That I am employed as, or engaged in the business of _____ with _____
(Type of Business)   (Name of concern)

at _____
(Street and Number)   (City)   (State)   (Zip Code)

I derive an annual income of *(if self-employed, I have attached a copy of my last income tax return or report of commercial rating concern which I certify to be true and correct to the best of my knowledge and belief. See instructions for nature of evidence of net worth to be submitted.)* $ _____

I have on deposit in savings banks in the United States $ _____

I have other personal property, the reasonable value of which is $ _____

OVER

Additional pages not shown.

Question 11: This question needs to be filled in, because it addresses the degree to which your sponsor is willing to support you. Your chances of getting a visa will improve if the sponsor checks the first box (before the word "intend"), indicating that he or she will make specific contributions of support. For example, if you've estimated your total expenses while you visit the United States, the sponsor could agree, in this question, to give you this lump sum. Showing this may help persuade the consulate or INS that the sponsor knows what he's getting into and is serious about supporting you.

"Oath or Affirmation of Deponent." Here is a lovely example of excruciating legalese. Don't try to puzzle this out; just take it to a notary public to sign. A notary public is someone who is legally authorized by a state government to check a person's identification and make sure that the person signing the document is the one who is named as the person who should sign. To convince a notary of his or her identity, the sponsor should bring a driver's license or other form of photo identification. The notary will then ask the sponsor to sign the form, and will place a stamp on it. In the United States, the notary shouldn't charge more than $15 for this service. In the United States you can find notaries easily by looking in the Yellow Pages of your phone book. Outside the United States, the sponsor can take this form to the U.S. consulate, who will provide a notary.

Grand Canyon
Arizona

5. Finding Documents to Match Unique Life Situations

Although we've suggested likely ways to document your plans, your life may not match our suggestions. In that case, you will need to be creative as well as organized about showing that your trip—and your return—will happen in just the way that you describe to the consular officer.

Below are examples of how some tourists might document their cases. Use these to help you think about what evidence would make *your* application strong.

> **EXAMPLE 1:** Aydin wants to visit the United States to attend the wedding of an old friend, then stay another month to do a cross-country road trip. He isn't married and lives with his parents in Turkey. About all he owns is a motorbike. Aydin helps out in his dad's business. The following table suggests documents Aydin could show the consulate (note that some of these items prove more than one thing):

Needs to Show	Documents That Will Show It
Purpose of trip: pleasure	Friend's wedding invitation, copies of correspondence with U.S. friends whom Aydin plans to visit, a map showing Aydin's route across the United States, copies of motel reservations
Limited-time visit	Round-trip plane ticket, a one-month contract with a car rental company
Ties to home country	Letter from Aydin's father explaining that he expects him back at work by a certain day, copy of the receipt for his motorbike, copy of health club membership contract
Financial support	Bank statement showing that Aydin has enough money to cover his trip

EXAMPLE 2: Federico wants to visit his girl-friend, a U.S. citizen, in New York. He truly intends a short trip; he and his girlfriend have logged a lot of flight mileage visiting each other. Federico has a full-time job in Italy and has promised his mother he will be with her for her surgery the following month.

Need to Show	Documents That Will Show It
Purpose of trip: pleasure	Correspondence with Federico's girlfriend talking about events or activities they will attend during his stay, receipts for concert tickets, a contract with a Bed and Breakfast in New Hampshire for a weekend's stay
Limited-time visit	Round-trip plane ticket, copies of Federico's passport showing his previous entries and, more importantly, exits from the United States (Federico's good record of leaving on time will be a point in his favor)
Ties to home country	A letter from Federico's employers confirming his time off and that they expect him back for long-term employment, and a letter from his mother's doctor confirming the scheduled surgery and the importance that he and the family attach to Federico's being there to support her
Financial support	Bank statement showing enough money to cover Federico's trip

EXAMPLE 3: Leihua, age 12, lives in a small Chinese village and suffers from a rare form of cancer. Her uncle in the United States, who is very successful in the real estate business, has offered to pay for her to travel to the United States and for her treatment.

Need to Show	Documents That Will Show It
Purpose of trip: medical treatment	A very detailed letter from the doctor who will be treating Leihua, explaining her condition and the fact that she won't be a health risk to others
Limited-time visit	Round-trip plane ticket, plus a section in the doctor's letter explaining the length of time the treatment will take and the expectation that she'll be well enough to travel afterward
Ties to home country	A letter from Leihua's parents stating that they have no intention of giving Leihua up and they expect her to return home following treatment (with an English translation attached)
Financial support	The doctor's letter should include the cost of the treatment and the payment arrangements. In addition, Leihua's uncle should provide a letter describing his willingness to pay the cost of treatment and to provide Leihua with food, housing and spending money while she's in the United States. He should attach to his letter a copy of his most recent income tax return and bank statement

⚠️ **Do not bother with "guarantees" of your return.** Some applicants go through the effort of having a family member or friend in the United States prepare a sworn, notarized statement promising that they will make sure you leave on time. Don't waste your time on this. The consulate isn't going to entrust your return to someone they've never heard of—they want to form their own opinion about your true intentions.

Now try planning what documents you will bring:

Need to Show	Documents That Will Show It
Purpose of trip: (pleasure or medical treatment)	
Limited-time visit	
Ties to home country	
Financial support	

D. How to Use the Tourist Visa Checklist

Use this Checklist as your organizational tool. Make a copy and attach the Checklist to the envelope of items that you'll be bringing to the consulate. As soon as you have found or finished an item, check the appropriate box and put it in the envelope. Do not go to the consulate until every box is checked off and you are sure you have everything ready. In all cases, bring original documents to the consulate to show them, but also bring photocopies for them to keep.

You'll find a tear-out version of this Checklist in Appendix E.

Tourist Visa Checklist

Here are all the items you'll need to present for your tourist visa application:

- ☐ Form OF-156
- ☐ valid passport
- ☐ two photographs
- ☐ application fee; currently $45
- ☐ documents showing the purpose of your trip
- ☐ documents showing your plan to remain in the United States for a limited time period
- ☐ documents showing that you have a residence in your home country and other binding ties that will draw you back
- ☐ documents showing that you will be able to support yourself financially while you are in the United States

---

Once you've completed your tourist visa application, go to Chapter 9, which discusses how to successfully present it at a U.S. consulate. ∎

Applying for a Change to Tourist Status in the U.S.

Applying to become a tourist in the United States is fairly straightforward. You fill out a single form, assemble some supporting documents, submit them to a U.S. INS office and receive a written answer within a few weeks or months. Unlike overseas applicants, you can include your spouse and children in your application (so long as they currently have the same type of visa that you do).

Don't let the simplicity of the application process fool you, however. Unless you have carefully thought out how you will prepare and present your application, it could be denied faster than you can say "official discretion." Below we give you line-by-line instructions on filling out the application form, as well as detailed descriptions of what documents might be appropriate for you to submit. At the end of this section is a Checklist covering all the forms and documents. Use this Checklist to help organize and complete the application process.

A. The Application Form

Only one government form is required for your application to change to tourist status. It's called the INS Form I-539, Application to Extend/Change Non-immigrant Status, pictured below. See subsection 1, below, for details on how to fill out this form, and subsection 2 for instructions on filling out the supplemental portion for your spouse and children.

1. Line-by-Line Instructions for Form I-539

 You'll find a tear-out version of this form in Appendix D.

If you choose to print this form out from the INS site, it's normally printed out double-sided, head to foot. When you're ready with a copy of Form I-539 in hand, follow these instructions on how to fill it out.

Instructions page 5, box at bottom of page: Fill in your name and U.S. address (this will be used to mail the form back to you).

Part 1. Information About You: Mostly self-explanatory. You probably won't have a Social Security number unless you are changing from a visa or status that allowed you to work. If you don't have a number, enter "None."

Did you have a Social Security number when you shouldn't have? If you have a Social Security number but haven't been on a visa that allows you to be employed in the United States, your answer to this question could send the INS a message that you've worked illegally. If there is an explanation for your having a number that dispels any question of illegality, attach a letter giving the details. If not, you may want to consult a lawyer.

You will only have an **"A-number"** (an eight-digit number following the letter "A" for Alien) if you have been in deportation or removal proceedings or submitted certain immigration applications, particularly for permanent residence. If you were in such proceedings or had any applications denied, see a lawyer.

Your **"I-94 number"** is on the small white card that you received at the border. If the date on that card has passed, you are no longer in status and cannot file this application. Under INS policy, an exception may be made for you if you are within one week of the expiration date, but try to avoid relying on this exception.

If your I-94 card is green, stop now. A green I-94 card means that you entered on the Visa Waiver Program and are not allowed to apply for a Change of Status in the United States.

For **"Current nonimmigrant status,"** enter your visa status, such as "F-1 student" or "G-2, family member of foreign government representative." The date your status **"Expires on"** is found on your I-94 card.

Part 2. Application Type:
Question 1: As a first-time applicant for tourist status, you should check box **1b** and enter the code "B-2."

Form I-539, Application to Extend/Change Nonimmigrant Status—Page 1

U.S. Department of Justice Immigration and Naturalization Service	OMB No. 1115-0093; Expires 7/31/04

Application to Extend/Change Nonimmigrant Status

START HERE - Please Type or Print.	FOR INS USE ONLY

Part 1.   Information about you.

Family Name	Given Name	Middle Initial

Address -
In care of -

Street Number and Name		Apt. #

City	State	Zip Code	Daytime Phone #

Country of Birth	Country of Citizenship

Date of Birth (MM/DD/YYYY)	Social Security # (if any)	A # (if any)

Date of Last Arrival Into the U.S.	I-94 #

Current Nonimmigrant Status	Expires on (MM/DD/YYYY)

FOR INS USE ONLY

Returned   Receipt

Date

Resubmitted

Date

Reloc Sent

Date

Reloc Rec'd

Date

☐ Applicant Interviewed on

_____ Date

☐ Extension Granted to (Date): _____

Change of Status/Extension Granted
New Class: From (Date): _____
_____ To (Date): _____

If Denied:
☐ Still within period of stay
☐ S/D to: _____
☐ Place under docket control

Remarks:

Action Block

Part 2. Application type. *(See instructions for fee.)*

1. I am applying for: *(Check one.)*
   a. ☐ An extension of stay in my current status.
   b. ☐ A change of status. The new status I am requesting is: _____
   c. ☐ Other: *(Describe grounds of eligibility.)* _____
2. Number of people included in this application: *(Check one.)*
   a. ☐ I am the only applicant.
   b. ☐ Members of my family are filing this application with me.
       The total number of people (including me) in the application is: _____
       (Complete the supplement for each co-applicant.)

Part 3. Processing information.

1. I/We request that my/our current or requested status be extended until
   (MM/DD/YYYY): _____
2. Is this application based on an extension or change of status already granted to your
   spouse, child or parent?
   ☐ No ☐ Yes, Receipt # _____
3. Is this application based on a separate petition or application to give your spouse,
   child or parent an extension or change of status? ☐ No ☐ Yes, filed with this I-539.
   ☐ Yes, filed previously and pending with INS. INS receipt number: _____
4. If you answered "Yes" to Question 3, give the name of the petitioner or applicant:

   If the petition or application is pending with INS, also give the following information:

   Office filed at _____ Filed on (MM/DD/YYYY) _____

Part 4. Additional information.

1. For applicant #1, provide passport information: Country of Issuance	Valid to: (MM/DD/YYYY)

2. Foreign Address: Street Number and Name	Apt. #

City or Town	State or Province

Country	Zip/Postal Code

To be Completed by
Attorney or Representative, if any

☐ Fill in box if G-28 is attached to represent the applicant

ATTY State License

Additional pages not shown.

Question 2: This is where you have an opportunity to include any spouse and children in your application. Check box **2b**, and then write in the total number of them plus you. (For example, a husband wanting to bring his wife and child would enter "3.") Also fill out the Form I-539 Supplement-1 page, where you list their names and other information; complete instructions are in subsection 2, below.

Part 3. Processing Information:

Question 1: Answer this question even though it seems to only mention extensions. Enter the date you'd like to leave—the maximum would be six months from the expiration date of your current stay (found on your I-94 card).

Question 2 to 4: As the primary applicant, your answer to these questions is "no."

Part 4. Additional Information:

Questions 1 and 2: Self-explanatory questions based on the information in your passport and calling for your overseas address.

⚠ When does your passport expire? If the expiration date in your passport is within the next six months, you should have it renewed. You can usually do this at a consulate of your home country in the United States. If there isn't a consulate in the city where you're living, you can usually locate one in the phone books for Washington, D.C., Los Angeles, San Francisco or Chicago, or on the Internet at http://www.embassy.org/embassies/index.html or http://www.embpage.org.

Question 3: These questions are designed to see whether you are inadmissible. Think carefully before entering your answers, and keep reading for details. If there isn't a good solution below, you'll need to see a lawyer.

Question 3a: If you (or any members of your family included in your application) have applied for an **"immigrant visa,"** it indicates that you're seeking a green card. The INS will probably conclude that you have no intention of returning home after your visit and will deny this Change of Status application accordingly. There isn't a solution for

this—and hiding the other application is impossible.

Question 3b: This is similar to the question above except that instead of referring to an application that you filed yourself, it asks whether someone else has filed a petition to start the process of your acquiring permanent residence to the United States. For example, some petitions filed by family members will only place you on a waiting list that will last many years before you see an immigrant visa. Nevertheless, the INS may deny your application if your answer to this question is yes.

Question 3c: See advice for question 3a. Form I-485 is simply the U.S. version of a green card application.

Question 3d: If you were simply arrested and not charged (for example, the police picked up the wrong person), you are safe entering "yes" here and attaching a written explanation and a copy of the police report. But for more serious arrests, you must consult a lawyer before going any farther. Most criminal convictions will make you inadmissible to the United States. If you were later found innocent (acquitted) or your case was dismissed by the judge, it will probably not affect your immigration status—but consult a lawyer anyway. This is a tricky area—for example, the INS merely has to suspect that you are guilty of drug trafficking in order to find you inadmissible. An acquittal might not help with that.

Question 3e: To determine whether you have violated your current immigration status, you must consider the type of visa you are on and what you agreed to do to get that visa. For example, if you came to the United States as a student but worked without INS authorization, this would be a status violation. The INS will probably deny your application if you have violated your visa terms.

Question 3f: If you are now in **"removal proceedings"** (formerly known as exclusion or deportation proceedings), you should talk to a lawyer immediately—it's likely that the INS has no power over this Change of Status application because your immigration situation is in the hands of the courts.

Question 3g: If you have been employed in the United States, your work needs to have been permissible under the visa or status that you had at the time. You may also have been required to obtain a work permit card from the INS. If your work wasn't permitted, talk to a lawyer before continuing with this application. If your work was permitted, look at the paragraph below the question to see what additional information you'll need to supply (do so on a separate piece of paper and don't forget to put your name at the top in case it gets separated from the rest of the application). Also add a photocopy of both sides of your INS work permit (EAD) if you had one.

Part 5. Signature: Self-explanatory.

Part 6. Signature of person preparing form if other than above: This is where a lawyer or legal assistant would sign. If you simply had some typing help, the person does not need to sign.

2. Line-by-Line Instructions for Form I-539 Supplement-1

This is a one page, single-sided form that can be attached to Form I-539. As you'll see, it has repeating blocks for information about your spouse and children, allowing them to apply for a Change of Status along with you. Most of this form is self-explanatory.

➡️ If you don't have a spouse or children, or they won't be accompanying you in the United States, you can skip this subsection.

📄 You'll find a tear-out version of this form in Appendix D.

For **"Date of Arrival,"** enter the date of each family member's most recent arrival into the United States (many people mistakenly put the first arrival date). Their **"Current nonimmigrant status"** is the name of the visa that your family member is currently on. **"Expires on"** refers to the date his or her status expires, found on the I-94 card in your family member's passport. **"Country where passport issued"** is self-explanatory. When you enter the **expiration**

date of the passport, make sure that it is at least six months into the future. If not, get the passport renewed before completing this application. However, if waiting for the renewal will so delay your filing this application that you might lose your very eligibility to apply, simply submit the application, write in the current passport expiration date, and then add the words "renewal pending."

B. Documents You'll Need

Almost anyone can fill out a form—but what will enhance your chances for tourist status is the quality of your supporting documentary evidence. Along with the form itself, you'll need to provide copies of your official and personal papers that will give the INS a clear, strong idea of who you are, what your plans are and why they can trust you with a longer stay in the United States.

In general, use the most official-sounding documents or letters whenever possible. Letters you gather from family and friends can be useful in combination with other documents, but the INS knows that your family and friends are on your side. The officer will be more impressed by records that were not created at your request, solely in order to get you a visa. Medical or school records and letters from people with a professional reputation, like doctors, employers and teachers, will be the most convincing. Don't forget to obtain translations, word-for-word, of any documents that are not in English.

You'll need to assemble the following items. If you have a spouse and children included in the application, they will also need to assemble their own sets of the same or similar documents, except where noted. You'll need:

- a copy of the primary pages of your valid passport, with an expiration date at least six months beyond the current date
- the application fee, currently $120 (one fee only—your family members need not pay extra). Pay by check or money order, payable to the USINS. Do not pay cash
- your original I-94 card (make a separate copy for yourself and keep it with you)

Form I-539, Supplement-1

Supplement -1
Attach to Form I-539 when more than one person is included in the petition or application.
(List each person separately. Do not include the person named in the form.)

Family Name	Given Name	Middle Name	Date of Birth (MM/DD/YYYY)
County of Birth	County of Citizenship	Social Security # (if any)	A # (if any)
Date of Arrival (MM/DD/YYYY)		I-94 #	
Current Nonimmigrant Status:		Expires On (MM/DD/YYYY)	
Country Where Passport Issued		Expiration Date (MM/DD/YYYY)	

Family Name	Given Name	Middle Name	Date of Birth (MM/DD/YYYY)
County of Birth	County of Citizenship	Social Security # (if any)	A # (if any)
Date of Arrival (MM/DD/YYYY)		I-94 #	
Current Nonimmigrant Status:		Expires On (MM/DD/YYYY)	
Country Where Passport Issued		Expiration Date (MM/DD/YYYY)	

Family Name	Given Name	Middle Name	Date of Birth (MM/DD/YYYY)
County of Birth	County of Citizenship	Social Security # (if any)	A # (if any)
Date of Arrival (MM/DD/YYYY)		I-94 #	
Current Nonimmigrant Status:		Expires On (MM/DD/YYYY)	
Country Where Passport Issued		Expiration Date (MM/DD/YYYY)	

Family Name	Given Name	Middle Name	Date of Birth (MM/DD/YYYY)
County of Birth	County of Citizenship	Social Security # (if any)	A # (if any)
Date of Arrival (MM/DD/YYYY)		I-94 #	
Current Nonimmigrant Status:		Expires On (MM/DD/YYYY)	
Country Where Passport Issued		Expiration Date (MM/DD/YYYY)	

Family Name	Given Name	Middle Name	Date of Birth (MM/DD/YYYY)
County of Birth	County of Citizenship	Social Security # (if any)	A # (if any)
Date of Arrival (MM/DD/YYYY)		I-94 #	
Current Nonimmigrant Status:		Expires On (MM/DD/YYYY)	
Country Where Passport Issued		Expiration Date (MM/DD/YYYY)	

If you need additional space, attach a separate sheet(s) of paper.
Place your name, A # if any, date of birth, form number and application date at the top of the sheet(s) of paper.

Form I-539 (Rev. 09/04/01)Y Page 4

- documents showing that you have not fallen out of lawful immigration status (by overstaying or violating the conditions of your visa) since arriving in the United States; normally your I-94 will be enough for this
- documents showing the purpose of your stay (see subsection 1 below)
- documents showing your plan to remain in the United States for a limited time period (see subsection 2 below)
- documents showing that you have a residence in your home country and other binding ties that will draw you back (see subsection 3 below)
- documentation showing that you will be able to support yourself financially while you are in the United States (see subsection 4 below).

For more specific information on providing these documents, see the subsections below. Then move on to subsection 6, which explains how to pull all the documents together, gives example cases and provides a sample worksheet for your use.

1. Showing Your Purpose

Think about what documents would answer the question, "Why do you want to spend time as a visitor in the United States?" You might have a specific purpose, such as a conference or event, or you might simply wish to see the sights. A combination of purposes is fine, too—such as going to a wedding and then travelling to other cities. In any case, gather documents to demonstrate that your plans are serious ones, not just empty talk intended to get you a visa. You'll also need to show that the purpose of your trip matches the type of visa—in other words, your plans must be entirely for pleasure (or medical treatment), not for business or an effort to stay in the United States permanently. Examples of documents to show your purpose might include:

- an invitation to an event, such as a printed wedding invitation
- a detailed travel itinerary, showing where you'll visit, what hotels you'll stay in and how you'll get around, such as the kind prepared by a travel agent

- appointment with a doctor, evidenced by an appointment slip or letter
- registration for a conference, as shown by your ticket to the event or your cancelled check, or
- a whirlwind tour of the United States, as evidenced by your "See the U.S." bus ticket that will take you anywhere during a limited time.

2. Showing Your Plans to Stay for a Limited Time

Think of this category as answering the question "How much time will you need to accomplish the purpose of your visit?" Every well-thought-out plan should have an ending—and you'll need to demonstrate that yours does, too. One of the best forms of evidence is a plane or other ticket out of the United States. You could also include items showing that you need or plan to return home by a specific time, such as a letter from your employer saying, "We approve your additional one month leave and expect to see you back on June 21, 200x."

3. Showing Your Residence in and Ties to Your Home Country

Think about finding documents that will answer the question, "Why would you want to return home after your trip?" This requirement may sound patronizing to you—but the U.S. government makes no secret of believing that this is the best country in the world, and that everyone is angling for a way to stay forever.

Your home, family and employment situations will probably be the best sources of proof that you will return. Possible documents might include:

- a copy of your home title deed or rental agreement showing that you have a stable place to live
- a letter from your employer like the one below, indicating that you have a job to return to or, if you're self-employed, a business license or other proof that the business is ongoing
- copies of your most recent pay stubs

- birth or marriage certificates showing your ties to family that lives in your home country
- letters from family in your home country confirming that they live there and explaining any special reasons that you are likely to return to them, and
- evidence of any special arrangements you've made relating to your extended U.S. stay, such as an extended one-month lease with the person subletting your home or apartment.

Sample Overseas Employer Letter

TIVOLI PRODUCTIONS, INC.
TIVOLI ALLE 100
2000 COPENHAGEN

June 11, 200x

To Whom It May Concern:

We have authorized our employee, Dag Moller, an additional one month's leave in addition to the one year's leave that he is just completing. Moller is the head of events planning at our office and a valued employee. We hired a temporary substitute in his absence, and the substitute has agreed to stay on for one more month. However, we eagerly await Mr. Moller's return, as he is the creative mind behind our planned anniversary celebration for this December. We expect him back at work on August 28th, 200x.

Very truly yours,

Karl Follerup

Karl Follerup
Director

4. Showing Your Ability to Pay for Your Trip

If you have the funds to pay for your trip, this will be the easiest category to document. A copy of your bank statement will be sufficient. If your trip will be funded by some other source (for example, a scholarship to attend a conference), include copies of the award letter and any other documents showing proof of the amount. If you don't have your own source of funds, you'll need to show that someone else is able and willing to support you. See subsection 5, below, on how your friends and family can help.

5. How Your Friends and Family Can Help

If they're willing to help, offers of financial support from your friends or family in the United States or abroad can make all the difference in getting you a tourist visa. There are two ways in which friends or family members can support your application: one, by writing a letter describing your visit and/or their financial support for you (see subsection a, below), and two, by signing a form promising financial support (see subsection b, below).

Having family in the United States may also hurt. If you have close family members in the United States who could potentially apply for a green card for you, the INS may think that your secret plan is to take advantage of this and never leave. That doesn't mean that you should hide your family's existence— just be especially careful in documenting the reasons that you would choose to return. For information on which family members could apply for green cards for you, see the Immigration and Green Cards section of Nolo's Legal Encyclopedia at http://www.nolo.com.

Your U.S. relatives or sponsors may wonder how far their obligation will go after they sign a support letter or Form I-134. If you take a tumble in the Grand Canyon and are in the hospital for six weeks, will they get stuck with the hospital bill? Unfortunately, we can't give you any clear guidance on this. On the one hand, you can reassure your sponsors that their obligation will be more moral than legal— no immigration attorney whom we know has ever heard of the INS going after a sponsor for support money (or, more likely, reimbursement for any benefits you received from the U.S. government) for a tourist. Most lawyers think that Form I-134 is a flawed legal contract and that it wouldn't hold up in court if the INS tried to enforce it. On the other hand, there's no guarantee that the INS would never try and pressure the family of a foreign visitor or take them to court. And, of course, the hospital or other service provider would still have a right to demand that you find a way to pay. They couldn't demand that your sponsor pay, but the practical reality is that you might look to your sponsor for help. Since accidents or other medical issues are the most likely source of out-of-control expenses, you might want to look into traveler's insurance to cover this risk.

a.   The Support Letter

The easiest way for your friends or family to demonstrate their willingness to fund your trip is to write a letter explaining this. The letter should discuss the purpose of your planned visit, how long you will be staying with them or where you will stay and how much of your expenses, if any, they plan to cover. If they will be covering expenses, it is also helpful if they attach copies of their most recent tax returns, bank statements and a letter from their employer confirming their income.

A sample of a family support letter is below. Of course, this is just a sample—you don't need to match the facts described. Use this sample to get yourself thinking and to help format your letter. Note how the personal details supplied by the writer are much more convincing than fancy legal language.

Hollywood Sign
California

Sample Support Letter

555 Sunnyside Way
Palo Alto, CA 9xxxx
May 1, 200x

Re: Application of Gundars Mann for B-2
    visitor status

To Whom It May Concern:

We are U.S. permanent residents living at the above address. We would like to help our nephew, Gundars, celebrate having finished high school in the United States. We've invited him to spend some time with us after his graduation.

Our plan is that Gundars will spend the first three weeks of his six-week vacation with us in California. During this time, we will be responsible for his food, lodging, transportation and all other daily expenses. We plan to take him on various car trips in the California area.

After those three weeks, Gundars will leave us to travel with a friend. It is our understanding that he and his parents will be responsible for supporting him financially during this time. However, we are helping him plan and budget this part of his trip. Also, if he has any problems, we will be available to help out financially and in other ways. In fact, he is free to stay in our house for as much of his time in the U.S. as he likes.

To prove our capacity to provide support to Gundars, we are enclosing a copy of our last year's tax return and a bank statement.

Thank you for your consideration of Gundars' application. We look forward to spending time with him.

Very truly yours,

Eric Mann
Eric Mann

Karen Blakely-Mann
Karen Blakely-Mann
Encl.

b. Affidavit of Support on Form I-134

If your friends and family would rather sign a form as a way of showing that they will support you, use INS Form I-134 (pictured below). (You have a choice of whether to include it with your application—but if the INS is in doubt about your financial resources, it may later notify you that you must submit a Form I-134.) Before your sponsor begins filling it out, they should understand that it was originally designed for people applying for green cards (permanent U.S. residence), though it will cover the basic information that you need to show the INS in order to get your tourist visa. Because the form wasn't designed for tourist visas, a letter is probably an easier and clearer way of presenting the information. Still, if your family or friends are more comfortable presenting the information on a form, or if the INS actually notifies you that they will require it, you will find Form I-134 in this book—our line-by-line instructions are next.

 You'll find a tear-out version of this form in Appendix D.

If you choose to print this form out from the INS website, print the instructions to Form I-134 as a separate page. The rest is traditionally printed out double-sided, head to foot. See Chapter 4, Section B, for general information on printing and filling out INS forms.

Paragraph 1: The financial sponsor fills in his or her name and address.

Question 1: The financial sponsor fills in his or her date and place of birth. If the sponsor lives outside the United States, he or she is probably not a citizen or permanent resident of the United States. That's fine; the sponsor can simply ignore parts a, b, c and d of this question.

Question 2: Self-explanatory for U.S. citizens or residents. If the sponsor is not a resident of the United States, he or she can simply enter "N/A" for the second half of this question.

Question 3: This is for information about you, the foreign visitor. The questions are self-explanatory. Enter only the names of any spouse and children who will actually be accompanying you to the United States.

Items 4 through 6: This is where you'll notice that the form is primarily used for permanent immigrants, not for tourists. The language about posting a bond and holding the sponsor responsible for three years is meant to prevent immigrants from becoming "public charges" (going on welfare) in the United States. It is highly unlikely that your sponsor will be asked to post a bond.

Question 7: The sponsor must enter information about his or her place of employment. For "type of business" it is appropriate to put one's position (such as "secretary" or "accountant") or a more generic description such as "medicine" or "sales."

On the next set of lines, the sponsor enters information about his or her income and assets. The question about the amount **"on deposit in savings banks in the United States"** is a little misleading—it's okay to include amounts in savings or checking accounts, as well as amounts in the sponsor's home country. For **"personal property,"** the sponsor does not need to be completely scientific and can enter an approximate total value for his or her cars, jewelry, appliances (stereo, television, refrigerator), automobiles, cameras and other equipment. The sponsor should also supply proof of ownership, such as a deed or sales receipt.

Question 8: A sponsor living in the United States will list the people who were named as dependents on the sponsor's income tax forms. If the sponsor lives outside the United States and that country has a tax system comparable to the United States, in which a taxpayer lists dependents on tax returns, the names of these dependent persons should be entered here.

Question 9: This question attempts to find out whether the sponsor would be overextending himself by supporting you. If he or she has filled out this form, or a Form I-864 (another version of the Affidavit of Support, used only in applications of people seeking permanent residence) for any other U.S. immigrant, these lines should be filled in. Otherwise, the sponsor can simply enter "N/A."

Question 10: This question applies only to a sponsor who is a U.S. citizen or permanent resident (green card holder). It attempts to find out whether the sponsor is planning to sponsor anyone else,

Form I-134, Affidavit of Support—Page 1

U.S. Department of Justice
Immigration and Naturalization Service

OMB No. 1115-0062

Affidavit of Support

(Answer All Items: Fill in with Typewriter or Print in Block Letters in Ink.)

I, _____ residing at _____
       (Name)   (Street and Number)

_____
  (City)   (State)   (Zip Code if in U.S.)   (Country)

BEING DULY SWORN DEPOSE AND SAY:

1. I was born on _____ at _____
             (Date)   (City)   (Country)

    If you are **not** a native born United States citizen, answer the following as appropriate:
    a. If a United States citizen through naturalization, give certificate of naturalization number _____
    b. If a United States citizen through parent(s) or marriage, give citizenship certificate number _____
    c. If United States citizenship was derived by some other method, attach a statement of explanation.
    d. If a lawfully admitted permanent resident of the United States, give "A" number _____

2. That I am _____ years of age and have resided in the United States since (date) _____
3. That this affidavit is executed in behalf of the following person:

Name			Gender	Age
Citizen of (Country)	Marital Status	Relationship to Sponsor		
Presently resides at (Street and Number)	(City)	(State)	(Country)	

    Name of spouse and children accompanying or following to join person:

Spouse	Gender	Age	Child		Gender	Age
Child	Gender	Age	Child		Gender	Age
Child	Gender	Age	Child		Gender	Age

4. That this affidavit is made by me for the purpose of assuring the United States Government that the person(s) named in item 3 will not become a public charge in the United States.
5. That I am willing and able to receive, maintain and support the person(s) named in item 3. That I am ready and willing to deposit a bond, if necessary, to guarantee that such person(s) will not become a public charge during his or her stay in the United States, or to guarantee that the above named person(s) will maintain his or her nonimmigrant status, if admitted temporarily and will depart prior to the expiration of his or her authorized stay in the United States.
6. That I understand this affidavit will be binding upon me for a period of three (3) years after entry of the person(s) named in item 3 and that the information and documentation provided by me may be made available to the Secretary of Health and Human Services and the Secretary of Agriculture, who may make it available to a public assistance agency.
7. That I am employed as, or engaged in the business of _____ with _____
                                         (Type of Business)   (Name of concern)

    at _____
      (Street and Number)   (City)   (State)   (Zip Code)

    I derive an annual income of (*if self-employed, I have attached a copy of my last income tax return or report of commercial rating concern which I certify to be true and correct to the best of my knowledge and belief. See instructions for nature of evidence of net worth to be submitted.*) $_____

    I have on deposit in savings banks in the United States $_____

    I have other personal property, the reasonable value of which is $_____

OVER

Additional pages not shown.

having submitted a visa petition on that person's behalf.

Question 11: This question needs to be filled in, and it will probably look best if the sponsor checks the box in front of the word "intend," indicating that he or she will make specific contributions of support. For example, if you've estimated your total expenses while you visit the United States, the sponsor could agree, in this question, to give you this lump sum. Showing this may help persuade the INS that the sponsor knows what he or she is getting into and is serious about supporting you.

"Oath or Affirmation of Deponent." Here is a lovely example of excruciating legalese. Don't try to puzzle this out; just take it to a notary public to sign. A notary public is someone who is legally authorized by a state government to check a person's identification and make sure that the person signing the document is the one who is named as the person who should sign. To convince a notary of his or her identity, the sponsor should bring a driver's license or other form of photo identification. The notary will then ask the sponsor to sign the form, and will place a stamp on it. In the United States, the notary shouldn't charge more than around $15 for this service. You can easily find notaries in the United States by looking in the Yellow Pages of your phone book. Outside the United States, the sponsor can take this form to the U.S. consulate, who will provide a notary.

6. Finding Documents to Match Unique Life Situations

Although we've suggested likely ways to document your plans, your life may not match our suggestions. In that case, you will need to be creative as well as organized about showing that your trip—and your return—will happen in just the way that you describe to the INS.

Below are examples of how some fictional tourists might document their cases. Use these to help think about what evidence would make your application strong.

EXAMPLE 1: Aydin's student visa is about to run out, but he wants to continue his stay in the United States to attend the wedding of a friend, then stay another month to do a cross-country road trip. He isn't married, and lived with his parents in Turkey before he started college. About all he owns in Turkey is a motorbike. Aydin hasn't found a job for after graduation, but plans to help out in his dad's business. The following table suggests documents Aydin could include in his application (note that some of these items prove more than one thing):

Need to Show	Documents That Will Show It
Purpose of stay: pleasure	Friend's wedding invitation, copies of correspondence with friends whom Aydin plans to visit, a map showing his route across the United States, copies of motel reservations
Limited-time visit	Return plane ticket, a one-month contract with a car rental company
Ties to home country	Letter from Aydin's father explaining that he expects him at work by a certain day, copies of cover letters and rejection notices sent between Aydin and prospective employers in Turkey, copy of the receipt for Aydin's motorbike
Financial support	Bank statement showing that Aydin has enough money to cover his trip

EXAMPLE 2: Federico's H-1B visa is about to run out. He wants to stay longer to spend time with his girlfriend, a U.S. citizen, in New York. He truly intends to leave afterward. Federico has a full-time job awaiting him in Italy and has promised his mother he will be with her for her surgery the following month.

Need to Show	Documents That Will Show It
Purpose of stay: pleasure	Copies of correspondence between Federico and his girlfriend planning the events or activities they will attend during this time period, receipts for upcoming concert tickets, a contract with a Bed and Breakfast in New Hampshire for a weekend's stay
Limited-time visit	A return plane ticket to Italy
Ties to home country	A job offer letter from Federico's employers confirming the date they expect him to report for work, and a letter from his mother's doctor confirming the scheduled surgery and the importance that he and the family attach to Federico's being there to support her
Financial support	Bank statement showing enough money to cover Federico's continued stay

EXAMPLE 3: Leihua, age 12, has been in the U.S. with her diplomat parents. She suffers from a rare form of cancer. Her parents' tour of duty is ending and they must return to China. However, her uncle in the United States, who is very successful in the real estate business, has offered to pay for Leihua to stay longer and receive treatment.

Need to Show	Documents That Will Show It
Purpose of stay: medical treatment	A very detailed letter from the doctor who will be treating Leihua, explaining her condition, and the fact that she won't be a health risk to others
Limited-time visit	Return plane ticket to China, plus a section in the doctor's letter explaining the length of time the treatment will take and the expectation that she'll be well enough to travel afterward
Ties to home country	A letter from Leihua's parents stating that they have no intention of giving Leihua up and they expect her to return home following treatment (with an English translation attached)
Financial support	The doctor's letter should also mention the cost of the treatment and the payment arrangements. In addition, Leihua's uncle should provide a letter describing his willingness to pay the cost of treatment and to provide Leihua with food, housing and spending money during her stay. He should attach to his letter a copy of his most recent income tax return and bank statement.

Do not bother with "guarantees" of your return. Some applicants go through the effort of having a family member or friend in the United States prepare a sworn, notarized statement promising that they will make sure you leave on time. Don't waste your time on this. The INS isn't going to entrust your return to someone they've never heard of—they want to form their own opinion about your true intentions.

Now try planning what documents you will include in your application:

Need to Show	Documents That Will Show It
Purpose of trip: (pleasure or medical treatment)	
Limited-time visit	
Ties to home country	
Financial support	

C. How to Use the U.S. Change of Status Checklist

Use this Checklist as your organizational tool. Keep the Checklist next to the envelope of items that you'll be sending to the INS. As soon as you have found or finished an item, check the appropriate box and put the item in the envelope. Do not submit your application until every box is checked off. In all cases except your I-94 card, send photocopies rather than original documents.

This Checklist is also available as a tear-out in Appendix E.

U.S. Change of Status Checklist

Here are all the items you'll need to present for your application to change to tourist status within the United States:

☐ INS Form I-539
☐ original I-94 card
☐ documents showing you have not fallen out of status
☐ copy of valid passport
☐ application fee; currently $120
☐ documents showing the purpose of your stay
☐ documents showing your plan to remain in the United States for a limited time period
☐ documents showing that you have a residence in your home country and other ties that will draw you back
☐ documents showing that you will be able to support yourself financially while you are in the United States

---

D. Where to Send Your Application

Once you've filled out Form I-539 and prepared the accompanying documents, make a complete copy for your records. Then send the packet of forms and documents to an INS Service Center—the address is in Appendix B, and you can double-check it on the INS website at http://www.ins.usdoj.gov/graphics/fieldoffices/statemap.htm or by calling the INS information number at 800-375-5283.

INS Service Centers are different than the local INS offices that you can actually visit. All contact with the Service Center will have to be by mail. Certified mail with return receipt requested is highly recommended—these Service Centers receive a huge volume of mail. When you request a return receipt, you will prepare a little postcard that is attached to your envelope. It will be signed by the person at the INS who physically receives your envelope. The postcard will be mailed to you, which will be your proof that the INS received your petition. You can use this postcard to convince the INS to look for the petition if it gets misplaced.

E. What Happens After You Submit Form I-539

Once your application is received and the INS Service Center has reviewed it to see that you've included all the appropriate documents and fee, you'll get a receipt notice, usually within six weeks. If you don't receive a receipt notice within that time, see Chapter 13, Dealing With Bureaucrats, Delays and Denials, for suggestions on what to do. If, in the meantime, your old visa expires, don't worry too much—as long as your application was submitted in good faith, the time you spend waiting for a decision is legal, up to 120 days.

The receipt notice will tell you how long the Service Center is likely to take to approve or deny your application—and the Center won't want to hear from you until that date goes by. If you don't get an answer by the predicted time, again see Chapter 13.

With any luck at all, the Service Center will approve your change of status by mail. However, in rare cases you may be called in for an interview at a local INS office. This probably means the INS has some doubts about your application. If this happens, take a careful look at your paperwork— maybe ask a friend to look it over as well—and try to identify and fill any gaps. Then read Chapter 9 for tips on how to handle the interview.

After your application is approved, go to Chapter 10 for information on enjoying and protecting your status as a visitor to the United States. ■

Applying for a Student Visa From Overseas

This chapter gives you the "nuts and bolts" of putting together your student visa application from overseas. The application requirements are nearly identical for F-1 (academic) and M-1 (vocational) visa applicants, so we address both in this chapter.

You'll start the process by getting admitted to a school and receiving some paperwork from them. Then you'll fill out and assemble some more paperwork of your own and take or send it all to a nearby U.S. consulate for a decision. Once you've been approved, the consulate will stamp a visa into your passport and you will be ready for travel to the United States.

This chapter tells you what you need to know as you begin your quest for a student visa. It covers:

- tips on choosing a U.S. school (Section A)
- contacting your consulate (Section B)
- filling out the visa form and collecting the documents that will accompany it (Sections C and D)
- using the Checklist to help you stay organized (Section E), and
- how to bring family member with you (Section F).

A. Before the Visa Application: School Admission

You can't start the immigration process until you have been admitted to an INS-approved school. In addition, that school must have filled out and sent you a form called an I-20 (which we'll discuss further on in this section).

This book does not go into depth about how to find the right U.S. school or program or how to get accepted to it. Some good resources to consult about schools and admissions processes include http://www.studyusa.com, http://www.embark.com and http://www.ies-ed.com (the International Education Service). Also, most U.S. consulates have a library where you can look at materials about schools in the United States. Some colleges actually recruit overseas. If you're in high school but your school can't tell you about local college fairs or recruiting

activities, contact the nearest American School (a school that caters to overseas American students or those learning English), which is usually a popular destination for recruiters.

If you'd like to know which schools most foreign students choose, see the sidebar below, "U.S. Colleges and Universities With High Foreign Student Attendance." Attending a school with many other foreign students has certain advantages. The school administration is likely to be expert in dealing with the immigration aspects of your stay. The administration as well as the students may have developed culturally sensitive practices concerning daily life issues—depending on where you're from, you might want to know that you'll find such amenities as vegetarian food or all-women dormitories. And, you might find it a relief to be able to speak to other students in your own language once in awhile. Of course, this list shouldn't be your only guide. You'll need to take a number of factors into account in choosing a school, including the focus or quality of the academic program, the location, the cost and more.

1. When to Start Applying to Schools

If you are applying to academic programs, start contacting schools at least a year before you plan to start your studies. Competition for entry to schools in the United States can be fierce, especially if they are big-name schools like Harvard or Stanford. You'll probably want to submit between five and ten applications to a mix of schools, including some that you know you have a good chance of being admitted to.

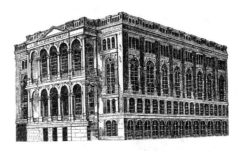

Cooper Union
New York, New York

U.S. Colleges and Universities With High Foreign Student Attendance

This list ranks the U.S. colleges and universities, both public and private, with the highest percentages of foreign student attendance in 1998-99. The initials after the school's name indicate which state it is located in. Source: U.S. News and World Report, Inc., at http://www.usnews.com/usnews/edu/college/rankings/natl_int.htm.

College or University	Percentage of Foreign Students	College or University	Percentage of Foreign Students
U.S. International University (CA)	34%	Brown University (RI)	7%
Florida Institute of Technology (FL)	28%	Columbia University (NY)	7%
New School University (NY)	24%	Cornell University (NY)	7%
Illinois Institute of Technology (IL)	16%	Drexel University (PA)	7%
Andrews University (MI)	14%	Florida International University (FL)	7%
American University (DC)	13%	Georgetown University (DC)	7%
Eckerd College (FL)	12%	Harvard University (MA)	7%
Mount Holyoke College (MA)	12%	Northeastern University (MA)	7%
Clark University (MA)	11%	Nova Southeastern University (FL)	7%
Beloit College (WI)	11%	Pepperdine University (CA)	7%
Knox College (IL)	11%	University of Oregon (OR)	7%
Macalester College (MN)	11%	University of Southern California (CA)	7%
Ohio Wesleyan University (OH)	11%	Yale University (CT)	7%
University of Tulsa (OK)	10%	Bethany College (WV)	7%
Goshen College (IN)	10%	Bryn Mawr College (PA)	7%
California Institute of Technology (CA)	9%	Lake Forest College (IL)	7%
Carnegie Mellon University (PA)	9%	Lawrence University (WI)	7%
University of Miami (FL)	9%	Middlebury College (VT)	7%
University of Pennsylvania (PA)	9%	Randolph-Macon Women's College (VA)	7%
Bennington College (VT)	9%	Swarthmore College (PA)	7%
Boston University (MA)	8%	Bard College (NY)	6%
Johns Hopkins University (MD)	8%	Franklin and Marshall College (PA)	6%
Massachusetts Institute of Technology (MA)	8%	Manhattanville College (NY)	6%
Stevens Institute of Technology (NJ)	8%	Oberlin College (OH)	6%
Tufts University (MA)	8%	Smith College (MA)	6%
University of San Francisco (CA)	8%	Washington College (MD)	6%
College of Wooster (OH)	8%	Wellesley College (MA)	6%
Connecticut College (CT)	8%	Williams College (MA)	6%
Grinnell College (IA)	8%		

Why Are Some Schools "Public" and Others "Private"?

The entire U.S. school system is split between public and private schools. Public schools are funded all or in part by the U.S. or local governments. For students who are U.S. citizens or residents, public schools are free through the 12th grade (the end of high school), and cost less than private schools at the university level. Private schools (all grades and college) are not funded by the government, and usually charge tuitions of many thousand's of dollars per year.

As discussed in Chapter 3, foreign students are not allowed to attend public elementary or middle schools (kindergarten through 8th grade) at all. You are allowed to attend one year of a U.S. public high school (9th through 12th grade)—but no more than one year, and you'll have to pay for it.

Foreign students are allowed to attend U.S. public colleges and universities. There are usually a few in every state, such as the "University of California" or "State University of New York" systems. However, you will have to pay a higher tuition than people who live in the state where the school is located—that's because you, along with U.S. students from other states, will be considered a "nonresident." (The reasoning is that nonresidents' families didn't help fund the university with their taxes, and therefore shouldn't benefit from the government's funding.) Even at nonresident tuition rates, however, public universities may be more affordable than the private ones. And they're usually larger, which may increase your chances of gaining admission.

There is no barrier to your attending private U.S. schools, colleges and universities—you must simply meet the school's own admissions standards. Some of America's most prestigious colleges and universities are private, including Yale, Harvard, Stanford, Smith, Williams, Brown and others. Many of them make a special effort to attract foreign students. The tuition will be the same no matter where you're coming from.

Some schools will give you an answer right away, but most academic programs require at least a few months to make a decision about accepting you. Applications for undergraduate programs, for example, are usually due around January; and acceptances and rejections come anywhere between April and June of that year. For more information, contact the schools directly, or see websites such as http://www.studyusa.com.

It's less easy to generalize about vocational programs. Some will follow an academic calendar, others are on shorter schedules of weeks or months. Just remember to start planning ahead with enough time to allow for an acceptance by your program as well as a visa decision by the U.S. consulate.

2. After You're Admitted: The Form I-20

Once a school or program has admitted you and you've indicated that you will attend (usually by paying a deposit), the school will prepare a Form I-20 Certificate of Eligibility. You won't have to supply them with the blank Form I-20—they'll have it on hand and know how to fill it out before they send it to you. F-1 students will get what's called an I-20AB, and M-1 students will get an I-20MN. Take good care of this form, because you'll be submitting it as part of your visa application. The school should not charge you any money for issuing the I-20.

The I-20 is nothing mysterious. It is the school's statement to the U.S. government that you have submitted all the right paperwork and financial documents, the school has evaluated your application and it meets their standards and you have been accepted for enrollment in a full course of study. There's a sample blank form I-20AB below. The I-20MN for M-1 students is similar.

When you receive the I-20, you'll see that the front has been signed by the school's Designated Student Officer ("DSO," the school's link between international students and the INS). You'll need to sign the back of the form. If you are under age 18, one of your parents will have to sign as well. Then hang onto the form until you're ready with the rest of your visa application, coming up later in this chapter.

I-20, Certificate of Eligibility for Nonimmigrant (F-1) Student Status—Page 1

| **U.S. Department of Justice**
Immigration and Naturalization Service
Please Read Instructions on Page 2 | Certificate of Eligibility for Nonimmigrant (F-1) Student
Status - For Academic and Language Students | OMB No. 1115-0051

Page 1 |

This page must be completed and signed in the U.S. by a designated school official.

1. Family Name (surname)

   First (given) name (do not enter middle name)

Country of birth	Date of birth (mo./day/year)
Country of citizenship	Admission number (Complete if known)

   For Immigration Official Use

Visa issuing post	Date Visa issued

   Reinstated, extension granted to:

2. School (school district) name

   School official to be notified of student's arrival in U.S. (Name and Title)

   School address (include zip code)

   School code (including 3-digit suffix, if any) and approval date

   _____ 214F_____ approved on _____

3. This certificate is issued to the student named above for:
   (Check and fill out as appropriate)
   a. ☐ Initial attendance at this school
   b. ☐ Continued attendance at this school
   c. ☐ School transfer.
      Transferred from _____
   d. ☐ Use by dependents for entering the United States.
   e. ☐ Other _____

4. Level of education the student is pursuing or will pursue in the United States:
   (check only one)
   a. ☐ Primary   e. ☐ Master's
   b. ☐ Secondary   f. ☐ Doctorate
   c. ☐ Associate   g. ☐ Language training
   d. ☐ Bachelor's   h. ☐ Other

5. The student named above has been accepted for a full course of study at
   this school, majoring in_____
   The student is expected to report to the school no later than (date)
   _____ and complete studies not later than (date)_____
   The normal length of study is _____

6. ☐ English proficiency is required:
   ☐ The student has the required English proficiency
   ☐ The student is not yet proficient, English instructions will be given at
      the school.
   ☐ English proficiency is not required because_____

7. This school estimates the student's average costs for an academic term of
   _____ (up to 12) months to be:
   a. Tuition and fees $ _____
   b. Living expenses $ _____
   c. Expenses of dependents $ _____
   d. Other(specify): $ _____
      Total $ _____

8. This school has information showing the following as the students means of
   support, estimated for an academic term of _____ months (Use the same
   number of months given in item 7).
   a. Student's personal funds $ _____
   b. Funds from this school $ _____
      (specify type)   _____
   c. Funds from another source $ _____
      (specify type and source)   _____
   d. On-campus employment (if any) $ _____
      Total $ _____

9. Remarks: _____
   _____
   _____
   _____
   _____

10. School Certification: I certify under penalty of perjury that all information provided above in items 1 through 8 was completed before I signed this form and is true and correct; I executed this form in the United States after review and evaluation in the United States by me or other officials of the school of the student's application, transcripts or other records of courses taken and proof of financial responsibility, which were received at the school prior to the execution of this form; the school has determined that the above named student's qualifications meet all standards for admission to the school; the student will be required to pursue a full course of study as defined by 8 CFR 214.2(f)(6); I am a designated official of the above named school and I am authorized to issue this form.

| Signature of designated school official | Name of school official (print or type) | Title | Date issued | Place issued (city and state) |

11. Student Certification: I have read and agreed to comply with the terms and conditions of my admission and those of any extension of stay as specified on page 2. I certify that all information provided on this form refers specifically to me and is true and correct to the best of my knowledge. I certify that I seek to enter or remain in the United States temporarily, and solely for the purpose of pursuing a full course of study at the school named on page 1 of this form. I also authorize the named school to release any information from my records which is needed by the INS pursuant to 8 CFR 214.3(g) to determine my nonimmigrant status.

| Signature of student | Name of student | Date |

| Signature of parent or guardian
if student is under 18 | Name of parent/guardian (Print or type) | Address(city) | (State or province) | (Country) | (Date) |

Form I20 A-B/I20ID(Rev 04-27-88)N

| For official use only
Microfilm Index Number |

I-20 SCHOOL

I-20, Certificate of Eligibility for Nonimmigrant (F-1) Student Status—Page 4

Page 4

IF YOU NEED MORE INFORMATION CONCERNING YOUR F-1 NONIMMIGRANT STUDENT STATUS AND THE RELATING IMMIGRATION PROCEDURES, PLEASE CONTACT EITHER YOUR FOREIGN STUDENT ADVISOR ON CAMPUS OR A NEARBY IMMIGRATION AND NATURALIZATION SERVICE OFFICE.

THIS PAGE, WHEN PROPERLY ENDORSED, MAY BE USED FOR ENTRY OF THE SPOUSE AND CHILDREN OF AN F-1 STUDENT FOLLOWING TO JOIN THE STUDENT IN THE UNITED STATES OR FOR REENTRY OF THE STUDENT TO ATTEND THE SAME SCHOOL AFTER A TEMPORARY ABSENCE FROM THE UNITED STATES.

For reentry of the student and/or the F-2 dependents (EACH CERTIFICATION SIGNATURE IS VALID FOR ONLY ONE YEAR.)

Signature of Designated School Official	Name of School Official(print or type)	Title	Date
Signature of Designated School Official	Name of School Official(print or type)	Title	Date
Signature of Designated School Official	Name of School Official(print or type)	Title	Date
Signature of Designated School Official	Name of School Official(print or type)	Title	Date
Signature of Designated School Official	Name of School Official(print or type)	Title	Date
Signature of Designated School Official	Name of School Official(print or type)	Title	Date

Dependent spouse and children of the F-1 student who are seeking entry/reentry to the U.S.

Name family (caps) first	Date of birth	Country of birth	Relationship to the F-1 student

Student Employment Authorization and other Records

Before signing your I-20, review it carefully for errors. If there are errors, send it back to the school for correction. It's better to have the school fix any errors now than to have to explain them to a consular or INS officer later.

B. Contact Your Local U.S. Consulate

You will be applying for your student visa at a U.S. embassy or consulate. Start by locating the nearest one. Your country's capital city probably has at least one embassy, and other major cities may have smaller consulates. You can locate consulates in different countries by checking the State Department's website at http://www.state.gov/www/regions_missions.html or by calling the U.S. State Department in Washington, D.C., at 202-663-1225.

1. If You Live Outside Your Native Country or Your Country Has No U.S. Consulate

If you live in a country other than your country of citizenship, go to the consulate in the country where you live. If the country where you live has no U.S. consulate, there will most likely be a consulate in an adjoining country that has been chosen by the State Department to handle visa requests from your country.

Although you can, in theory, apply for your student visa at any consulate in the world, in reality consulates are reluctant to accept applications from stray travelers. If you are in this predicament, go ahead and try to apply to the consulate in the country where you are. Be prepared for questions about why you could not go to your home country's U.S. consulate. You will not be hurt by the fact that you were turned down for a visa if the only reason for the refusal was that you went to the wrong consulate.

2. Ask About Local Consular Procedures

Once you've identified the proper consulate, you'll need to figure out its procedures for taking your application. In some countries, you can to go straight to the consulate, present your application and paperwork and receive your visa within a day. In other countries, the decision will take several weeks, even after a walk-in appointment. The State Department warns that the months of June, July and August tend to be especially busy with visa applications. Check with your local U.S. consulate via telephone or their website to see whether you can just walk in, or whether you need to make an appointment or mail in your application.

Your application will be a combination of forms and documents. The ones which require explanation are covered in Sections C and D, coming up. All the items are summarized on the Checklist in Section E.

C. The Application Form

Once you have your I-20, you'll only be responsible for filling out one form for your student visa application, the State Department Form OF-156 (pictured below). This is a standard form used by the consulates to gather information about all applicants for temporary visas.

You'll find the standard version of Form OF-156 as a tear-out in Appendix D. However, it's best to use the form that you get from your local consulate, as it may be slightly different (many consulates have their own version).

When you've got a copy of Form OF-156 in hand, follow these line-by-line instructions on filling it out.

Questions 1-5: Self-explanatory.

Question 6: Your **"nationality"** refers to the country whose passport you carry. Even if you apply for your student visa at a U.S. consulate in a country other than the one that gave you a passport, the consulate will evaluate your application in part on the likelihood that you will return to your country of nationality. If your country of nationality has severe economic or civil difficulties, or if it offers few career opportunities in the field which you'll be studying, your chances of an approval are reduced.

OF-156, Nonimmigrant Visa Application—Page 1

PLEASE TYPE OR PRINT YOUR ANSWERS IN THE SPACE PROVIDED BELOW EACH ITEM.

1. SURNAMES OR FAMILY NAMES (*Exactly as in Passport*)

2. FIRST NAME AND MIDDLE NAME (*Exactly as in Passport*)

3. OTHER NAMES (*Maiden, Religious, Professional, Aliases*)

4. DATE OF BIRTH (*mm-dd-yyyy*)

8. PASSPORT NUMBER

5. PLACE OF BIRTH
City, Province   Country

DATE PASSPORT ISSUED (*mm-dd-yyyy*)

6. NATIONALITY

7. SEX
☐ MALE
☐ FEMALE

DATE PASSPORT EXPIRES (*mm-dd-yyyy*)

9. HOME ADDRESS (*Include apartment no., street, city, province, and postal zone*)

10. NAME AND STREET ADDRESS OF PRESENT EMPLOYER OR SCHOOL (*Postal box number unacceptable*)

11. HOME TELEPHONE NO.

12. BUSINESS TELEPHONE NO.

13. MARITAL STATUS
☐ Married ☐ Single ☐ Widowed ☐ Divorced ☐ Separated
If married, give name and nationality of spouse

14. NAMES AND RELATIONSHIPS OF PERSONS TRAVELING WITH YOU
(NOTE: *A separate application must be made for a visa for each traveler, regardless of age.*)

15. HAVE YOU EVER APPLIED FOR A U.S. NONIMMIGRANT VISA?
☐ NO ☐ YES
HAVE YOU EVER APPLIED FOR A U.S. IMMIGRANT VISA?
☐ NO ☐ YES
WHERE? _____
WHEN? _____
VISA WAS ISSUED ☐   VISA WAS REFUSED ☐

16. HAS YOUR U.S. VISA EVER BEEN CANCELED?
☐ NO ☐ YES
WHERE? _____
WHEN? _____
BY WHOM? _____

17. Bearers of visitor visas may generally not work or study in the U.S.
DO YOU INTEND TO WORK IN THE U.S.? ☐ NO ☐ YES
If YES, explain.

18. DO YOU INTEND TO STUDY IN THE U.S.? ☐ NO ☐ YES
If YES, write name and address of school as it appears on Form I-20.

DO NOT WRITE IN THIS SPACE
B-1/B-2 MAX   B-1 MAX   B-2 MAX

OTHER_____ MAX
Visa Classification

MULT OR_____
Number Applications

MONTHS_____
Validity

L.O. CHECKED

ON_____ BY _____

ISSUED/REFUSED

ON_____ BY _____

UNDER SEC.   214(b)   221(g)

OTHER:_____ INA

REFUSAL REVIEWED BY _____

19. PRESENT OCCUPATION (*If retired, state past occupation*)

20. WHO WILL FURNISH FINANCIAL SUPPORT, INCLUDING TICKETS?

21. AT WHAT ADDRESS WILL YOU STAY IN THE U.S.A.?

22. WHAT IS THE PURPOSE OF YOUR TRIP?

23. WHEN DO YOU INTEND TO ARRIVE IN THE U.S.A.?

24. HOW LONG DO YOU PLAN TO STAY IN THE U.S.A.?

25. HAVE YOU EVER BEEN IN THE U.S.A.?
☐ NO ☐ YES
WHEN? _____
FOR HOW LONG? _____
COMPLETE ALL QUESTI...
REVERSE OF F...

NONIMMIGRANT VISA APPLICATION

OPTIONAL FORM 156   PAGE 1   50156-108   NS...
10-2000   PREVIOUS EDITIONS OBSOLETE

U.S. Department of State

Additional pages not shown.

Question 7: Self-explanatory.

Question 8: This information should be found on your passport. Note that the expiration date needs to be at least six months beyond the date of your visa approval.

Question 9: Your **"Home Address"** is important not only for identifying you, but to make sure that you're applying at the correct consulate for your area.

Question 10: Your **"Work Address"** is important because the fact that you are employed hopefully adds to your reason to want to return to your home country. (Even if you do not plan to return to this job, it shows at least that you are employable.) Bring documents to verify this work, such as a letter from your employer and copies of pay stubs.

Question 11: Self-explanatory.

Question 12: Self-explanatory.

Question 13: Self-explanatory.

Question 14: This is where you write the names of your spouse and children if they will be accompanying you to the United States. After their name(s), list their relationship to you, such as "husband," "wife" or "child." Each of your family members will also have to fill out a separate Form OF-156, but if you are granted the student visa, they have a good chance of being granted visas as well (the F-2 or M-2 visa for spouses and children of students). See Section F, below, for more on bringing your family with you.

Question 15: If you have ever applied for any other visa to the United States, whether nonimmigrant (temporary) or immigrant (permanent), you'll need to supply the details here. A previous visa denial doesn't mean that the consulate will deny this one, but the officer will definitely look into why the previous one was denied.

Question 16: This question asks about whether you have had a visa "cancelled"—meaning that you received a visa, but a consul or INS official later made a formal decision that you didn't deserve it. As in the last question, a cancellation doesn't automatically mean that your present student vis will be denied. However, the consulate will loo hard at the reason for the cancellation

Question 17: You should enter "No" here. A limited amount of work may be allowed under your visa, but a "Yes" answer will look like working is part of your primary plan in getting the student visa. The exception would be if you already know that your study program will require you to perform curricular practical training. In that case, you should answer Yes and attach an explanation.

Questions 18-19: Self-explanatory.

Question 20: List your sources of support, such as "myself, parents (Mr. and Mrs. *[Name]*), scholarship from the *[country]* government." If you can find room on the form, enter the words "please see attached documentation of support"—you will, in accordance with our instructions later in this chapter, be attaching documents.

Question 21: You should have some arrangement for temporary or permanent housing upon your arrival in the United States, even if it's just a hotel reservation. Your school should be able to help you with this.

Question 22: The **"Purpose of Your Trip"** is to "study."

Question 23: Your arrival date cannot be earlier than 90 days before your study program starts.

Question 24: The length of your stay should correspond to the DSO's notation on your I-20, which states how long it should take you to complete your studies.

Question 25: You will need to list all of your previous trips to the United States, the dates of those trips and how long each trip lasted. You will probably be asked more about these trips at your consular interview, and should bring any previous passports and visas to show the consular officer, if possible. One of the most important issues will be whether you have ever stayed past the date that your visa or authorized stay expired (see Chapter 2, Can You Enter the U.S. at All? for the consequences of having stayed too long).

Questions 26(a)-(c): A "Yes" answer to any of these questions will lead the consul to wonder whether your true intention in entering the United States is to wait until an immigrant visa becomes available to you. You'll need to answer honestly, but provide an explanation for any Yes answers.

Question 27: Self-explanatory. As you can imagine, the more family members you list, the more proof the consulate will want that you don't plan to stay with your family permanently in the United States.

Question 28: You must provide this list of residences so that the consulate can run security checks on you. They'll ask the appropriate government whether you have a police record.

Question 29: All of these questions refer to the grounds of inadmissibility discussed in Chapter 2. If the answer to any of these is "Yes," you are likely to be denied the visa and should consult a lawyer before going any farther. The lawyer may find that you can honestly answer "No," or may help you qualify for an exception or waiver forgiving the problem (waivers are not covered in this book).

D. Documents You'll Need

Almost anyone can fill out a form—but what will set you apart from the thousands of other people applying for student visas and increase your chances of getting one is the quality of your documentary evidence. You'll need to assemble copies of your official and personal papers that confirm your intent to return home at the end of your visit and attest to your ability to support yourself during your stay. Here is a full list of the required documents, with references to discussions below that provide further explanation where needed:

- your passport (valid for at least six months after your consular appointment)
- documents showing that you will return to your home country (see subsection 1, below)
- documents showing that you have the academic credentials to attend the school or program of your choice, including diplomas, transcripts and scores from standardized tests required by the school that you'll be attending
- documents showing that you can pay your tuition, fees and living expenses, including

Form I-134 if necessary (see subsection 2, below)
- fee (currently $45) for a machine-readable visa plus a "reciprocity fee" (charged only in countries that charge U.S. students a fee to get a visa), and
- two passport-style photos. (Although technically only one photo is required, some consulates want one photo for your visa and another for their file.)

1. Proving Your Intent to Return Home

One of your most important tasks in applying for your student visa is to prove that you plan to return home when your studies are over. Explaining your plans to the consular officer is a good start, but she is not likely to be convinced until she sees some evidence of those reasons on paper.

Start assembling your proof before you meet the consular officer. Look for documents from official sources. For example, a deed showing that you own a house will be considered stronger evidence than a letter from your mother saying she wants you to come home. There is no limit on how many documents you can submit—though you wouldn't want to irritate the officer by showing up with a box-full. It's best to put together a combination of credible documents from different sources.

The following are examples of types of documents that you could include in your visa application. Don't feel limited by this list. You may have a special reason for wanting to return home that no one but you could think of and which may be the most convincing reason of all. In general, consider including:

- a copy of your home title or rental agreement, either of which shows that you have a stable place to live
- a sworn affidavit from your parents listing all the family members who live in your home country, and including details to show that they are all firmly settled there; even better is to include a statement of why you, too, are

likely to return (especially if there is a family business or property)

- evidence that you are leaving a spouse and children behind, such as copies of marriage and birth certificates; leaving your family behind is not a requirement of the visa, but if you do plan to leave them, make the most of this information
- documentation of an existing business or employment that you will return to, such as a business license or a letter from your employer and copies of recent pay stubs
- documentation of your career potential in your home country, including statistics from a reputable source, such as your government, showing that people with your skills are in high demand; or a letter from a potential employer
- documentation of any monetary bonds that you paid to government scholarship funders in order to guarantee your return (copies of your receipts and correspondence will be best), and
- a prepaid, round-trip plane ticket to and from the United States. Some consulates routinely ask for this, despite the fact that the regulations do not require it.

2. Proving Your Ability to Pay

You are expected to prove that you can cover your tuition and living expenses not only for yourself, but for your spouse and children if they will be accompanying you to the United States. You'll have to do this without relying on any employment that you might pick up in the United States—and without your spouse or children working at all.

If you will be on an F-1 visa, your existing financial resources must clearly cover a 12-month academic term, and you must be prepared to prove that your further years of study will be covered as well. The government doesn't expect you to be able to pay for all your years of education the day you get your visa, but they do expect you to show where the money will come from. If you are on an M-1 visa,

your resources must cover your entire 12-month (or shorter) study term.

Your sources of financial support can include personal funds, personal assets or property that are readily convertible to cash, pay from work that you will do in the United States as part of a fellowship or scholarship or specified funds from other persons or organizations. To establish your source of support, try to provide a combination of the following documents:

- evidence of personal or family funds, such as copies of bank statements or stock certificates. Combine this with a list summarizing your total cash assets. Note that if a bank statement shows a recent deposit but a low average balance, the U.S. government will want an explanation. Attach something in writing (your own statement or an official document showing the source of the new cash) to the copy of the bank statement. Your goal is to overcome any suspicion that the money was borrowed from a friend to pad the account and make the financial situation look better than it is
- evidence that family members who will support you from your home country are employed, such as a letter (on company letterhead) from their employer (see the Sample Letter From Family Member's Employer, below), or copies of their income tax statements (if any)
- evidence that you or your family members possess assets that can be readily converted to cash (in a country whose currency is traded on the international exchange). For example, real estate (land) is a good asset to show. The consulate will want to see whether the property is owned free and clear, or whether it carries any debt or lien—include papers that show to what extent any loans or mortgages have been paid off. If the ownership papers don't make the value clear, or show a value that seems too low, you can hire a professional appraiser to prepare an estimate and report
- if your family members will be supporting you, you can use an INS Form I-134 (see subsection 3, below) to indicate that they not only have the income and assets you've shown, but

they are willing to spend them on your studies and living expenses

- documentation of any scholarships, fellowships, assistantships, grants or loans from your school, government or private sources. Although these will also be listed on your I-20, you must provide independent confirmation of them. A copy of the notification letter you received is best.

If individuals who are not members of your family are willing to support you, use any of the types of evidence mentioned above for family members, including a Form I-134 Affidavit of Support. The consulate will wonder, however, why someone who is not related to you would want to support your getting an expensive U.S. education. For that reason, non-family members should also write a sworn statement explaining why they are so willing, able and motivated. The statement should mention that the person understands that she is not just a "backup" if other sources fail, but that she will be immediately responsible for paying all or part of your tuition, fees and expenses. Don't be shocked if the consular officer doubts the person's sincerity and denies your application accordingly.

Should Your Family Be Nervous About Agreeing to Support You?

Family members kind enough to pledge money toward your studies hopefully understand and are prepared for the costs of your tuition, books and living expenses. However, two issues might cause them additional concern: the chances that unexpected and uncontrollable costs may arise, and the implications of signing an INS form that promises the family's support to you.

We're assuming that you're not going to go on a spending spree at the local U.S. mall and present the bills to your family. But what if you have a bike accident and spend a few weeks in the hospital? Or what if you become pregnant and need prenatal and other medical care? Medical bills are your most likely source of unexpected costs. The United States has no system of national health insurance, and medical care can be staggeringly expensive. Your school will probably have an infirmary to deal with minor health issues (like the flu or a localized infection) for free or at low cost. Talk to your DSO about whether you need additional student health insurance to cover more serious health matters, and whether such insurance is offered through the school—if so, it's well worth the investment.

The second possible concern for families is the fact that they may be asked to sign a government form in connection with supporting you (INS Form I-134, discussed in more detail below). Families wonder just how bound they'll be by this form and how far the U.S. government will go in demanding their support. Unfortunately, there are no clear answers to these questions. On the one hand, you can reassure your sponsors that their obligation will be more moral than legal. Most lawyers think that Form I-134 is a flawed legal contract that wouldn't hold up in court if the INS tried to enforce it. If your family is unable to support you over the long haul, the most likely consequence is that you'll have to apply for an emergency work permit (discussed in Chapter 12) or you'll have to drop out of school and leave the United States.

On the other hand, there's no guarantee that the INS would never try to pressure the family of a foreign student or take the family to court—particularly if you use U.S. government assistance or welfare and the INS wants it reimbursed. And, of course, anyone from whom you purchase goods or services will have a right to demand that you find a way to pay. They couldn't demand that your sponsor pay, but the practical reality is that you might look to your sponsor for help.

Sample Letter From Family Member's Employer

City Medical Group
111 Vermeer Road
Amsterdam, Holland

September 4, 200x

To Whom It May Concern:

This letter is to confirm the employment of Mr. Tiemo Terwilliger with our office. Mr. Terwilliger is employed full-time as a radiology technician. He earns a salary of 70,000 guilders per year (approximately $26,000 U.S. at current exchange rates). His position is permanent and his prospects for advancement are excellent.

Very truly yours,

Laurentius-Petrus Van Slyke

Laurentius-Petrus Van Slyke
Director of Personnel

3. Line-by-Line Instructions for Form I-134

Form I-134 (pictured below) can be used by your friends or family to indicate their agreement to provide financial support. If you choose to print this form yourself from the INS website, print the instructions as a separate page but don't turn them in to the consulate. Print the rest double-sided, head to foot. In the instructions below, we'll refer to the person filling out the form as the "sponsor."

If you have a spouse or children accompanying you to the United States, they won't need a separate Form I-134—listing them in Question 3 is sufficient.

You'll find a tear-out version of this form in Appendix D.

When the sponsor has a copy of this form in hand, he or she should follow these line-by-line instructions for filling it out.

Paragraph 1: Self-explanatory, calling for the sponsor to fill in his or her name and address.

Question 1: Self-explanatory. If the sponsor lives outside the United States, he or she is probably not a citizen or permanent resident of the United States. That's fine, he or she can simply ignore parts a, b, c and d of this question.

Question 2: If the sponsor is not a resident of the United States, he or she can simply enter "N/A" for the second half of this question.

Question 3: This is for information about you. The questions are self-explanatory. Enter the names of your spouse and children (if any) only if they will be accompanying you to the United States.

Question 7: Back to the sponsor, who must enter information about his or her place of employment. For **"type of business,"** the sponsor may enter his or her position (such as "secretary" or "accountant") or a more generic description such as "medicine" or "sales."

On the next set of lines, the sponsor enters information about his or her income and assets. The question about the amount **"on deposit in savings banks in the United States"** is a little misleading— it's okay to also include amounts in savings *or* checking accounts, as well as amounts in the sponsor's home country. For **"personal property,"** the sponsor doesn't need to consider the exact value of everything he owns. An approximate total value on his or her cars, jewelry, appliances (stereo, television, refrigerator), automobiles, cameras and other equipment will do. Your sponsor should also supply proof of ownership of the largest items, such as a title for real property (land) or a sales receipt for a car.

Question 8: If the sponsor lives in the United States, he or she will list the same people who were named as dependents on the sponsor's income tax form. If the sponsor lives overseas in a country with a tax system comparable to the United States, in which a taxpayer lists dependents on a tax return, the names of these dependent persons should be entered here.

Question 9: This question attempts to find out whether the sponsor would be overextending him or herself financially by supporting you. If he or

I-134, Affidavit of Support—Page 1

U.S. Department of Justice
Immigration and Naturalization Service

OMB No. 1115-0062

Affidavit of Support

(Answer All Items: Fill in with Typewriter or Print in Block Letters in Ink.)

I, _____ residing at _____
  (Name)   (Street and Number)

_____
  (City)   (State)   (Zip Code if in U.S.)   (Country)

BEING DULY SWORN DEPOSE AND SAY:

1. I was born on _____ at _____
   (Date)   (City)   (Country)

   If you are **not** a native born United States citizen, answer the following as appropriate:

   a. If a United States citizen through naturalization, give certificate of naturalization number _____

   b. If a United States citizen through parent(s) or marriage, give citizenship certificate number _____

   c. If United States citizenship was derived by some other method, attach a statement of explanation.

   d. If a lawfully admitted permanent resident of the United States, give "A" number _____

2. That I am _____ years of age and have resided in the United States since (date) _____

3. That this affidavit is executed in behalf of the following person:

Name		Gender	Age
Citizen of (Country)	Marital Status	Relationship to Sponsor	
Presently resides at (Street and Number)	(City)	(State)	(Country)

Name of spouse and children accompanying or following to join person:

Spouse	Gender	Age	Child	Gender	Age
Child	Gender	Age	Child	Gender	Age
Child	Gender	Age	Child	Gender	Age

4. That this affidavit is made by me for the purpose of assuring the United States Government that the person(s) named in item 3 will not become a public charge in the United States.

5. That I am willing and able to receive, maintain and support the person(s) named in item 3. That I am ready and willing to deposit a bond, if necessary, to guarantee that such person(s) will not become a public charge during his or her stay in the United States, or to guarantee that the above named person(s) will maintain his or her nonimmigrant status, if admitted temporarily and will depart prior to the expiration of his or her authorized stay in the United States.

6. That I understand this affidavit will be binding upon me for a period of three (3) years after entry of the person(s) named in item 3 and that the information and documentation provided by me may be made available to the Secretary of Health and Human Services and the Secretary of Agriculture, who may make it available to a public assistance agency.

7. That I am employed as, or engaged in the business of _____ with _____
   (Type of Business)   (Name of concern)

   at _____
      (Street and Number)   (City)   (State)   (Zip Code)

   I derive an annual income of (*if self-employed, I have attached a copy of my last income tax return or report of commercial rating concern which I certify to be true and correct to the best of my knowledge and belief. See instructions for nature of evidence of net worth to be submitted.*) $ _____

   I have on deposit in savings banks in the United States $ _____

   I have other personal property, the reasonable value of which is $ _____

   OVER

Additional pages not shown.

she has filled out this form, or a Form I-864 (another type of affidavit of support), on behalf of any other U.S. immigrant, these lines should be filled in. If not, the sponsor can enter "N/A."

Question 10: This question also looks for sponsors who are overextending themselves, but it applies only to a sponsor who is a citizen or permanent resident (green card holder) of the United States. It asks whether the sponsor has filed a visa petition on behalf of anyone. The implication here is that the sponsor will eventually have to promise financial support to that other person, which would (depending on the timing) reduce the sponsor's ability to support you. Non-U.S. citizen or non-U.S. permanent resident sponsors can enter "N/A."

Question 11: This question is important to fill in, because it addresses the degree to which your sponsor is willing to support you. Your chances of getting a visa will improve if the sponsor checks the box in front of the word "intend" to indicate that the sponsor will make specific contributions of support. For example, if you can estimate what your living expenses and tuition will come to on a monthly basis, the sponsor could agree, in this question, to send you this monthly amount. Showing this may help persuade the consulate that the sponsor knows what he or she is getting into and is serious about fulfilling the obligation.

"Oath or Affirmation of Deponent." This is a lovely example of excruciating legalese. Don't try to puzzle this out; just take it to a notary public to sign. A notary public is someone who is legally authorized by a state government to check a person's identification and make sure that the person signing the document is the one who is named as the person who should sign. To convince a notary of his or her identity, the sponsor should bring a driver's license or other form of photo identification. The notary will then ask the sponsor to sign the form and will place a stamp on it. In the United States, the notary shouldn't charge more than $15 for this service. You can easily find notaries in the United States by looking in the Yellow Pages of your local phone book. Outside the United States, the sponsor can take this form to the U.S. consulate, who will provide a notary.

Harvard University
Cambridge, Massachusetts

E. How to Use the Checklist for Student Visa Application

The following Checklist will help you organize your student visa application. By marking an "X" in the box next to each item as you have prepared or obtained it, you'll ensure that nothing is overlooked or forgotten.

 You'll find a tear-out version of this Checklist in Appendix E.

Checklist for Student Visa Application

Here is what you will need to apply for your student visa.

- ☐ Form I-20 from your school
- ☐ Form OF-156, Nonimmigrant Visa Application
- ☐ valid passport
- ☐ documents showing that you will return to your home country
- ☐ documents showing your academic credentials
- ☐ documents showing that you can pay your tuition, fees and living expenses
- ☐ fee (currently $45 plus any reciprocity fee)
- ☐ two passport-style photos

F. Applying to Bring Your Family Members Along

Your spouse and minor children (under 18) may request visas to come and stay in the United States with you. They are eligible for visas (F-2 and M-2) simply by virtue of being your spouse and children—in other words, they won't have to prove that they're coming to the United States for a specific purpose, such as to travel or study.

Your family members will not get visas automatically, however. First, you'll have to prove that they are really your spouse and children, as discussed in Section 1, below. (For how to bring unmarried partners or other family members, also see Section 1, below.)

Your family members will also have to fill out a separate set of application forms, summarized on the Checklist in subsection 2, below. We don't take your family members step-by-step through the forms and documents as we did for you, but the basic principles are the same. Once you've filled out your own form and prepared your documents, helping your family members with their applications should be no problem. In fact, you have probably covered some of the requirements for your family members' applications already—in the previous sections concerning your own visa, we covered such necessities as proving that your financial resources were enough to cover your accompanying family along with yourself.

Finally, don't forget our discussion of inadmissibility in Chapter 2: *Every* applicant for a U.S. visa, your family members included, must prove that they don't present such a high health, security or other risk that they cannot be admitted to the United States. If one of them is inadmissible, their visa could be denied even if the other family members' visas are granted.

! Your visa could be granted, but your family members' denied. Certain consulates, particularly those in Southeast Asia, have been known to deny student visas to family members in order to ensure the return of the student.

1. Who Counts As a Family Member?

The F-2 and M-2 visas were specially created for the legal spouse and children of F-1 and M-1 students. If you want to bring your spouse and children to the United States while you study, you will have to prove that they are in fact your spouse and children. To do so, use official marriage and birth certificates.

Other Family Members May Be Able to Come Along As Tourists

Family members who are not your spouse and children don't get the same recognition when it comes to visas. Your live-in domestic partner for example, will not qualify for an F-2 visa if you haven't actually gotten married.

However, such family members may not be left completely out in the cold. A B-2 (tourist) visa may be given to family or household members with close ties to you, such as elderly parents or domestic partners of the same or opposite sex. See Chapters 3 and 5 for details on how they can obtain a tourist visa.

2. Using the Overseas Family Members' Checklist

Although your family members' applications are dependent on yours, your family will need to be just as careful as you are to prepare complete applications. Your spouse or children's visas may be rejected if the applicant doesn't prepare a satisfactory application, is inadmissible or doesn't appear likely to return to your home country. Your family's applications will be similar to yours, including the items on the following Checklist.

 You'll find a tear-out copy of the Overseas Family Members' Checklist in Appendix E.

Overseas Family Members' Checklist

☐ Form OF-156, Nonimmigrant Visa Application.
☐ proof of family member's relationship to you (copy of marriage or birth certificate)
☐ copy of your Form I-20AB or Form I-20 MN
☐ passport (valid for at least six months after the consular appointment)
☐ documents showing that your family members will return to your home country
☐ copies of your documents showing that you can pay your tuition, fees and the whole family's living expenses
☐ fee (currently $45)
☐ two passport-style photos

After you have prepared visa applications for yourself and any accompanying family members, see Chapter 9 to prepare for your consular interview. ■

Applying for a Change to Student Status in the U.S.

This chapter is for people who are presently in the United States on a valid visa, but want to enter school and switch their immigration status to "student." For example, if you're a tourist who's found a school to admit you and classes will start soon, you're a worker whose H-1B visa will soon expire or you are married to a U.S. citizen but the marriage and green card application are failing, spending some time studying in the United States may be a natural next step. Assuming that you've read Chapters 1 and 3 to make sure that you're eligible to change to student status, it's time to be guided through the process of putting together your application form and documents.

The application requirements are nearly identical for F-1 (academic) and M-1 (vocational) applicants, so we address both in this chapter. You'll start by getting some paperwork from the school that admits you. After that, you'll fill out and assemble some more paperwork of your own (a "Change of Status" application) and send it all to an INS Service Center for a decision. This chapter takes you through this entire process, including:

- tips on choosing a U.S. school (Section A)
- filling out the application form and collecting the documents that will accompany it (Sections B and C)
- using the Checklist to help stay organized (Section D)
- how to apply for family members to accompany you (Section E), and
- how to track the INS's processing of your application (Section F).

A. Before the Immigration Application: School Admission

You can't start the immigration process until you have been admitted to an INS-approved school and that school has filled out a form called an I-20 (which we'll discuss further on in this section).

This book does not go into depth about how to find the right U.S. school or program and how to get accepted to it. Some good resources to consult about schools and admissions processes include http://www.studyusa.com, http://www.embark.com, and http://www.ies-ed.com (the International Education Service). Also, a local U.S. library should have materials about schools.

If you'd like to know which schools most foreign students choose, see the Sidebar below, "U.S. Colleges and Universities With High Foreign Student Attendance." Attending a school with many other foreign students has certain advantages. The school administration is likely to be expert in dealing with the immigration aspects of your stay. The administration as well as the students may have developed culturally sensitive practices concerning daily life issues— depending on where you're from, you might want to know that you'll find such amenities as vegetarian food or all-women dormitories. And, you might find it a relief to be able to speak to other students in your own language once in awhile. Of course, this list shouldn't be your only guide. You'll need to take a number of factors into account in choosing a school, including the focus or quality of the academic program, the location, the cost and more.

1. When to Start Applying to Schools

If you are applying to academic programs, start contacting schools at least a year before you plan to start your studies. Competition for entry to schools in the United States can be fierce, especially if they are big-name schools like Harvard or Stanford. You'll probably want to submit between five and ten applications to a mix of schools, including some that you know you have a good chance of being admitted to.

Some schools will give you an answer right away, but most academic programs require at least a few months to make a decision about accepting you. Applications for undergraduate programs, for example, are usually due around January and acceptances and rejections come anywhere between April and June of that year. For more information, contact the schools directly, or see websites such as http://www.studyusa.com.

Vocational programs follow their own schedules. Some follow the academic calendar explained

U.S. Colleges and Universities With High Foreign Student Attendance

This list ranks the U.S. colleges and universities, both public and private, with the highest percentages of foreign student attendance in 1998-99. The initials after the school's name indicate which state it is located in. Source: U.S. News and World Report, Inc., at http://www.usnews.com/usnews/edu/college/rankings/natl_int.htm.

College or University	Percentage of Foreign Students	College or University	Percentage of Foreign Students
U.S. International University (CA)	34%	Brown University (RI)	7%
Florida Institute of Technology (FL)	28%	Columbia University (NY)	7%
New School University (NY)	24%	Cornell University (NY)	7%
Illinois Institute of Technology (IL)	16%	Drexel University (PA)	7%
Andrews University (MI)	14%	Florida International University (FL)	7%
American University (DC)	13%	Georgetown University (DC)	7%
Eckerd College (FL)	12%	Harvard University (MA)	7%
Mount Holyoke College (MA)	12%	Northeastern University (MA)	7%
Clark University (MA)	11%	Nova Southeastern University (FL)	7%
Beloit College (WI)	11%	Pepperdine University (CA)	7%
Knox College (IL)	11%	University of Oregon (OR)	7%
Macalester College (MN)	11%	University of Southern California (CA)	7%
Ohio Wesleyan University (OH)	11%	Yale University (CT)	7%
University of Tulsa (OK)	10%	Bethany College (WV)	7%
Goshen College (IN)	10%	Bryn Mawr College (PA)	7%
California Institute of Technology (CA)	9%	Lake Forest College (IL)	7%
Carnegie Mellon University (PA)	9%	Lawrence University (WI)	7%
University of Miami (FL)	9%	Middlebury College (VT)	7%
University of Pennsylvania (PA)	9%	Randolph-Macon Women's College (VA)	7%
Bennington College (VT)	9%	Swarthmore College (PA)	7%
Boston University (MA)	8%	Bard College (NY)	6%
Johns Hopkins University (MD)	8%	Franklin and Marshall College (PA)	6%
Massachusetts Institute of Technology (MA)	8%	Manhattanville College (NY)	6%
Stevens Institute of Technology (NJ)	8%	Oberlin College (OH)	6%
Tufts University (MA)	8%	Smith College (MA)	6%
University of San Francisco (CA)	8%	Washington College (MD)	6%
College of Wooster (OH)	8%	Wellesley College (MA)	6%
Connecticut College (CT)	8%	Williams College (MA)	6%
Grinnell College (IA)	8%		

above, others are on shorter schedules of weeks or months. Just remember to start planning ahead with enough time for an admission decision by your program (ask the school for a time estimate) as well as a Change of Status decision by the U.S. INS (allow for at least three months).

2. After You're Admitted: Form I-20

Once a school or program has admitted you and you've indicated that you will attend (usually by paying a deposit), the school will prepare a Form I-20 Certificate of Eligibility. F-1 students will get what's called an I-20AB, and M-1 students will get an I-20MN. Take good care of this form, because you'll be submitting it as part of your application for student status. The school should not charge you any money for issuing the I-20.

The I-20 is nothing mysterious. It is the school's statement to the U.S. government that you have submitted all the right paperwork and financial documents, the school has evaluated your application and it meets their standards and you have been accepted for enrollment in a full course of study.

Rutgers University
New Brunswick, New Jersey

Why Are Some Schools "Public" and Others "Private"?

The entire U.S. school system is split between public and private schools. Public schools are funded all or in part by the U.S. or local governments. For students who are U.S. citizens or residents, public schools are free through the 12th grade (the end of high school), and cost less than private schools at the university level. Private schools (all grades and college) are not funded by the government, and usually charge tuitions of many thousand's of dollars per year.

As discussed in Chapter 3, foreign students are not allowed to attend public elementary or middle schools (kindergarten through 8th grade) at all. You are allowed to attend one year of a U.S. public high school (9th through 12th grade)—but no more than one year, and you'll have to pay for it.

Foreign students are allowed to attend U.S. public colleges and universities. There are usually a few in every state, such as the "University of California" or "State University of New York" systems. However, you will have to pay a higher tuition than people who live in the state where the school is do—that's because you, along with U.S. students from other states, will be considered a "nonresident." (The reasoning is that nonresidents' families didn't help fund the university with their taxes, and therefore shouldn't benefit from the government's funding.) Even at non-resident tuition rates, however, public universities tend to be more affordable than the private ones. And they're usually larger, which may increase your chances of gaining admission.

There is no barrier to your attending private U.S. schools, colleges and universities—you must simply meet the school's own admissions standards. Some of America's most prestigious colleges and universities are private, including Yale, Harvard, Stanford, Amherst, Williams, Brown and others. Many of them make a special effort to attract foreign students. The tuition will be the same no matter where you're coming from.

I-20, Certificate of Eligibility for Nonimmigrant (F-1) Student Status—Page 1

U.S. Department of Justice
Immigration and Naturalization Service
Please Read Instructions on Page 2

Certificate of Eligibility for Nonimmigrant (F-1) Student Status - For Academic and Language Students

OMB No. 1115-0051

Page 1

This page must be completed and signed in the U.S. by a designated school official.

1. Family Name (surname)

   First (given) name (do not enter middle name)

   Country of birth

   Date of birth (mo./day/year)

   Country of citizenship

   Admission number (Complete if known)

For Immigration Official Use

Visa issuing post | Date Visa issued

Reinstated, extension granted to:

2. School (school district) name

   School official to be notified of student's arrival in U.S. (Name and Title)

   School address (include zip code)

   School code (including 3-digit suffix, if any) and approval date

   _____ 214F_____ approved on _____

3. This certificate is issued to the student named above for:
   (Check and fill out as appropriate)
   a. ☐ Initial attendance at this school
   b. ☐ Continued attendance at this school
   c. ☐ School transfer.
      Transferred from _____
   d. ☐ Use by dependents for entering the United States.
   e. ☐ Other _____

4. Level of education the student is pursuing or will pursue in the United States:
   (check only one)
   a. ☐ Primary   e. ☐ Master's
   b. ☐ Secondary   f. ☐ Doctorate
   c. ☐ Associate   g. ☐ Language training
   d. ☐ Bachelor's   h. ☐ Other

5. The student named above has been accepted for a full course of study at this school, majoring in_____

   The student is expected to report to the school no later than (date) _____ and complete studies not later than (date)_____
   The normal length of study is _____

6. ☐ English proficiency is required:
   ☐ The student has the required English proficiency
   ☐ The student is not yet proficient, English instructions will be given at the school.
   ☐ English proficiency is not required because_____

7. This school estimates the student's average costs for an academic term of
   _____ (up to 12) months to be:
   a. Tuition and fees $_____
   b. Living expenses $_____
   c. Expenses of dependents $_____
   d. Other(specify): $_____
      Total $_____

8. This school has information showing the following as the students means of support, estimated for an academic term of _____ months (Use the same number of months given in item 7).
   a. Student's personal funds $_____
   b. Funds from this school $_____
      (specify type)   _____
   c. Funds from another source $_____
      (specify type and source) _____
   d. On-campus employment (if any) $_____
      Total $_____

9. Remarks: _____
   _____
   _____
   _____
   _____
   _____

10. School Certification: I certify under penalty of perjury that all information provided above in items 1 through 8 was completed before I signed this form and is true and correct; I executed this form in the United States after review and evaluation in the United States by me or other officials of the school of the student's application, transcripts or other records of courses taken and proof of financial responsibility, which were received at the school prior to the execution of this form; the school has determined that the above named student's qualifications meet all standards for admission to the school; the student will be required to pursue a full course of study as defined by 8 CFR 214.2(f)(6); I am a designated official of the above named school and I am authorized to issue this form.

Signature of designated school official | Name of school official (print or type) | Title | Date issued | Place issued (city and state)

11. Student Certification: I have read and agreed to comply with the terms and conditions of my admission and those of any extension of stay as specified on page 2. I certify that all information provided on this form refers specifically to me and is true and correct to the best of my knowledge. I certify that I seek to enter or remain in the United States temporarily, and solely for the purpose of pursuing a full course of study at the school named on page 1 of this form. I also authorize the named school to release any information from my records which is needed by the INS pursuant to 8 CFR 214.3(g) to determine my nonimmigrant status.

Signature of student | Name of student | Date

Signature of parent or guardian if student is under 18 | Name of parent/guardian (Print or type) | Address(city) | (State or province) | (Country) | (Date)

Form I20 A-B/I20ID(Rev 04-27-88)N

For official use only
Microfilm Index Number

I-20 SCHOOL

I-20, Certificate of Eligibility for Nonimmigrant (F-1) Student Status—Page 4

Page 4

IF YOU NEED MORE INFORMATION CONCERNING YOUR F-1 NONIMMIGRANT STUDENT STATUS AND THE RELATING IMMIGRATION PROCEDURES, PLEASE CONTACT EITHER YOUR FOREIGN STUDENT ADVISOR ON CAMPUS OR A NEARBY IMMIGRATION AND NATURALIZATION SERVICE OFFICE.

THIS PAGE, WHEN PROPERLY ENDORSED, MAY BE USED FOR ENTRY OF THE SPOUSE AND CHILDREN OF AN F-1 STUDENT FOLLOWING TO JOIN THE STUDENT IN THE UNITED STATES OR FOR REENTRY OF THE STUDENT TO ATTEND THE SAME SCHOOL AFTER A TEMPORARY ABSENCE FROM THE UNITED STATES.

For reentry of the student and/or the F-2 dependents (EACH CERTIFICATION SIGNATURE IS VALID FOR ONLY ONE YEAR.)

Signature of Designated School Official	Name of School Official(print or type)	Title	Date
Signature of Designated School Official	Name of School Official(print or type)	Title	Date
Signature of Designated School Official	Name of School Official(print or type)	Title	Date
Signature of Designated School Official	Name of School Official(print or type)	Title	Date
Signature of Designated School Official	Name of School Official(print or type)	Title	Date
Signature of Designated School Official	Name of School Official(print or type)	Title	Date

Dependent spouse and children of the F-1 student who are seeking entry/reentry to the U.S.

Name family (caps) first	Date of birth	Country of birth	Relationship to the F-1 student

Student Employment Authorization and other Records

There's a sample blank form I-20AB below. The I-20MN for M-1 students is similar.

When you receive the I-20, you'll see that the front has been signed by the school's Designated Student Officer ("DSO," the school's link between international students and the INS). Sign the back of the form. If you are under age 18, one of your parents will have to sign as well. Then hang onto the form until you're ready with the rest of your Change of Status application, coming up later in this chapter.

Before signing your I-20, review it carefully for errors. If there are errors, send it back to the school for correction. It's better to have the school fix any errors now than to have to explain them to a consular or INS officer later.

B. The Application Form

Once you have your I-20, you need to fill out one form for your Change of Status application—the INS Form I-539 (pictured below). Attach a Supplement-1 page if your spouse or children will be staying in the United States with you.

Form I-539 collects basic biographical information about you. The INS uses this information to determine whether you remain admissible to the United States and are eligible for the Change of Status. This form is normally printed out double-sided, head to foot. Form I-539 has more than one use—don't be confused by the presence of questions that don't apply to you.

 You'll find a tear-out version of this form in Appendix D.

1. Line-by-Line Instructions for Form I-539

When you've got Form I-539 in hand, follow these line-by-line instructions.

Instruction page 5, box at bottom of page: Enter your name and U.S. address (this will be used to mail the answer back to you).

Part 1. Information About You: Mostly self-explanatory. You probably won't have a Social Security number unless you are changing from a visa or status that allowed you to work. If you don't have a number, enter "None."

Did you have a Social Security number when you shouldn't have? If you have a Social Security number but haven't been on a visa that allows you to be employed in the United States, your answer to this question could send the INS a message that you've worked illegally. If there is an explanation for your having a number that dispels any question of illegality, attach a letter giving the details. If not, you may want to consult a lawyer.

You will have an **"A-number"** (an eight-digit number following the letter "A" for Alien) only if you have been in deportation or removal proceedings or submitted certain immigration applications, particularly for permanent residence. If you were in proceedings or had any applications denied, see a lawyer.

Your **"I-94 number"** is on the small white card that you received at the border. If the date on that card has passed, you are no longer in status and cannot file this application. Under INS policy, an exception may be made for you if you are within one week of the expiration date, but try to avoid relying on this exception.

If your I-94 card is green, stop now. A green I-94 card means that you entered on the Visa Waiver Program, and therefore are not allowed to apply for a Change of Status in the United States.

For **"Current nonimmigrant status,"** enter the type of visa you have now, such as "B-2 visitor." The date your status **"Expires on"** will be on your I-94 card.

Part 2. Application Type:
Question 1: As a first-time applicant for student status, you should check box **1b** and enter the code "F-1" for academic student status or "M-1" for vocational student status.

Form I-539, Application to Extend/Change Nonimmigrant Status—Page 1

U.S. Department of Justice
Immigration and Naturalization Service

OMB No. 1115-0093; Expires 7/31/04

Application to Extend/Change Nonimmigrant Status

START HERE - Please Type or Print.

FOR INS USE ONLY

Part 1.　Information about you.

Family Name	Given Name	Middle Initial

Address -
In care of -

Street Number and Name		Apt. #

City	State	Zip Code	Daytime Phone #

Country of Birth	Country of Citizenship

Date of Birth (MM/DD/YYYY)	Social Security # (if any)	A # (if any)

Date of Last Arrival Into the U.S.	I-94 #

Current Nonimmigrant Status	Expires on (MM/DD/YYYY)

Returned	Receipt
Date	
Resubmitted	
Date	
Reloc Sent	
Date	
Reloc Rec'd	
Date	

Part 2. Application type. (See instructions for fee.)

1. I am applying for: (Check one.)
   a. ☐ An extension of stay in my current status.
   b. ☐ A change of status. The new status I am requesting is: _____
   c. ☐ Other: (Describe grounds of eligibility.) _____

2. Number of people included in this application: (Check one.)
   a. ☐ I am the only applicant.
   b. ☐ Members of my family are filing this application with me.
   The total number of people (including me) in the application is: _____
   (Complete the supplement for each co-applicant.)

☐ Applicant Interviewed on
_____
Date

☐ *Extension Granted to (Date):*
_____

Change of Status/Extension Granted
New Class: From (Date): _____
_____ To (Date): _____

Part 3.　Processing information.

1. I/We request that my/our current or requested status be extended until (MM/DD/YYYY): _____

2. Is this application based on an extension or change of status already granted to your spouse, child or parent?
   ☐ No ☐ Yes, Receipt # _____

3. Is this application based on a separate petition or application to give your spouse, child or parent an extension or change of status? ☐ No ☐ Yes, filed with this I-539.
   ☐ Yes, filed previously and pending with INS. INS receipt number: _____

4. If you answered "Yes" to Question 3, give the name of the petitioner or applicant:

   If the petition or application is pending with INS, also give the following information:

Office filed at _____ Filed on (MM/DD/YYYY) _____

If Denied:
☐ Still within period of stay
☐ S/D to: _____
☐ Place under docket control

Remarks:

Action Block

Part 4.　Additional information.

1. For applicant #1, provide passport information: Country of Issuance	Valid to: (MM/DD/YYYY)

2. Foreign Address: Street Number and Name	Apt. #

City or Town	State or Province

Country	Zip/Postal Code

To be Completed by
Attorney or Representative, if any

☐ Fill in box if G-28 is attached to represent the applicant

ATTY State License

Additional pages not shown.

Question 2: This is where you have the opportunity to include any spouse or children who will be staying on with you in your application. Check box **2b**, and then write in the total number of them plus you. (For example, a husband wanting to bring his wife and child would enter "3.") Also, fill out the Form I-539 Supplement-1 page, discussed in subsection 2, below.

Part 3. Processing Information:

Question 1: Answer this question even though it seems to only mention extensions. Enter the same date as the one given on your I-20 for the expected completion of your program.

Questions 2 to 4: As the primary applicant, your answer to these questions is **"no."**

Part 4. Additional Information:

Questions 1 and 2: Self-explanatory questions based on the information in your passport and calling for your overseas address.

When does your passport expire? If the expiration date in your passport is within the next six months, you should have it renewed. You can usually do this at a consulate of your home country in the United States. If there isn't a consulate in the city where you're living, you can usually locate one in the phone books for Washington, D.C., Los Angeles, Chicago or San Francisco, or on the Internet at http://www.embassy.org/embassies/index.html or http://www.embpage.org.

Question 3: These questions are designed to see whether you are inadmissible. Think carefully before entering your answers and keep reading for details. If there isn't a good solution below, you'll need to see a lawyer.

Question 3a: If you (or any members of your family) have submitted an application for an **"immigrant visa,"** this indicates that you're seeking a green card. The INS may naturally conclude that you have no intention of returning home after your student stay and will deny your Change of Status application accordingly. There isn't a solution for this—and hiding the other application is impossible.

Question 3b: This is similar to the question above except that instead of referring to an application that you filed yourself, it asks whether someone else has filed a petition to start the process of you obtaining permanent U.S. residence. For example, some petitions filed by family members will place you on a waiting list that will last many years before you see an immigrant visa. Nevertheless, the INS may deny your application if your answer to this question is Yes.

Question 3c: See advice for question 3a. Form I-485 is simply the U.S. version of a green card application.

Question 3d: If you were simply arrested and not charged (for example, the police picked up the wrong person), you are safe entering "Yes" here and attaching a written explanation and a copy of the police report. But for more serious arrests, you must consult a lawyer before going any farther. Most criminal convictions will make you inadmissible to the United States. If you were later found innocent (acquitted) or your case was dismissed by the judge, it will probably not affect your immigration status—but consult a lawyer anyway. This is a tricky area—for example, the INS merely has to suspect that you are guilty of drug trafficking in order to find you inadmissible. An acquittal might not help with that.

Question 3e: To determine whether you have violated your current immigration status, you must consider the type of visa you are on and what you agreed to do to get that visa. For example, if you came to the United States as a tourist, but worked for pay, this would be a status violation. The INS will probably deny this Change of Status application if you have violated your visa terms.

Question 3f: If you are now in **"removal proceedings"** (formerly known as exclusion or deportation proceedings), talk to a lawyer immediately—it's likely that the INS has no power over your application because your immigration situation is in the hands of the courts.

Question 3g: If you have been employed in the United States, your work needs to have been permissible under the visa or status that you had at the time. You may also have been required to obtain a work permit card from the INS. If your work wasn't permitted, talk to a lawyer before continuing with this application. If your work was permitted, look at the paragraph below the question to see what additional information you'll need to supply (do so on a separate piece of paper—and don't forget to put your name at the top in case it gets separated from the rest of the application). Also add a photocopy of both sides of your INS work permit (EAD) if you had one.

Part 5. Signature: Self-explanatory.

Part 6. Signature of person preparing form if other than above: This is where a lawyer or legal assistant would sign. If you simply had some typing help, the person does not need to sign.

2. Line-by-Line Instructions for Form I-539 Supplement-1

Form I-539 Supplement-1 is a one-page, single-sided form (pictured below). As you'll see, it has repeating blocks for information about your spouse and children. Most of it is self-explanatory.

 You'll find a tear-out version of this form in Appendix D.

 If you don't have a spouse or children, or they won't be accompanying you in the United States, you can skip this subsection.

For **"Date of Arrival,"** enter the date of each family member's most recent arrival into the United States (many people mistakenly put the first arrival date). Their **"Current Nonimmigrant Status"** is the name of the visa that they are currently on, such as Visitor. **"Expires on"** refers to the date that person's status expires, which will be on the I-94 card in your family member's passport. When you enter the expiration date of the passport, make sure that it is at least six months into the future. If not, get the passport renewed before completing this application.

However, if waiting for the renewal will so delay your filing this application that you might lose your very eligibility to apply, simply submit the application, write in the current passport expiration date and then add the words "renewal pending."

C. Documents You'll Need

Almost anyone can fill out a form—but what will set you apart from the thousands of other people applying for student status and increase your chances of success is the quality of your documentary evidence. You'll need to assemble copies of your official personal papers that confirm your ability to support yourself during your studies and attest to your intent to return home at the end. Below is a full list of the required documents, with references to discussions below that provide further explanation where needed. You'll need:

- a copy of the primary pages of your passport, which must be valid for at least six months longer
- your original I-94 card (which you received at the U.S. border); make a copy to keep with you
- documentation that you have not fallen out of lawful immigration status (by overstaying or violating the conditions of your visa) since arriving in the United States; normally your I-94 will be enough to show that you have maintained lawful status
- documents showing that you will return to your home country (see subsection 1, below)
- documents showing that you have the academic credentials to attend the school or program of your choice, including diplomas, transcripts and scores from standardized tests required by the school that you'll be attending
- documents showing that you can pay your tuition, fees and living expenses, including a Form I-134 Affidavit of Support if necessary (see subsections 2 and 3, below)
- Fee (currently $120, but check for updates on the INS website at http://www.ins.gov). Pay by check or money order, payable to the USINS. Do not send cash.

Form I-539, Supplement-1

Supplement -1
Attach to Form I-539 when more than one person is included in the petition or application.
(List each person separately. Do not include the person named in the form.)

Family Name	Given Name	Middle Name	Date of Birth (MM/DD/YYYY)
County of Birth	County of Citizenship	Social Security # (if any)	A # (if any)
Date of Arrival (MM/DD/YYYY)		I-94 #	
Current Nonimmigrant Status:		Expires On (MM/DD/YYYY)	
Country Where Passport Issued		Expiration Date (MM/DD/YYYY)	

Family Name	Given Name	Middle Name	Date of Birth (MM/DD/YYYY)
County of Birth	County of Citizenship	Social Security # (if any)	A # (if any)
Date of Arrival (MM/DD/YYYY)		I-94 #	
Current Nonimmigrant Status:		Expires On (MM/DD/YYYY)	
Country Where Passport Issued		Expiration Date (MM/DD/YYYY)	

Family Name	Given Name	Middle Name	Date of Birth (MM/DD/YYYY)
County of Birth	County of Citizenship	Social Security # (if any)	A # (if any)
Date of Arrival (MM/DD/YYYY)		I-94 #	
Current Nonimmigrant Status:		Expires On (MM/DD/YYYY)	
Country Where Passport Issued		Expiration Date (MM/DD/YYYY)	

Family Name	Given Name	Middle Name	Date of Birth (MM/DD/YYYY)
County of Birth	County of Citizenship	Social Security # (if any)	A # (if any)
Date of Arrival (MM/DD/YYYY)		I-94 #	
Current Nonimmigrant Status:		Expires On (MM/DD/YYYY)	
Country Where Passport Issued		Expiration Date (MM/DD/YYYY)	

Family Name	Given Name	Middle Name	Date of Birth (MM/DD/YYYY)
County of Birth	County of Citizenship	Social Security # (if any)	A # (if any)
Date of Arrival (MM/DD/YYYY)		I-94 #	
Current Nonimmigrant Status:		Expires On (MM/DD/YYYY)	
Country Where Passport Issued		Expiration Date (MM/DD/YYYY)	

If you need additional space, attach a separate sheet(s) of paper.
Place your name, A # if any, date of birth, form number and application date at the top of the sheet(s) of paper.

Form I-539 (Rev. 09/04/01)Y Page 4

1. Proving Your Intent to Return Home

One of your most important tasks in applying for student status is to prove that you plan to return home when your studies are over. Your written evidence of this can make or break your application. Since you're already in the United States, the INS will be particularly suspicious that you are merely looking for a way to stay as long as possible, with no real intent to study.

Look for documents that come from official sources. A deed, for example, showing that you own a house, will be considered stronger evidence than a letter from your mother saying she wants you to come home. There is no limit on how many documents you can submit. It's best to put together a combination of credible documents from different sources.

The following are examples of types of documents that you could include in your Change of Status application. Don't feel limited by this list. You may have a special reason for wanting to return home that no one but you could think of and which may be the most convincing reason of all. Consider providing:

- a copy of a home title or rental agreement, either of which shows that you have a stable place to live in your home country
- a sworn affidavit from your parents listing all the family members who live in your home country, including details to show that they are all firmly settled there; even better is to include examples of why you, too, are likely to return (especially if there is a family business or property)
- evidence that you are leaving a spouse and children in your home country, such as copies of marriage and birth certificates; leaving your family behind is not a requirement, but if you do plan to leave them, make the most of this information
- documentation of an existing business or employment that you will return to, such as a business license or a letter from your employer
- documentation of your career potential in your home country, including statistics from a reputable source, such as your government, showing that people with your skills are in high demand; or a letter from a potential employer
- documentation of any monetary bonds that you paid to government scholarship funders in order to guarantee your return (copies of your receipts and correspondence will be best), and
- a copy of a prepaid plane ticket out of the United States.

2. Proving Your Ability to Pay

You are expected to prove that you can cover your tuition and living expenses not only for yourself, but for your spouse and children if they will be staying on with you in the United States. You'll have to do this without relying on any employment that you might pick up in the United States while you're a student—and without your spouse or children working at all.

If you will be on F-1 status, your financial resources must clearly cover a 12-month academic term—and you must show indications that your additional years of study will be covered as well. The government doesn't expect you to be able to pay for all your years of education right away, but they do expect you to show where the money will come from. Similarly, if you will be on M-1 status, your resources must cover your entire 12-month (or shorter) study term.

Your sources of financial support can include personal funds; personal assets or property that are readily convertible to cash; pay from work that you do as part of a fellowship or scholarship; or specified funds from other persons or organizations. Try to provide a combination of documents that will supply evidence of:

- personal or family funds, such as copies of bank statements or stock certificates. Combine this with a list summarizing your total cash assets. Note that if a bank statement shows a recent deposit but a low average balance, the U.S. government will want an explanation. Attach something in writing (your own statement or an official document showing the source of the new cash) to the copy of the bank statement. Your goal is to overcome any suspicion that the money was borrowed from a friend to pad the account and make the financial situation look better than it is.

- the employment status of family members who will support you, such as a letter, on company letterhead, from their employer (see the sample below); or copies of their income tax statements.

- assets held by you or your family members that can be readily converted to cash. (The conversion must be done in a country whose currency is traded on the international exchange.) For example, real estate (land) is a good asset to show. The INS will want to see whether the property is owned free and clear or whether it carries any debt or lien (attach bank or other receipts that show to what extent loans or mortgages have been paid off). If the ownership papers don't make the value clear, or show a value that seems too low, you can hire a professional appraiser to prepare an estimate and report.

- any scholarships, fellowships, assistantships, grants or loans from your school, government or private sources. Although these will also be listed on your I-20, you must provide independent confirmation of them. Usually a copy of the notification letter you received is best.

If your family members will be supporting you, they can use an INS Form I-134 (see subsection 3, below) to indicate that they not only have the income and assets you've shown, but they are willing to spend them on your studies and living expenses.

If individuals who are not members of your family are willing to support you, use any of the types of evidence mentioned above for family members, including a Form I-134 Affidavit of Support. The INS will wonder, however, why someone who is not related to you will want to pay for you to get an expensive U.S. education. For that reason, non-family members should also write a sworn statement explaining why they are so willing, able and motivated. The statement should mention that the person understands that she is not just a "backup" if other

sources fail, but that she will be immediately responsible for paying all or part of your tuition, fees and expenses. Don't be shocked if the INS doubts the person's sincerity and denies your application accordingly. (We'll talk later about what to do if your application is denied, in Chapter 9, Section C.)

Sample Letter From Family Member's Employer

City Medical Group
111 Vermeer Road
Amsterdam, Holland

September 4, 200x

To Whom It May Concern:

This letter is to confirm the employment of Mr. Tiemo Terwilliger with our office. Mr. Terwilliger is employed full-time as a radiology technician. He earns a salary of 70,000 guilders per year (approximately $26,000 U.S. at current exchange rates). His position is permanent and his prospects for advancement are excellent.

Very truly yours,

Laurentius-Petrus Van Slyke

Laurentius-Petrus Van Slyke
Director of Personnel

3. Line-by-Line Instructions for Form I-134, Affidavit of Support

The Form I-134 Affidavit of Support (pictured below) can be used by your friends or family if they agree to sponsor you financially. If you choose to print it out from the INS website, print the instructions as a separate page. Print the rest double-sided, head to foot. We'll refer to the person filling out the form as the "sponsor." You, the student, won't have to fill out any of this form, but should work with the sponsor to make sure that it is filled out correctly.

You'll find a tear-out version of this form in Appendix D.

Once you have a copy of Form I-134 in hand, follow these line-by-line instructions. If you have a spouse or children staying on with you in the United States, they won't need a separate Form I-134—listing them in Question 3 is sufficient.

Paragraph 1: Self-explanatory, calling for the sponsor to fill in his or her name and address.

Question 1: Self-explanatory. If the sponsor lives outside the United States, he or she is probably not a citizen or permanent resident of the United States. That's fine, the sponsor can simply ignore parts a, b, c and d of this question.

Question 2: If the sponsor is not a resident of the United States, he or she can simply enter "N/A" for the second half of this question.

Question 3: This is for information about you. The questions are self-explanatory. Enter only the names of your spouse and children (if any) if they will be staying on with you in the United States.

Question 7: Back to the sponsor, who must enter information about his or her place of employment. For "type of business" the sponsor may enter his or her position (such as "secretary" or "accountant") or a more generic description such as "medicine" or "sales."

On the next set of lines, the sponsor enters information about his or her income and assets. The question about the amount **"on deposit in savings banks in the United States"** is a little misleading— it's okay to also include amounts in savings or checking accounts in the sponsor's home country. For **"personal property,"** the sponsor doesn't need to consider the exact value of everything he owns. An approximate total value on his or her cars, jewelry, appliances (stereo, television, refrigerator), automobiles, cameras and other equipment will do. He should also supply proof of ownership, such as a title deed or sales receipt, of the largest items.

Question 8: If the sponsor's country has a tax system comparable to the United States, in which a person lists people who are dependent on him or her on his or her tax returns, the names of these persons should be entered here.

Question 9: This question attempts to find out whether, by offering to sponsor others beside you, the sponsor is overextending him or herself financially. If he or she has filled out this form or a Form I-864 (another type of affidavit of support), on behalf of any other U.S. immigrant, these lines should be filled in.

Question 10: This question also looks for sponsors who are overextending themselves, but it applies only to a sponsor who is a citizen or permanent resident (green card holder) of the United States. It asks whether the sponsor has filed a visa petition on behalf of anyone. The implication is that the sponsor will eventually have to promise financial support to that other person, which would (depending on the timing) reduce the sponsor's ability to support you. Noncitizen or non-permanent resident sponsors can enter "N/A."

Question 11: This question is important to fill in. It will look best if the sponsor checks the box indicating that they "do intend" to provide specific contributions of support. For example, if you can estimate what your living expenses and tuition will come to on a monthly basis, the sponsor could agree, in this question, to send you this monthly amount. Showing this may help persuade the INS that the sponsor knows what he or she is getting into and is serious about fulfilling the obligation.

"Oath or Affirmation of Deponent." Here is a lovely example of excruciating legalese. Don't try to puzzle this out; just take it to a notary public to sign. A notary public is someone who is legally authorized by a state government to check a person's identification and make sure that the person signing the document is the one who is named as the person who should sign. To convince a notary of his or her identity, the sponsor should bring a driver's license or other form of photo identification. The notary will then ask the sponsor to sign the form, and will place a stamp on it. In the United States, the notary shouldn't charge more than $15 for this service. You can easily find notaries in the United States by looking in the Yellow Pages of your local phone book.

I-134, Affidavit of Support—Page 1

U.S. Department of Justice
Immigration and Naturalization Service

OMB No. 1115-0062

Affidavit of Support

(Answer All Items: Fill in with Typewriter or Print in Block Letters in Ink.)

I, _____ residing at _____
　　　　　　(Name)　　　　　　　　　　　　　　　　　　　　(Street and Number)

_____
(City)　　　　　　　　　(State)　　　　　(Zip Code if in U.S.)　　　　(Country)

BEING DULY SWORN DEPOSE AND SAY:

1. I was born on _____ at _____
　　　　　　　　　　(Date)　　　　　　　　　　(City)　　　　　　　　(Country)

　 If you are **not** a native born United States citizen, answer the following as appropriate:
　 a. If a United States citizen through naturalization, give certificate of naturalization number _____
　 b. If a United States citizen through parent(s) or marriage, give citizenship certificate number _____
　 c. If United States citizenship was derived by some other method, attach a statement of explanation.
　 d. If a lawfully admitted permanent resident of the United States, give "A" number _____

2. That I am _____ years of age and have resided in the United States since (date) _____
3. That this affidavit is executed in behalf of the following person:

Name			Gender	Age
Citizen of (Country)		Marital Status	Relationship to Sponsor	
Presently resides at (Street and Number)	(City)	(State)	(Country)	

　 Name of spouse and children accompanying or following to join person:

Spouse	Gender	Age	Child		Gender	Age
Child	Gender	Age	Child		Gender	Age
Child	Gender	Age	Child		Gender	Age

4. That this affidavit is made by me for the purpose of assuring the United States Government that the person(s) named in item 3 will not become a public charge in the United States.
5. That I am willing and able to receive, maintain and support the person(s) named in item 3. That I am ready and willing to deposit a bond, if necessary, to guarantee that such person(s) will not become a public charge during his or her stay in the United States, or to guarantee that the above named person(s) will maintain his or her nonimmigrant status, if admitted temporarily and will depart prior to the expiration of his or her authorized stay in the United States.
6. That I understand this affidavit will be binding upon me for a period of three (3) years after entry of the person(s) named in item 3 and that the information and documentation provided by me may be made available to the Secretary of Health and Human Services and the Secretary of Agriculture, who may make it available to a public assistance agency.
7. That I am employed as, or engaged in the business of _____ with _____
　　　　　　　　　　　　　　　　　　　　　　　　(Type of Business)　　　　　　(Name of concern)

　 at _____
　　　　(Street and Number)　　　　　(City)　　　　　(State)　　　(Zip Code)

　 I derive an annual income of *(if self-employed, I have attached a copy of my last income tax return or report of commercial rating concern which I certify to be true and correct to the best of my knowledge and belief. See instructions for nature of evidence of net worth to be submitted.)*　　$ _____

　 I have on deposit in savings banks in the United States　　$ _____

　 I have other personal property, the reasonable value of which is　　$ _____

OVER

Additional pages not shown.

Outside the United States, the sponsor can take this form to a U.S. consulate and they should provide a notary.

D. How to Use the Checklist for Applying for Change of Status to Student

The following Checklist will help you organize your Change of Status application. By marking an "X" in the box next to each item as you have prepared or obtained it, you'll be able to ensure that nothing is overlooked or forgotten.

 You'll find a tear-out version of this Checklist in Appendix E.

Checklist for Applying for Change of Status to Student

☐ Form I-539, Application to Extend/Change Nonimmigrant Status

☐ Form I-20 A-B for F status applicants, and Form I-20 M-N for M status applicants (from your school)

☐ your I-94 card

☐ document showing that you will return to your home country

☐ documents showing your academic credentials

☐ documents showing that you can pay your tuition, fees and living expenses for you and any accompanying spouse or children

☐ documentation of any scholarships, fellowships, assistantships, grants or loans from your school, government or private sources

☐ documents showing that you have not fallen out of lawful immigration status in the United States

☐ fee (currently $120)

E. Applying for Family Members to Stay With You

Your spouse and minor children (under 18) may be included in your Change of Status application and allowed to stay in the United States with you. There is no additional fee for including family members in your Change of Status application. You will have to prove that they are:

- your legal spouse and children (see subsection 1, below, for details on who qualifies as a family member and how to bring unmarried partners and others who don't qualify)
- not inadmissible to the United States (see Chapter 2), and
- that you can support them financially without having to work in the United States.

We don't take your family members step-by-step through the forms and documents as we did for you, but the basic principles are the same. Once you've filled out your own form and prepared your documents, their applications should be no problem. In fact, you have probably covered some of the requirements for your family members' applications already—in the previous sections concerning your documents, we covered such necessities as proving that your financial resources were enough to cover your accompanying family along with yourself. What your family members will need to complete their application need is summarized on the Checklist in subsection 2, below.

The INS can pick and choose whom to approve. If the INS doubts that your family members will return to your home country—or wants to ensure your return by sending your family back without you—it could grant your student status but deny your family the right to stay with you.

1. Who Counts As a Family Member?

F-2 status and M-2 status was specially created to allow the legal spouses and children of F-1 and M-1 students to stay with them in the United States. To avail yourself of this opportunity, you will have to prove your spouse and children's relationships to you using marriage and birth certificates.

Other family members don't get the same recognition. Your live-in domestic partner for example, will not qualify for F-2 status if you haven't actually gotten married. However, such family members may not be left completely out in the cold. B-2 (tourist) status may be given to family or household members with close ties to you, such as elderly parents or domestic partners of the same or opposite sex. The application form is the same, but there are a few differences in the accompanying documents. See Chapter 6 for details on how to apply for tourist status from within the United States.

2. Using the Checklist for Family Members in the U.S.

The procedure for including your spouse and children in your Change of Status application (in order to obtain F-2 or M-2 status for them) is fairly simple. You'll need to mention them on your Form I-539 (Question 2), complete a Form I-539 Supplement-1 for each of them and include documents showing that they are each separately eligible to stay in the United States. See instructions for filling out this form in Section B2, above.

Although your family members' applications are largely dependent on yours, they will need to be just as careful as you to prepare complete documentation. Any one of your spouse's or children's requests could be rejected because they are inadmissible or don't appear likely to return to your home country. Their applications will include the items on the Checklist below.

 You'll find a tear-out version of this Checklist in Appendix E.

Checklist for Family Members in the U.S.

☐ Form I-539 Supplement-1
☐ proof of family member(s) relationship to you, such as copies of marriage certificate and/or birth certificate(s)
☐ family member(s) I-94 cards
☐ documents showing that they have not fallen out of lawful immigration status
☐ separate proof of reasons that they'll return to their home country

---

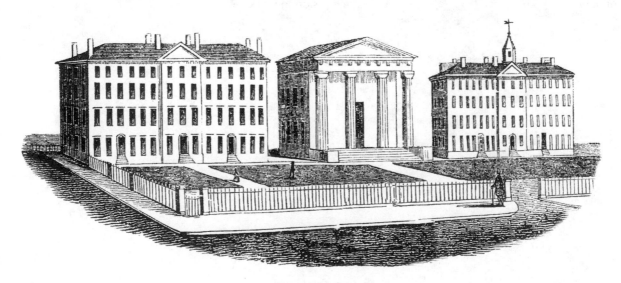

Brown University
Providence, Rhode Island

F. Processing Your Change of Status Application

Send your Change of Status application by mail to the INS Service Center that serves the geographic area of the school you will be attending. (See Appendix B for a list of Service Center addresses or check the INS website at http://www.ins.gov.) Use certified mail with a return receipt. (This means that you fill out a small postcard, which is attached to your letter, signed by the INS upon receipt and mailed by to you.) The return receipt postcard will assure you that the INS received your application, and you can use it to track the application if it's lost.

1. When to Send the Application

When you send the application is important. You are not permitted to apply for a Change of Status until 30 days have passed since you entered the United States. On the other hand, you cannot apply later than the expiration date of your current stay and should allow for at least three months for the INS to make a decision. Your "window" for applying depends on how much time your current stay is good for, but the safest course is to apply no later than three months before the expiration of your current stay.

2. What Happens After You Submit Change of Status Application

After you've mailed your Change of Status application, the INS should send you a receipt notice within about six weeks. The receipt notice will predict how long the INS will take to approve or deny your application. If the receipt notice doesn't come within that time, or if the final answer doesn't come within the time predicted on the receipt notice, see Chapter 13, Dealing With Bureaucrats, Delays and Denials. The INS may or may not ask you to attend an interview. If it does, see Chapter 9.

What if classes have started and you still haven't gotten an answer from the INS? It's best to start attending class. Otherwise, if your approval comes and you haven't been attending school, you'll find that you have violated your student status before getting to enjoy it—and you could be deported as a result. The school's DSO will understand this dilemma, and should be able to make sure the school doesn't hold up your registration over your lack of immigration status.

If you are called in for an interview, see Chapter 9 on how to prepare. If you are approved without an interview, go straight to Chapters 11 and 12 to learn how to maintain your status, deal with your changing needs or circumstances and apply for permission to work. ∎

Meetings With Government Officials

Before receiving your visa or change of status, whether you are applying to be a student or tourist, you will probably be required to meet with an official of the U.S. government. Overseas applicants will attend a visa interview at a local U.S. consulate. In addition, when they enter the United States, overseas applicants will have to present their visa and other paperwork to a U.S. border patrol official for a final review. Applicants in the United States may, although it's less common, be called to a local U.S. INS office for a Change of Status interview.

This chapter covers interviews for tourist as well as student (F-1 and M-1) visas and status changes. Both would-be students and tourists will have to convince government officials that they are eligible for their visa or status, that they are not inadmissible, that they can pay for their stay and that they are likely to return home at the end.

 If you are applying from within the United States, skip ahead to Sections C and D.

A. The Overseas Visa Interview

Finally, after all your careful preparation, you'll have the chance to speak with an official at the U.S. consulate and hand over your forms and documents. (A few consulates may require you to do everything by mail, but most will want to meet you personally before granting you a visa.) If you're a student visa applicant, look at your calendar before you choose a day to go to the consulate—you are not allowed to apply earlier than 90 days before the start of classes.

⚠ Beware of crime around U.S. consulates. Criminals know where the U.S. consulates are, and they know that some people going for interviews are carrying large sums of money (for visa fees). Take whatever precautions you think are appropriate in your country. Also watch out for con artists who hang around the consulate trying to convince people that they won't get through the front door unless they hand over some money first.

1. Homework

Before you go to the consulate, carefully look through your materials one last time. Make sure everything on your Checklist is really there. Read over your forms and documents to make sure all the information is clear in your head. (If you spot any mistakes or inconsistencies, fix them fast.) Then engage in a little role-playing: Knowing that the official will approach your case—and every case—with a bias against you, put yourself in his starched shirt and think of any reason he may have to conclude that you won't return home after your visit to the United States. Be sure that you have convincing answers before you head for the consulate and your interview.

One way to test your papers is to ask a trusted friend to look them over. Ask the friend to imagine that he is the interviewer, and that he has already denied 20 other applicants that day. Then ask your friend questions like, "Are you convinced that the applicant will really be able to pay her expenses?" and "Does it seem that this person is really going to return to her country after she completes her stay?" If your friend isn't convinced, the consular officer isn't likely to be either. Fix your paperwork accordingly.

If you're applying for a student visa and you're not entirely comfortable in English, practice it as much as possible in the days before you go to the consulate. The more smoothly you can speak, the less likely the officer is to hold up the application on the grounds that you are not ready to study in the United States. (The exception, of course, would be if you are applying for an F-1 visa for the sole purpose of studying the English language.)

2. What to Wear

The interviewing officer's decision rests in large part on whether he or she believes that you're telling the truth. You'll come across as more sincere if you're dressed neatly, professionally and even conservatively. Avoid t-shirts or jewelry with slogans or symbols that might make the officer wonder about your lifestyle or morals. In a word, we suggest that you dress as if you were going to visit your grandmother. Think about what you'll wear to your interview earlier than the night before, so that you're not up late with your ironing board.

EXAMPLE: Jon showed up at his interview wearing expensive leather shoes and, around his neck, a solid gold chain with a marijuana leaf dangling from it. The officer took one look at this and went right into questioning him as to whether he had ever tried, abused or sold drugs. When Jon wouldn't admit to anything, she referred him for a medical exam. The doctor found evidence of drug use in Jon's bloodstream and he was denied the visa.

3. What Will Happen When You Get There

Each consular office has its own procedure for reviewing applications. You may have to ask for an appointment for your visa interview, or you may be able to arrive when you'd like and wait in line. Often a clerk will be the first person to meet with you. The clerk's job is to simply review your paperwork to make sure that everything is in order. Presenting the clerk with a well-organized file will go a long way toward getting a "Yes" answer to your visa request.

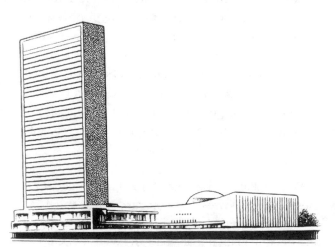

United Nations
New York City, New York

After these preliminaries, a consular officer will meet with you, place you under oath (where you raise your right hand and swear to tell the truth) and review the contents of your entire application. Don't expect a cozy fireside chat in the official's office. Many consulates now conduct interviews through bulletproof glass windows, which make you feel like you're in a bank or a prison. And don't count on much privacy—to make sure that the officer can hear you, some consulates have installed microphones that broadcast your conversation to everyone within hearing range.

4. What They'll Ask

Some consular officers report that visa applicants come in with memorized speeches—answers to questions the applicants felt sure they'd be asked. Although we can tell you what the consular officer is most likely to ask, don't assume that you'll get these—and only these—questions. You may get different questions, or you may get far fewer questions —most consular interviews are conducted within minutes. Listen carefully to the precise questions you're asked. The officer wants to talk to a responsive human being, not a preprogrammed robot. You will be less believable if you appear to avoid the officer's questions.

The officer will probably start by reviewing your forms and documents. He or she may ask you questions that are identical to the ones on your forms. Since you will have reviewed these carefully, you should be able to supply the answers—but if you can't remember something, it's much better to say so than to guess at the answer. If you're a student visa applicant, the officer may test your English by handing you a book, newspaper or INS form and asking you to read aloud from it. Even if you already passed a language exam such as the TOEFL, the officer wants to make sure that you didn't send an English-speaking friend to take the exam for you.

The biggest area of discussion will probably be your intention to return to your home country after your travels or studies are through. The officer may ask questions such as, "What do you plan to do after you have finished your stay," "Do you have a job here (in your home country) that you will come back to?" "Do you own a home, and where?" and "Where do your closest family members (parents, spouse, and children) live?" If you have close family who are U.S. citizens or permanent residents, the officer will wonder whether your true intention is to have them start the process of applying for a green card for you in the United States. You'll need to come up with a convincing reason why you aren't inclined to take advantage of this possibility.

The officer will probably consider him or herself to be an expert on your country, and you may also get some surprising questions. There's a story about one consular officer in Eastern Europe who maintained that people from that country would always return if they owned cows. Later, when the applicants got wise and started claiming cow ownership, he began quizzing them on the names of those cows. Applicants who faltered or didn't supply "cow-type" names were denied the visas.

If things are going badly—for example, the officer is acting displeased or obsessively focusing on a difficult area of your application—do not just sit quietly waiting for the officer to ask the right question. Speak up and explain what she has overlooked. If the issue is whether you'll return home after your stay, you might also ask the officer what further evidence she'll accept—a nonrefundable airplane ticket or a "maintenance bond" (a sum of money that you submit to the U.S. government that will be forfeited by you if you do not leave the U.S. when you say that you will) are two possibilities.

EXAMPLE 1: Sven has applied for a tourist visa. His wife happens to be a U.S. citizen. At the interview, the officer hints that Sven must be looking for a way to get into the United States in order to apply for a green card there. Sven says, "I know you might think I would want to stay with my wife in the United States, but our goals are different. I have a great job here in Sweden—I'm the director of an important art museum. I fly all over the world on arts tours, and my salary is good. I would not want to leave—I could never find such a job in the

United States. My wife too has a job she does not want to leave yet, as a management trainee in a large company. But once her training is over and she has some experience (in about three years), she will come to Sweden to live with me. Life is saner here in Sweden and the big cities are safer places to raise children. I am remodeling my house in preparation for this."

EXAMPLE 2: Rashiva has been accepted to a medical school in the United States. At her student visa interview, the consular officer finds out that her parents already live in the United States, that she is unmarried and that her employer isn't willing to hold a job open for her for the many years it will take her to finish medical school. She can see from the consul's face that he is dubious about granting her application. Rather than waiting for him to fish for helpful information, Rashiva says, "I know you are concerned that I might not have enough ties in my home country. But consider this: I was eligible to get a green card to the United States at the same time that my parents did, but I chose not to. I have never regretted that choice. I am 24 years old, an adult, and I am not interested in living with my parents. The medical school that I will be attending is 2,000 miles away from them. My goal is to become an expert in communicable diseases and return to my country to treat people living in poverty. I have spent the last four years as a community health educator; here is a letter from the agency with which I worked, talking about my commitment to improving health in this country and their role in persuading me that a medical degree was the next step for me." The consul grants Rashiva's application.

You probably won't match the facts in either of these example cases, but you can, with enough thought, match their use of logic. Also think about any documentation that you can use to back up your logic, such as the health agency letter that Rashiva provided.

Truth and Consequences

Here is a former consular officer's description of visa decision-making. Don't let this happen to you!

"As point man on the visa line, it was up to me to decide who was lying and who was telling the truth. In one case a man said his brother 'Bob' had just died in America and that his family had to fly at once to the United States. The unemployed man claimed he would pay for all ten tickets himself. Sensing that something didn't quite ring true, I called his U.S. family and was informed that Bob couldn't come to the phone since he was bowling. I returned to the grieving man with 'some good news and some bad news.' The good news, of course, was that Bob was not dead yet. The bad news was that I would be unable to issue the visas since he had attempted to commit fraud."

Source: "Till the Cows Come Home," by Michael J. Labriola, *California Lawyer* p. 96, March 2001.

5. Is It Harder to Get a Visa From Certain Countries?

Unfortunately, it is no secret that the consulate's decision will depend in large part on two factors you cannot control: what country you're from, and how many people from your country have violated the terms of their visa and not returned home. Sven, in the example from the previous subsection, had luck on his side: He was born in Sweden, a relatively prosperous country to which it's easy to imagine he would want to return. Not everyone comes from such comfortable places.

If you're from a developing nation, you've got an uphill battle ahead. The consular officer may look at you as just another person anxious to get into the "land of opportunity." Consular officials in Asia and Russia, where economic crises have made life very hard, believe that many applicants are really looking for a way to earn money in the United States, not to visit or study. In addition, it is widely reported that

the U.S. consulates in Asian countries frequently deny student visas for high school programs. Officers figure that since some Asian countries' pre-college entrance exam preparation is so rigorous, any student who would miss it must not be planning to return.

Although it seems unfair, you will also be judged on the basis of those from your country who have gone before you: The State Department keeps statistics on how many visitors to the United States return home. If the statistics look bad at a certain consulate, the State Department will put pressure on that consulate to get tougher in its visa decisions.

6. Your Visa Approval

Your visa may be approved on the spot, or you may have to wait days or weeks for a decision. If your interview went badly, the officer is more likely to simply deny your visa than allow you a second chance. Most of them have many visa applications to decide every day, so the likelihood that yours will get special treatment is slim. But if, during your interview, you can name a specific item or document that you would like to bring that might change the consular officer's mind, explain this and ask for time to submit it later. The officer may say no, but it doesn't hurt to ask.

The final step before approval of your visa is for you to pay any visa processing or reciprocity fees. The consular officer will place a visa stamp in your passport. On the stamp, he or she will write the visa's date of issuance, an expiration date and the number of times you're allowed to use the visa to enter the United States—either a specific number or an unlimited number, indicated by the statement "multiple entry." A multiple entry visa is one that you can use for many U.S. trips, up until its expiration date. If this is your first time applying for a tourist visa, it's more likely that you'll receive a single entry visa, good for only one trip. However, if you come back a second time without a problem you may be granted a multiple entry visa—a sign that the consular officer believes that you are a low-risk applicant. In fact if you have a multiple entry visa this sends a clear message to the INS at the border that the

Consul believes that you are low risk, and it may it easier for you when you arrive at the port of entry.

If you're entering as a student, the officer will also write the name of the school you'll be attending. The officer may also give you some of your visa application materials, in a sealed envelope, to show to the border patrol officer when you enter the United States. Do not open the envelope, or the border officer may assume you tampered with the contents.

Unless your visa states "multiple entry," you'll have to keep track of how many times you leave and return to the United States. If you run out of permitted entries, you'll need to revisit the consulate and request a new visa (there is no place to submit a visa renewal within the United States). Being issued a visa with a limited number of entries is also usually a sign that while the consul was willing to issue you a visa, they weren't entirely convinced about you—so be prepared for heavy questioning at the U.S. border.

Student visas will normally be issued for as long as the consulate thinks is appropriate to finish your studies, with a maximum possible time of 60 months for academic visas and one year for vocational visas.

Tourist visas usually have a maximum life of ten years, though nationals of a few countries may be given visas that have no expiration date. Remember, the expiration date on your visa is not the same as the length of time you can stay in the United States. The officer who meets you at the border will tell you how long you can actually stay. Read more about what happens at the border in Section B, below.

Now you're ready for travel to the United States. You can go anytime between the date you got your visa and the date it expires. If you're a student, you won't have been given the visa until you're within 90 days of the start of classes.

7. What to Do If You Are Denied

If the consulate denies your visa, that's final. There is no appeal process. But make sure that you ask the consular officer for the exact reason that they denied the visa. If you can correct the problem, you can start over and submit a new application. Also ask for the rules on reapplying. Some consulates have special procedures to reduce your paperwork if you are reapplying within one year.

Then the question is, can you correct the underlying problem? If the problem had to do with your basic eligibility, such as whether you have enough money to cover your stay or whether you will return home afterwards, you may be able to fix it yourself. Re-read the portions of this book covering how to establish your eligibility in the first place. Then think about what additional forms of evidence you can come up with to tip the balance in your favor. The consulate will, however, want to see something new, such as a source of financial support that you did not mention before, your recent wedding or a home purchase indicating your plans to live permanently in your home country.

The more difficult problems to correct are those having to do with fraud and inadmissibility, especially for security or health reasons. These are problems that would stop you from getting any kind of visa, not just the one you're applying for now. If one of these was the reason, we suggest consulting with an immigration lawyer in the United States to discuss whether you can overcome this ground of inadmissibility or whether a waiver is available. See Chapter 14 for tips on finding a lawyer.

In rare cases, the consular officer may have actually misapplied the law to your case. For example, an officer who mistakenly believed that time you spent illegally in the United States before 1997 counted toward the Three- and Ten-Year Bars could deny you a visa on that basis. In such a case, ask the officer for the exact section number of the law under which you're being denied—then consult a lawyer.

B. At the Border

After you've gotten your visa (or decided to use a Visa Waiver) and have endured a long ride or flight to the United States, you'll find yourself at a border or airport in a long line of people. At the front of that line is a U.S. border patrol official, waiting to have another look at your passport and immigration paperwork. If everything is in order, this meeting should not be a problem. But you should be very careful with this meeting nonetheless. This section gives you information on how to:

- prepare for your encounter (subsection 1)
- conduct yourself during the meeting (subsection 2)
- react if things go wrong (subsection 3), and
- what to expect if you're approved (subsection 4).

1. Avoiding Expedited Removal

We suggest that you think of your meeting with the border official as a second interview—in spite of the fact that you already passed the one at the consulate. Before you begin your trip, pack a carry-on bag or backpack with your important papers, which should include the following:

- your passport
- a visa stamp; or, if you're on a Visa Waiver, Form I-94W
- Form I-20 (students only), and
- evidence of financial support.

Try to wake yourself up before your plane is due to land—ask for coffee if you have to! Retrieve all of your paperwork from your bag. Review your paperwork and your plans so that they are fresh in your mind when you arrive. With any luck, the border officer will be satisfied that your visa is in order and that your intention is truly to enjoy a temporary stay in the United States.

There's a reason for all this preparation. U.S. border patrol officials have what are called expedited removal powers, meaning they can stop you from entering the United States if they think you have used fraud or were not really eligible for your visa. For example, if they think you lied about your intentions to return home after your trip, they could close the border on you right there. You would be placed on the next flight home. In the meantime, you would probably be placed in handcuffs and not allowed to move about.

2. Conduct Yourself Carefully

The official at the border will be making a snap judgment about your character. How you're dressed, how you carry yourself and how confidently you answer his questions will all figure in to whether he thinks you can be trusted with entry to the United States. As with the consular interview, it's best to err on the conservative side. You don't need to do something amazing to impress the officer; you simply need to avoid doing something inappropriate that will make him doubt you.

In the "body language" of the United States, it's very important to look a person in the eyes when you speak with him. Looking away or at the floor may be perceived as a sign that you're hiding something. Try to look straight at the border patrol officer when the two of you speak—even if this would be impolite in your country or culture. If you find this difficult, try looking at the officer's forehead or nose. Other ways of making yourself appear honest and confident include keeping your hands away from your face and answering questions in a loud, strong voice. Try to keep your answers short and to the point.

Now that we've made you nervous, try to relax! Think about all of the positive aspects of your application: you understand the entry requirements, you've prepared your paperwork carefully, and you are, we hope, the real thing. It's the drug-smuggling ex-spy in the next line over who should be worried.

3. Difficulties at the Border

No matter what, there is a risk that the border patrol officer will believe that you lied to get your entry visa or that it's not the real thing. It's unlikely that this will happen to you, but you should read this section now, just in case—you won't have time if the officer is hustling you onto a plane heading home.

If the border officer decides to use his expedited removal powers on you, you will not be allowed a hearing in front of a judge (unless you fear persecution in your home country and ask to apply for political asylum). You might be able to get a second review from another immigration officer, if you can convince the officer that you deserve it. If you think the first border officer made a mistake, ask for this second interview.

If you have lied or used fraud to get the visa however, do the opposite—ask to withdraw (take back) your application and go home without a fight. Why? Because once you have been kept out of the United States through expedited removal, you are not allowed to reenter for a full five years. If you push things when you don't deserve entry, you are likely to get a negative decision. But you can avoid this five-year prohibition on reentry by withdrawing your application before the border officer makes his or her final decision. Unfortunately, the officer does not have to grant your request to withdraw your application, so everything depends on how reasonable he or she is and how persuasive you are.

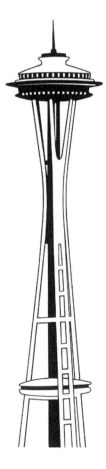

Space Needle
Seattle, Washington

What the Public Says About Expedited Removal

Expedited removal is relatively new and has been the subject of much concern by immigrants' rights groups and the media. There are charges that border officials act arbitrarily, keeping people out whom they should not. For example, in a prize-winning article for *The Oregonian* newspaper, journalists told the story of Japanese citizen Kiyoe Nakamine. Nakamine traveled to the United States intending to visit friends. She brought several copies of her resume with her, which she was going to show her friends and ask for editing help, with the eventual goal of applying for jobs with foreign companies in Japan. The border officer, however, searched her bags, found the resumes and concluded that Nakamine intended to look for work in the United States and had lied to get her visa. Nakamine was summarily removed and cannot return to the United States for many years. (Source: "Rejected Foreigners Have No Voice in Changing the System," by Richard Read, *The Oregonian*, Friday, December 15, 2000.)

Unfortunately, this was not an isolated case. In the year 2000, the Portland, Oregon, airport was making so many arbitrary decisions excluding people that people began calling it "Deportland." One major airline stopped flying to Portland. There are stories of border officers in Portland strip-searching a Chinese businesswoman and sending the German wife of a U.S. citizen back to Europe without her nursing baby. Luckily, these problems were made public, and Portland is cleaning up its act. But who knows where the next scandal will arise?

It may be wise to avoid certain cities. Talk to your friends, your travel agent and even your airline about which U.S. ports of entry tend to be friendlier.

4. When You're Approved

After you have satisfied the border official that you really are just an honest and ordinary tourist or student, she will stamp your passport to show that day's date. She will also insert a little card called an "I-94." The card will be white for regular visa holders, but green for people who enter under the Visa Waiver Program. This card is very important—and easy to lose, so take good care of it. There is a charge for this card, currently $8.

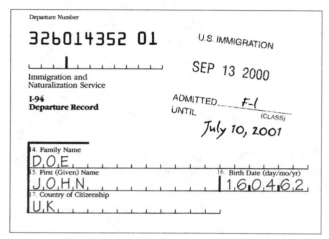

Departure Number

326014352 01   U.S. IMMIGRATION

Immigration and
Naturalization Service   SEP 13 2000

**I-94
Departure Record**   ADMITTED____ *F-1*
UNTIL   (CLASS)

                    July 10, 2001

4. Family Name
D,O,E
5. First (Given) Name   6. Birth Date (day/mo/yr)
J,O,H,N   1,6,0,4,6,2
7. Country of Citizenship
U,K

I-94, Arrival/Departure Card

The date shown on the I-94 card is the date by which you will have to leave the United States. How long you'll be allowed to stay depends on what type of visa you have, as follows:

- **Visa Waiver entrants** will be allowed a stay of no more than 90 days.
- **Tourists** are usually allowed a six months' stay, but in special circumstances, may be allowed up to a year.
- **M-1 students** will be allowed one year or the time needed to complete their studies (whichever is less) plus a 30-day period in which to pack their bags and head home.
- **F-1 students** will probably receive the notation "D/S" instead of a date—that means "duration of status," or the appropriate length of their studies as indicated on their Form I-20, including 60 days to pack their bags and head home.

(Luckily for students, it is easy for your school to adjust the date on your I-20 if you need more time to complete your studies.)

Don't make the mistake that many people do and assume that you can stay in the United States until your visa runs out—the I-94 is the document to look at. You can use the original visa to enter the United States more than once, up to its expiration date.

If you're a student (F-1 or M-1), the officer will also remove part of your Form I-20, which he will use to enter your information in the INS records and later send to your school. The other portion will be returned to you. Your portion is called an "I-20 ID." Keep this form with you at all times. The officer will enter your "admission number" on this form. This number is important for identifying you—you'll need to use it in any future correspondence with the INS. It's a good idea to make a few copies of the I-20 ID and keep them in safe places.

Your spouse and children will also have their passports stamped and will be given I-94 cards. Their I-94 will probably have the same expiration date as yours. However, if you are on different types of visas—for example, if you are an F-1 student but your domestic partner (unmarried) came on a B-2 visitor visa, the dates may differ. Your I-94 might say "D/S," but your partner's would have a time limit of one year at most. (Your partner would need to apply to extend his or her stay before the end of that one year if necessary to continue accompanying you.)

C. Interviews at a U.S. INS Office

 If you applied from overseas, skip ahead to Section D.

Being called for an interview at a U.S. INS office is rare. However, if you are called, it probably means that the INS had some doubts about your application to change status. In that case, you will want to prepare carefully. In addition, you may want to look for additional documentation of the sort we've already described, to strengthen your case.

1. Preparing for Your Interview

Before you go to the INS, carefully look through your materials one last time. Make sure everything on your Checklist is really there. Read over your forms and documents to make sure all the information is clear in your head and that the forms and documents contain no mistakes or inconsistencies. Then engage in a little role-playing. Knowing that the official will approach your case—and every case—with a bias against you, put yourself in his starched shirt and think of any reason he may have to conclude that you won't return home after your visit to the United States. Be sure that you have convincing answers before you head for your interview.

One way to test your papers is to ask a trusted friend to look them over. Ask the friend to imagine that he is the interviewer and that he has already denied 20 other applicants that day. Then ask your friend questions like, "Are you convinced of the applicant's ability to pay her expenses?" and "Does it seem that this person is really going to return to her country after she completes her stay?" If your friend isn't convinced, the INS officer isn't likely to be either. Fix your paperwork accordingly.

If you're applying for student status and you're not entirely comfortable in English, practice it as much as possible in the days before you go to the INS. The more smoothly you can speak, the less likely the officer is to hold up the application on the grounds that you are not ready to study at a U.S. school. (The exception, of course, would be if you are applying for an F-1 visa for the sole purpose of studying the English language.)

2. What to Wear

The interviewing officer's decision rests almost entirely on whether he or she believes that you're telling the truth. You'll come across as more sincere if you're dressed neatly, professionally and even conservatively. Avoid t-shirts or jewelry with slogans or symbols that might make the officer wonder about your lifestyle or morals. In a word, we suggest that you dress as if you were going to visit your grandmother. Think about what you'll wear to your interview earlier than the night before, so that you're not up late with your ironing board.

> **EXAMPLE:** Jon showed up at his interview wearing expensive leather shoes and, around his neck, a solid gold chain with a marijuana leaf dangling from it. The officer took one look at this and went right into questioning him as to whether he had ever tried, abused or sold drugs. When Jon wouldn't admit to anything, she referred him for a medical exam. The doctor found evidence of drug use in Jon's bloodstream and his Change of Status application was denied.

3. Arrange for an Interpreter

The INS doesn't provide interpreters at interviews in the United States. A few of their officers speak Spanish or other languages, but you can't count on getting a bilingual officer, nor can you request one. If you're not comfortable in English, you'll need to bring a friend or hire an interpreter to help. (If you're applying for F-1 student status in a program other than English, don't even consider bringing an interpreter. Proving your English language ability is part of the purpose of the interview.)

The interpreter must be over 18 and fluent in your language and in English. Some officers also require that the interpreter be a legal resident or citizen of the United States (of course, if they're here illegally, they'd be foolish to walk into an INS office).

4. What Will Happen When You Get There

Your visit to the INS office promises to be a long one. Don't forget to bring your interview notice with you—it will probably tell you what room to go to first. Check the office hours before you go—they tend to open before any of us are awake and close in mid-afternoon. Very long lines are not unusual. At some offices, people start camping out in line outside the night before. Often someone will come outside to escort the people with appointments in—keep your eyes open and ask any official-looking person that you see.

Even if you don't live in a city where camping out is a necessity, it's best to arrive well ahead of your interview time and pack a snack and a good book (a snack that you can eat discreetly; many of the offices prohibit food and drink, but they'll look away if you're eating something clean like an energy bar). Often a number of people will be scheduled for interviews at the same time as you and you'll have to wait.

The interview might be simply a stand-up conversation conducted over a counter, or a sit-down event at an INS officer's desk. In either event, the officer will probably place you under oath (in which you raise your right hand and swear to tell the truth). Try and take note of the interviewer's name in case you have to follow up or register a complaint.

5. What They'll Ask

Some officers report that international student applicants come in with memorized speeches—answers to questions they felt sure they'd be asked. Although we can tell you what the INS officer is most likely to ask, don't assume that you'll get these—and only these—questions. Be sure to listen carefully to the precise questions you're asked. The officer wants to talk to a responsive human being, not a preprogrammed robot. You will be far less believable if you appear to avoid the officer's questions.

The officer will probably start by reviewing your forms and documents. He or she may ask you questions that are identical to the ones on your forms. Since you will have reviewed these carefully, you should be able to supply the answers—but if you can't remember something, it's much better to say so than to guess at the answer. If you're a student visa applicant, the officer may test your English ability by handing you a book, newspaper or INS form and asking you to read aloud from it. Even if you already

passed a language exam such as the TOEFL, the officer wants to make sure that you didn't send an English-speaking friend to take the exam for you.

The biggest area of discussion will probably be your intention to return to your home country after your travels or studies are through. The officer may ask questions such as, "What do you plan to do after you have finished your stay?" "Do you have a job in your home country that you will go back to?" "Do you own a home, and where?" and "Where do your closest family members (parents, spouse, and children) live?" If you have close family who are U.S. citizens or permanent residents, the officer will wonder whether your true intention is to have them start the process of applying for a green card for you in the United States. You'll need to come up with a convincing reason why you aren't inclined to take advantage of this possibility.

If things are going badly, do not just sit quietly waiting for the officer to ask the right question: speak up, and explain what they have overlooked.

EXAMPLE 1: Sven has applied for tourist status. Sven's fiancée happens to be a U.S. citizen. At Sven's interview, the officer hints that Sven must be looking for a way to stay in the United States in order to get married and apply for a green card here. Sven speaks up: "I know you might think I would want to stay with my fiancée in the United States, but our goals are different. I have a great job in Sweden—I'm the director of an important art museum. I fly all over the world on arts tours and my salary is good. I would not want to leave permanently—I could never find such a job in the United States. My fiancée too has a job she does not want to leave yet, as a management trainee in a large company. But once her training is over and she has some experience (in about three years), we will get married and she will come to Sweden to live with me. Life is saner in Sweden and the big cities are safer places to raise children."

EXAMPLE 2: Rashiva has been accepted to a medical school in the United States. She comes to the U.S. as a tourist and applies for a change to student status. At her INS interview, the officer finds out that Rashiva's parents already live legally in the United States, that Rashiva is unmarried and that her employer isn't willing to hold a job open for her for the many years it will take her to finish medical school. Rashiva can see from the consul's face that he is dubious about granting her application. Rather than waiting for him to fish for helpful information, Rashiva says, "I know you are concerned that I might not have enough ties in my home country. But consider this: I was eligible to get a green card to the United States at the same time that my parents did, but I chose not to. I have never regretted that choice. I am 24 years old, an adult, and I am not interested in living with my parents. The medical school that I will be attending is 2,000 miles away from them. My goal is to become an expert in communicable diseases and return to my country to treat people living in poverty. I have spent the last four years as a community health educator; here is a letter from the agency with which I worked, talking about my commitment to improving health in this country and their role in persuading me that a medical degree was the next step for me." The INS officer grants Rashiva's application.

You probably won't match the facts in either of these example cases, but you can, with enough thought, match their use of logic. Also think about any documentation that you can use to back up your logic, such as the health agency letter that Rashiva provided.

6. Is It Harder to Get a Visa From Certain Countries?

Unfortunately, it is no secret that the INS's decision will depend in large part on two factors you cannot control: what country you're from, and how many people from your country have violated the terms of their visa and not returned home. Sven, in the example from the previous subsection, had luck on his side: He was born in Sweden, a relatively prosperous country to which it is easy to imagine that he would want to return. Not everyone comes from such comfortable places.

If you're from a developing nation, you've got an uphill battle ahead. The INS officer may look at you as just another person anxious to get into the "land of opportunity." The Asian and Russian economic crises have made getting visas particularly difficult for applicants from these countries—the INS is suspicious that the applicants are looking for a way to earn money in the United States, not to travel or study.

Although it seems unfair, you will also be judged on the basis of those from your country who have gone before you. The State Department keeps statistics on how many visitors to the United States return home. If the statistics from your country look bad, the INS may hold that information against you.

7. Your Change of Status Approval

Your Change of Status may be approved on the spot, or you may have to wait days or weeks for a decision. If your interview went badly, the officer is more likely to simply deny your application than allow you a second chance. Most of them have many applications to decide every day, so the likelihood that yours will get special treatment is slim. But if, during your interview, you can name a specific item or document that you would like to submit by mail that might change the INS officer's mind, explain this and ask for time to submit it. The officer may say no, but it doesn't hurt to ask.

When you are approved, you will be given a little white card called an "I-94." This card is very important—and easy to lose, so take good care of it. The date shown on the I-94 card is the date by which you will have to leave the United States. How long you'll be allowed to stay depends on what type of visa you have, as follows:

- **Tourists** are usually allowed a six months' stay, but, in special circumstances, may be allowed up to a year.
- **M-1 students** will be allowed one year or the time needed to complete their studies (which-

ever is less) plus a 30-day period in which to pack their bags and head home.

- **F-1 students** will probably receive the notation "D/S" instead of a date—that means "duration of status," or the appropriate length of their studies as indicated on their Form I-20, including 60 days in which to pack their bags and head home. (Luckily for students, it is easy for your school to adjust the date on your I-20 if you need more time to complete your studies.)

If you're a student (F-1 or M-1), the officer will remove part of your Form I-20, which he will use to enter your information in the INS records and later send to your school. The other portion will be returned to you. Your portion is called an "I-20 ID." Keep this form with you at all times. The officer will enter your "admission number" on this form. This number is important for identifying you—you'll need to use it in any future correspondence with the INS. It's a good idea to make a few copies of the I-20 ID and keep them in safe places.

If you have a spouse and children who applied and were interviewed with you, they will also be given I-94 cards, with the same expiration date as yours.

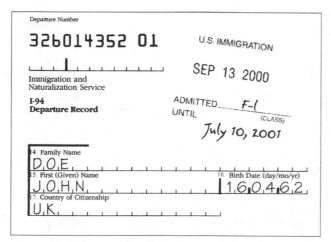

I-94, Arrival/Departure Card

8. What to Do If You Are Denied

There is no appeal from the denial of a Change of Status application. However, a lawyer can help you request that your application be reconsidered by the INS Regional Commissioner. The lawyer will need to argue that the INS incorrectly applied the law to the facts in your original application—not an easy argument to make unless the INS made an obvious error. See Chapter 14 for tips on finding a good lawyer.

If you decide to consult a lawyer or apply for reconsideration, you will need to act quickly. If your original visa status has run out, the INS will follow its denial of your application with a notice placing you in removal (deportation) proceedings. If you can't show that you have some separate basis for being allowed to stay in the United States (for example, political asylum or marriage to a U.S. citizen), you will be asked to voluntarily depart by a certain date or you will be ordered deported. Most people who are given a choice depart voluntarily, because once you've been deported, you cannot return to the United States legally for five years without special permission (a "waiver") from the U.S. government.

If your Change of Status application in the United States is denied and you leave within the time required (or voluntarily), you can always try applying for a visa at an overseas consulate. This could be tricky—by this time you may have spent more than six months in the United States unlawfully, which would make you unable to return for three or ten years (see Chapter 2 for details of the Time Bar penalties for illegal stays). Consult a lawyer if you're facing this issue.

If you are interested in reapplying overseas, you'll also need to consider whether you can correct the problem that led to your application being denied. If the denial had to do with your basic eligibility, such as whether you had enough money to cover your stay or whether you planned to return home afterwards, you may be able to fix the problem yourself. Re-read the portions of this book covering how to establish your eligibility. Then think about what additional forms of evidence you can come up with to tip the balance in your favor.

The more difficult problems to correct are those having to do with fraud and inadmissibility, especially for security or health reasons. These are problems that would stop you from getting any kind of visa, not just the one you're applying for now. If one of these was the reason for the denial, you could arrange for a consultation with an immigration lawyer to discuss whether you can overcome this ground of inadmissibility or whether a waiver is available.

D. The Long-Term Consequences If Your Application Is Denied

Having a visa or Change of Status application denied could have long-term consequences for your visits or eventual immigration to the United States. The U.S. government will keep a record of your visa denial. If you used fraud or they discovered that you were inadmissible for some other reason, this denial could affect your future visa applications. At the very least, having one application denied will mean that the U.S. government will look very hard at any other immigration application that you submit. Immigration authorities can consider this denial when making other visa decisions for you, no matter how long ago the denial happened. If you later try and hide the denial and are caught, it will probably destroy your chances of ever getting a U.S. visa or status. ■

In the U.S. As a Tourist

Once you are in the United States, you are pretty much free to travel as you please. You don't have to stick to your planned itinerary and you don't have to report back to any government officials. You just have to avoid trouble while you're here and leave on time.

But it's no secret that many people have stayed past the expiration date on their I-94, sometimes for years. In response to this, the immigration laws now include severe penalties for overstaying—ones that give you major incentives to leave by the expected date, as discussed in Chapter 2 and summarized in Section B, below. And in case you want to legally stay longer, we'll show you how in Section C.

A. How Long Can You Stay?

You can stay in the United States until the expiration date shown on the I-94 card that you got at the border. The maximum time you'll be given is usually six months or, in rare cases, a year. However, your visa (the original stamp in your passport that you received at the consulate) may have a later expiration date on it. That doesn't change the date you must leave the United States—but it does allow you, after leaving, to come back using that same visa, until it expires. You can reenter as often as you like before the visa's expiration date—limited only by your ability to convince the border patrol officer that you aren't attempting to live in the United States permanently and that you will leave on time.

EXAMPLE: Divitia is working on a book about ethical issues in art history and plans to spend six months doing research at museums and libraries around the United States. She applies for and receives a tourist visa. Looking at her visa stamp, Divitia sees that it is a multiple entry visa that will expire in ten years, on May 18, 2011.

Divitia flies to the United States on June 2, 2001. At the airport, the immigration officials give her an I-94 card with an expiration date of December 2, 2001. That means that Divitia can do as she planned and stay for six months. Toward the end of that time, Divitia feels that her research is unfinished. She could apply for an extension of her stay, but decides to return to Italy for her mother's birthday. However, since her visa has not yet expired, Divitia can return to the United States anytime and many times before May 18, 2011, to continue her research—or for other pleasure purposes—so long as the border officials don't get the idea that she's attempting to live in the United States permanently.

B. What Happens If You Break the Visa Rules

Your tourist visa or status comes with its own set of rules, although you won't see them written down for you. Whatever you promised when you obtained the visa becomes a rule you must follow now that you're here as a tourist. If you break the rules, in the eyes of the INS you have destroyed your status as a tourist. You could face immigration court proceedings and damage to any future hopes of coming to the United States.

The most common ways that people violate the terms of their visitor visa are to work illegally or to stay past their I-94 expiration date. Providing false information to the INS is also considered a violation of the rules. Not surprisingly, engaging in illegal or criminal acts is another violation—and will in all likelihood make it impossible for you to return to the United States in the future.

If you are caught breaking the rules (perhaps in a random INS raid or because someone tips the INS off) you will be placed in removal (deportation) proceedings. At this point you will need a lawyer. The lawyer could help you come to an arrangement with the court that is the least damaging to your immigration record.

Whatever you do, do not ignore a notice to appear in court. People who don't show up are given an automatic order of deportation. With this order in your file, you could be removed from the United States as soon as the INS finds you, no matter how sympathetic your situation is. You would also be prohibited from returning for ten years.

If you have any run-ins with the police during your visit, see an immigration lawyer as well as a criminal lawyer. Most people who are arrested for crimes consult only with a criminal lawyer. In fact, the state or federal government may provide free represen-tation (a "public defender") to low-income people con-victed of crimes, whether or not they're U.S. citizens. It is not uncommon for people to plead guilty to a crime (whether or not they're guilty) as part of a deal to avoid jail time. Unfortunately, criminal defense lawyers may not understand how a conviction may affect a person's immigration status. For example, seemingly minor details like the exact definition of your crime or the length of your jail sentence can make a huge difference in whether you are deportable or legally admissible to the United States in the future. This makes it extremely important that you consult with an immigration lawyer before you do anything definitive like pleading guilty. Unfortunately, the government never provides free immigration law services.

Whether or not you are deported, any time that you spend in the United States without permission or after violating your status will affect your right to come back to the United States later. Anyone who stays unlawfully in the United States for more than 180 days and then leaves isn't allowed to return to the United States for three years. Anyone who stays unlawfully for more than a year isn't allowed to come back for ten years. You'll need a lawyer's help to determine how much of your stay is considered unlawful, however—it all depends on INS interpre-tation and what an immigration court orders in your case. Also see Chapter 2, Section B, above, and I.N.A. § 212(a)(9)(B), 8 U.S.C. § 1182(a)(9)(B). This doesn't just mean you won't get a tourist visa for the three or ten years—you will not get any visa.

> **EXAMPLE:** Jacinto comes to the United States on a tourist visa, has a great time and ignores the expiration date on his I-94. He leaves seven months after he should have. The next year, he meets Lucinda, a U.S. citizen who is studying in the Phillipines, where he lives. They fall in love and get married. When Jacinto applies for a U.S. green card, however, his overstay is discovered.

He will not be allowed to move to the United States with Lucinda until three years past his last departure from the United States. (Fortunately, cases involving marriage to a U.S. citizen are among the few in which the immigrant can ask the consulate for a "waiver," or forgiveness of their illegal stay. Jacinto may get a break after all.)

A less serious, but highly inconvenient result of staying past the expiration date of your visa is that you lose your right to apply for an extension of that visa or for any other nonimmigrant (temporary) U.S. visa while you're in the United States. Only people who are in valid visa status in the U.S. can apply to extend their status or change to a new status. Once your permitted stay expires, you have no choice but to travel to the U.S. consulate in your home country —and not in any third country—to apply for a new visa. See 22 C.F.R. § 41.101.

C. Extending Your Stay

You may find that the time allotted on your I-94 is not sufficient to do all you want to do in the United States. As long as the expiration date on your I-94 has not yet passed, you can apply to extend your stay. If the expiration date has passed, you will have to return home and apply for a new tourist visa from there.

You will have to give a solid reason for wanting the extension. As with the original visa application, a desire to stretch your U.S. visit to the legal limits will get you nowhere. A simple change in your travel itinerary or a desire to see more places in the United States might be enough, but you'll have to explain why this is important to you and what happened to make you realize this.

If you are the principal wage earner for your family and you have left your spouse and children in your home country, the INS will be especially wary. You will have to come up with good reasons for this lengthy family separation, as well as evidence that your employer is aware that you'll be away from work for such a long time.

Extensions must be requested by mail. Most people wait until they are fairly close to the end of their stay to apply—because you are allowed to stay in the United States until the INS gives you a decision. The INS is not known for quick decisions, which means that simply by applying, you will probably buy yourself the right to stay at least a few more weeks. But your passport will need to remain valid. If it will expire, find a consulate from your home country and ask if they can renew it for you. If there isn't a consulate in the city where you're staying, you can usually locate one in the telephone directory for Washington, D.C., or San Francisco. Or, you can check the Internet at http://www.embassy.org/ embassies/index.html or http://www.embpage.org.

In the subsections that follow, we explain the forms and documents that you'll need to put together for your extension application. These are summarized in the Checklist in subsection 3.

1. Forms You'll Need for Your Extension Application

The extension application requires only one form, INS Form I-539, pictured below; with a Supplement page if you're bringing family members. Form I-539 gathers basic information about who you are and why you wish to extend your stay. This form is used by many different categories of applicants, so don't be disturbed by the existence of questions or sections that don't apply to you. Also, pay no attention to the advice on this form stating that you can turn it in late if you have an excuse—this was written before certain changes in the immigration laws, and is no longer true.

 You'll find a tear-out copy of this form in Appendix D.

If you choose to print out Form I-539 from the INS website, print it double-sided, head to foot. When you've got a copy of Form I-539 in hand, follow these line-by-line instructions.

Instructions page 5, box at bottom of page: Fill in your name and U.S. address (this will be used to mail the answer back to you).

Part 1: Information About You:
The address you put here should be the address at which you are staying in the United States (you will have a chance to insert your foreign address below). Make sure it's someplace where you can continue to receive mail if you move on—getting an answer from the INS may take awhile.

You probably won't have a **Social Security number** (unless you had some previous right to work in the United States). You probably won't have an **"A#"** (A-number) either—this refers to the Alien Registration number that is given to people who have applied for immigrant (permanent) visas or certain other immigration benefits, or have been in deportation proceedings. If you have been given an A-number, however, you will need to enter it here. And yes, the INS will check your file before they approve this extension. Your **"I-94 #"** is the number on the little card that was inserted into your passport when you entered the United States. Your **"current nonimmigrant status"** is "visitor (B-2)." **"Expires on"** is the date that your tourist status expires, that is, the expiration date in your I-94 card.

Part 2: Application Type:
Question 1: For an extension of your tourist visa, check **box a**.
Question 2: If you are traveling alone, check **box a**. If you have family members applying with you, check **box b** and be sure to complete the supplementary page to this form.

Part 3: Processing Information:
Question 1: Insert the date that you'd like to leave the United States. Note that this can be no more than six months from the expiration of your current stay, as shown on your I-94 card.
Question 2: You will probably check **No**. The only time you would need to check **Yes** here is if someone with whom you were travelling filed this form for an extension and forgot to include you.

Form I-539, Application to Extend/Change Nonimmigrant Status—Page 1

U.S. Department of Justice
Immigration and Naturalization Service

OMB No. 1115-0093; Expires 7/31/04

Application to Extend/Change Nonimmigrant Status

START HERE - Please Type or Print.

Part 1. Information about you.

Family Name		Given Name		Middle Initial

Address -
In care of -

Street Number and Name			Apt. #

City	State	Zip Code	Daytime Phone #

Country of Birth	Country of Citizenship

Date of Birth (MM/DD/YYYY)	Social Security # (if any)	A # (if any)

Date of Last Arrival Into the U.S.	I-94 #

Current Nonimmigrant Status	Expires on (MM/DD/YYYY)

Part 2. Application type. *(See instructions for fee.)*

1. I am applying for: *(Check one.)*
   a. ☐ An extension of stay in my current status.
   b. ☐ A change of status. The new status I am requesting is: _____
   c. ☐ Other: *(Describe grounds of eligibility.)* _____
2. Number of people included in this application: *(Check one.)*
   a. ☐ I am the only applicant.
   b. ☐ Members of my family are filing this application with me.
      The total number of people (including me) in the application is: _____
      (Complete the supplement for each co-applicant.)

Part 3. Processing information.

1. I/We request that my/our current or requested status be extended until (MM/DD/YYYY): _____
2. Is this application based on an extension or change of status already granted to your spouse, child or parent?
   ☐ No ☐ Yes, Receipt # _____
3. Is this application based on a separate petition or application to give your spouse, child or parent an extension or change of status? ☐ No ☐ Yes, filed with this I-539.
   ☐ Yes, filed previously and pending with INS. INS receipt number: _____
4. If you answered "Yes" to Question 3, give the name of the petitioner or applicant:

   If the petition or application is pending with INS, also give the following information:

   Office filed at _____ Filed on (MM/DD/YYYY) _____

Part 4. Additional information.

1. For applicant #1, provide passport information:
   Country of Issuance | Valid to: (MM/DD/YYYY)
2. Foreign Address: Street Number and Name | Apt. #

City or Town	State or Province

Country	Zip/Postal Code

FOR INS USE ONLY

Returned	Receipt
Date	
Resubmitted	
Date	
Reloc Sent	
Date	
Reloc Rec'd	
Date	

☐ Applicant Interviewed on
_____
Date

☐ *Extension Granted to (Date):*
_____

Change of Status/Extension Granted
New Class: From *(Date):* _____
_____ To *(Date):* _____

If Denied:
☐ Still within period of stay
☐ S/D to: _____
☐ Place under docket control

Remarks:

Action Block

To be Completed by
Attorney or Representative, **if any**

☐ Fill in box if G-28 is attached represent the applicant

ATTY State License

Additional pages not shown.

Question 3: You'll probably check **No**; see analysis of Question 2 above.

Question 4: Only needs to be filled in if you checked **Yes** to question 3.

Part 4, Additional Information:

Questions 1 and 2: Insert the requested information about your passport and your foreign address. For this extension to be granted, your passport will have to remain valid for the entire length of your stay. If your passport is due to expire, look for a consulate of your home country in the United States and see if they can renew it.

Question 3:

3a through 3c will look familiar. As with your original tourist visa application, the INS is interested in whether your underlying motive in staying longer is to apply for a green card.

3d: Not surprisingly, if you have been convicted of any crimes, you will be denied this extension and the INS will probably take steps to remove you from the United States immediately.

3e: If you have violated your nonimmigrant status (for example, by working), you will not be given an extension.

3f: If you are in **"removal proceedings"** (formerly known as exclusion or deportation proceedings, or being called to Immigration Court) you should speak to a lawyer. Your entire immigration situation is probably in the power of the immigration courts, which makes you ineligible for this extension.

3g: By now you probably know the significance of this question. Working in the United States while on a tourist visa is a violation of the visa. If you have been working, you will be denied this extension and could be called to Immigration Court.

Part 5: Signature.

Remember to sign and date the form. The INS will return it to you if you forget.

Part 6: Don't fill this in. If a lawyer or legal
assistant filled this form out for you, they will need to identify themselves here.

White House
Washington, District of Columbia

Form I-539 Supplement-1, Page 1

Supplement -1
Attach to Form I-539 when more than one person is included in the petition or application.
(List each person separately. Do not include the person named in the form.)

Family Name	Given Name	Middle Name	Date of Birth (MM/DD/YYYY)
County of Birth	County of Citizenship	Social Security # (if any)	A # (if any)

Date of Arrival (MM/DD/YYYY)		I-94 #	
Current Nonimmigrant Status:		Expires On (MM/DD/YYYY)	
Country Where Passport Issued		Expiration Date (MM/DD/YYYY)	

Family Name	Given Name	Middle Name	Date of Birth (MM/DD/YYYY)
County of Birth	County of Citizenship	Social Security # (if any)	A # (if any)

Date of Arrival (MM/DD/YYYY)		I-94 #	
Current Nonimmigrant Status:		Expires On (MM/DD/YYYY)	
Country Where Passport Issued		Expiration Date (MM/DD/YYYY)	

Family Name	Given Name	Middle Name	Date of Birth (MM/DD/YYYY)
County of Birth	County of Citizenship	Social Security # (if any)	A # (if any)

Date of Arrival (MM/DD/YYYY)		I-94 #	
Current Nonimmigrant Status:		Expires On (MM/DD/YYYY)	
Country Where Passport Issued		Expiration Date (MM/DD/YYYY)	

Family Name	Given Name	Middle Name	Date of Birth (MM/DD/YYYY)
County of Birth	County of Citizenship	Social Security # (if any)	A # (if any)

Date of Arrival (MM/DD/YYYY)		I-94 #	
Current Nonimmigrant Status:		Expires On (MM/DD/YYYY)	
Country Where Passport Issued		Expiration Date (MM/DD/YYYY)	

Family Name	Given Name	Middle Name	Date of Birth (MM/DD/YYYY)
County of Birth	County of Citizenship	Social Security # (if any)	A # (if any)

Date of Arrival (MM/DD/YYYY)		I-94 #	
Current Nonimmigrant Status:		Expires On (MM/DD/YYYY)	
Country Where Passport Issued		Expiration Date (MM/DD/YYYY)	

If you need additional space, attach a separate sheet(s) of paper.
Place your name, A # if any, date of birth, form number and application date at the top of the sheet(s) of paper.

Form I-539 (Rev. 09/04/01)Y Page 4

You'll find a tear-out copy of this supplement page to Form I-539 in Appendix D.

If you have family members traveling with you and they also want an extension of their stay, this is the place to enter their names and other information. This supplement will be self-explanatory once you have completed your portion of the form.

2. Documents and Other Items You'll Need for Your Extension Application

In addition to Form I-539, your application for an extension will need to include some supporting documents. Some will be easy to gather, such as your original I-94 card (this is one of few instances in which you cannot just send the copy of a document to the INS), and a copy of the page of your passport showing your picture and its expiration date (which should be at least six months into the future). And naturally you'll need to pay a fee, currently $120, but double-check it on the INS website at http://www.ins.gov. (Click on the entries regarding Forms and Fees, and look on the chart for Form I-539. That will be your total fee.) You do not need to pay extra for family members included in your application.

Other documents will require a bit more work to assemble. You'll need to write a statement or letter, explaining

- the reasons for your request
- why your extended stay would be temporary, including what arrangement you have made to depart the United States
- any effect of the extended stay on your foreign employment and residency. Take a look at the "Sample Letter in Support of Extension," below, to see how one applicant presented his case.

It will be helpful to gather any other documents that support your extension request. For example, if you need to stay for medical reasons, attach a letter from your doctor. If you were delayed by car trouble in the middle of the United States, attach a letter and receipt from the mechanic. If you've made a new plane reservation home, attach a copy of the ticket.

Sample Letter in Support of Extension

555 Sunnyside Way
Palo Alto, CA 9xxxx

May 1, 200x

Immigration and Naturalization Service
California Service Center
P.O. Box 10539
Laguna Niguel, CA 92607-0539
[See Appendix B for the address of the INS Service Centers serving your region.]

Dear Sir/Madam:

I would like to extend my stay in the United States. My visit has not quite gone as planned and I need four more weeks in order to accomplish my original plans.

When I first arrived, my aunt and uncle intended to show me around California. Unfortunately my aunt fell and broke her wrist the day before I arrived. As a result, she was house bound for three weeks, and I stayed and helped around the house.

After that I traveled with a friend who met up with me here. However, my aunt and uncle would still very much like to tour me around California, and I would like this as well.

I still have two months' time before I start college in my home country. I had not been planning to work in my country this summer anyway. I have arranged to change my flight home, as shown by the attached copy of my new plane ticket. I still have enough money to support myself. Attached is a photocopy of my remaining traveler's checks.

Thank you for your consideration of this request.

Very truly yours,

Gundars Mann

Gundars Mann

Encl.: Copies of new plane ticket and remaining traveler's checks

3. Using the Checklist for Extension of Visitor Stay

The Checklist below summarizes all the materials that you'll need to put together your extension application. By marking off the items as you've finished preparing or locating them, you'll be able to ensure that nothing is forgotten.

 You'll find a tear-out version of this Checklist in Appendix E.

Checklist for Extension of Visitor Stay

☐ Form I-539
☐ fee, currently $120
☐ your original I-94 card
☐ copy of the page of your passport showing your picture and the expiration date
☐ written statement in support of your request
☐ other documents that support your extension request

---

4. Mailing the Extension Application

When you have assembled everything for the application, make a complete copy of everything, including the check or money order. Keep the copy in a safe place. Mail the original application to the INS Service Center listed in Appendix B or on the INS website at http://www.ins.gov.

Use certified mail to send your application, with a return receipt requested. You can do this at any U.S. Post Office. This allows you to be sure that your application got to the INS (they will have to sign and return the receipt notice to you), and it gives you a way to pressure the INS to look harder for your application if they lose it.

For advice on how to track your application while it's being decided, see Chapter 13, Dealing With Bureaucrats, Delays and Denials.

5. Approval or Denial of Your Extension

The INS will respond to you by mail. If your application for an extension is approved, you will receive a new I-94 card showing the new date when your stay will expire. If your application is denied, you will receive a notice from the INS telling you to leave the United States by a certain date in the very near future. If you don't leave by that date, you could be placed in removal (deportation) proceedings. Consult a lawyer as soon as possible. Don't wait until close to the court date. The lawyer may be able to immediately help you protect against your current stay being considered "unlawful," for example, by negotiating with the INS for you to depart voluntarily by a certain date.

Independence Hall
Philadelphia, Pennsylvania

D. Changing to a New Immigration Status

While you are in the United States, you may have an opportunity or offer to stay longer. Perhaps you gain admission to a school, decide to get married to a U.S. citizen or are offered a job. So long as you have maintained your tourist status (not broken the rules) and your permitted stay has not yet expired, you may be able to apply to change to a new status without leaving the United States.

Changing from tourist to student status is covered in Chapter 8 of this book. Changing (or, more technically, "adjusting") to permanent resident status based on marriage to a U.S. citizen or permanent resident is covered in *Fiancé and Marriage Visas: A Couple's Guide to U.S. Immigration*, by Ilona Bray (Nolo). Neither book covers other potential changes of status, such as those based on job offers. You may wish to consult a lawyer who can help you determine your rights and apply for a new immigration status.

⚠ **U.S. green cards are given to limited categories of people.** If you're enjoying your visit and wondering if you can stay in the United States permanently, you should know one important thing: There is no "general" application for U.S. permanent residence (a "green card") or citizenship. Unless you fit into one of the categories described on the table in Chapter 3, Section D, there is no chance that you will be allowed to make your home in the United States. ■

In the U.S. As a Student

American colleges and study programs tend to be fun places. Most campuses offer much more than classes, including sports, social and cultural events and activities. For young people, college may be the first time they can socialize without their parents looking over their shoulders. And, schools have traditionally been the center of U.S. protest movements and political activism. Feel free to take part in all of this—the INS isn't watching your every move. But don't get carried away if you want to keep your visa. You'll want to remember your rights and responsibilities as a visa holder at all times. Otherwise, you risk being deported and having your future visa applications denied.

This chapter gives you information on how to stay within the time limits and other restrictions of your visa or status—and what will happen if you don't (see Sections A, B and C). If you've fallen out of student status (such as by violating your visa or dropping out of full-time study) see Section D on whether and how you can apply to get your status back. Changes in your choice of school or program or the length of time you take to finish studying are covered in Sections E, F and G.

You'll very likely want to travel outside the United States at some point during your studies—in that case, see Section H for what to bring in order to ensure a smooth return. If you have family members with you in the United States, read Section I for what they're allowed and not allowed to do while they're here, including travel rights. Whether and how you can be employed in the United States is covered in Chapter 12.

Depending on how helpful the Designated Student Officer, or "DSO" is at your school, that person may also be able to assist you with the applications described in this chapter.

⚠ The DSO is both friend and foe. Your school will have a "Designated School Official," or DSO, who is your information source and often your representative in dealing with the INS. (The DSO might also go by another name, such as "Foreign Student Advisor" or "Foreign Student Officer.") DSOs tend to be helpful and friendly, and will provide you with INS forms, initial approvals for visa extensions, program

changes and tips on dealing with complications. The DSO and the school have an interest in helping you overcome any temporary academic or financial problems—international students not only help the school's reputation, but also provide needed financial support. But beware: If you do something that violates your student status, the DSO has no legal choice but to report you to the INS.

No matter which procedure in this chapter you use, don't wait until the last minute. Getting approval from your DSO, assembling your application and getting a decision from the INS will all take time. Meanwhile, your school year is ticking by and you could find yourself unable to transfer schools, change programs or take other hoped-for action.

A. How Long You Can Stay

You can stay in the United States until the expiration date shown on the I-94 card that you got at the border. For M-1 students, that date is usually one year from when they entered the United States. For F-1 students it's a little more complicated. Their I-94s usually say "D/S" for "Duration of Status." If your I-94 has this notation, the expected completion date shown on your Form I-20 controls when you are supposed to leave. (As you know by now, the original visa stamp in your passport that you received at the consulate may have an earlier or later expiration date on it—but this date does not determine when you should leave the United States, only how long you can use that visa to enter.)

If you find that you need or want more time to complete your studies, you may be able to apply for an extension, discussed in Section F, below. Staying past your expiration date without an extension can have serious legal consequences, as described in Sections B, C and D, below.

B. How to Avoid Breaking the Visa Rules

Once you're in the United States, your right to stay depends not only on when your stay expires, but whether you are maintaining your student immigration status. You can maintain your status by following all of the rules of your student status—in other words, by doing everything you agreed to do when you received the visa or status change. If you violate these rules, you are said to "fall out of status," meaning that your right to be in the United States disappears automatically. Your accompanying spouse and children will simultaneously lose their right to be here. You and your family could be deported and your unlawful stay in the United States entered onto your permanent immigration records.

The most important rules are rather simple. You must:

- go to school as expected, and
- make sure that the DSO or INS approve any changes in your overall plan.

Many students break these rules and lose their student status by reducing their course load below full-time study (or just dropping out altogether), working without permission or switching schools or programs without advising the right people (your DSO or the INS). You'll also be violating your status if you lie or give false information to the INS or are convicted of a crime of violence.

Unfortunately, one violation tends to cause another. For example, if your expected completion date as shown on your Form I-20 passes by and you don't notice, and you continue working at your on-campus job, you will technically be working without authorization—on top of having overstayed your student status. In fact, any employment becomes unauthorized as soon as you fall out of student status. This compounding of violations can create problems because different violations may have different legal consequences.

 Staying beyond the expiration date on your original visa is not a status violation. Your student visa, unlike your I-20, is mainly an entry document. So the expiration date shows the last date you can use it to enter the United States, not the date by which you have to leave the United States. But if you do leave the United States with an expired visa, you will have to renew the visa at a U.S. consulate before returning. We'll discuss this further in Section H, below.

When in doubt about whether something you are planning to do will be a violation of your visa or student status, talk to your DSO. It is especially important to talk issues over with the DSO *before* you take action, because once you have violated your status, the DSO must report you to the INS.

1. Being Sick Is Not a Violation

The INS does not expect you to drag yourself to school if you come down with a serious illness or become pregnant. If this happens, talk to your DSO so that he or she understands the situation and doesn't report your absence from school to the INS. As soon as you are fully recovered, you are expected to resume a full-time course load. If your illness prevents you from completing your studies by the date on your I-20, you'll need to apply for an extension of time (see Section F, below for instructions).

2. School Vacations Are Not Usually Violations

Most foreign students don't have to worry about school vacations or exams breaking their status. For F-1 students, as long as your course of study extends into the next school term, scheduled school vacations (summer included) are not considered to break your full-time course of study or to violate your visa status. F-1 students whose school follows a quarter or a trimester calendar can shift their summer vacation to another season, so long as they study for a whole academic year first. Exam periods (when the school gives you a couple of weeks off from classes to study for exams) are similarly not considered to break your F-1 status.

If you are an M-1 student, exam periods and short vacations will not break your status. However, M-1 students are eligible for a summer vacation only if you have completed an academic year prior to that summer and are eligible and intend to register at the same school after the summer vacation. In addition, you'll maintain your status while taking a vacation only if vocational students at your school normally take a summer vacation. If, for example, your vocational program is only 12 weeks long, it is unlikely to include a summer vacation.

C. What Happens If You Break the Visa Rules

The consequences of violating your status depend on what you do and who finds out about it. A very minor violation, such as babysitting one night for cash, may go unnoticed and/or result in nothing. But don't take this example as permission to go out and try it! In fact, unauthorized employment is the worst sort of status violation, because it is the only one that you cannot overcome by applying to be returned to student status, through a process called reinstatement, discussed below.

If you have any run-ins with the police during your visit, see an immigration lawyer as well as a criminal lawyer. Most people who are arrested for crimes consult only with a criminal lawyer. In fact, the state or federal government may provide free representation (a "public defender") to low-income people convicted of crimes, whether or not they're U.S. citizens. It is not uncommon for the person to plead guilty to a crime (whether or not they're guilty) as part of a deal to avoid jail time. Unfortunately, criminal defense lawyers may not understand how a conviction may affect a person's immigration status. For example, seemingly minor details like the exact definition of your crime or the length of your jail sentence can make a huge difference in whether you are deportable or legally admissible to the United States in the future. This makes it extremely important that you consult with an immigration lawyer before you do anything definitive like pleading guilty. Unfortunately, the government never provides free immigration law services.

If the INS catches you in a status violation, it could place you and your spouse and children in removal proceedings. If you don't have a defense, you could be deported. On top of this, even if you avoid deportation, the judge will likely find that your violation caused some of your time in the United States to be "unlawful." To remind yourself what that could mean, go back and review Chapter 2, covering the three- and ten-year Time Bars. Briefly, once your "out of status" time has added up to six months or more, the first time you leave the United States you could find yourself prevented from reentering for three or ten years.

To avoid the deportation or Time Bar consequences described above, you may want to step up and apply for "reinstatement." Don't wait until you're caught in a violation, or the application will most likely be denied. If your request for reinstatement is approved, the INS will officially recognize that you have gotten back your student status (and are no longer accruing unlawful time) as of the date they reinstate you. For details on how to apply for reinstatement, see Section D, below.

To be eligible for reinstatement, you must show either that you fell out of status for reasons beyond your control (these reasons cannot be financial) or that you would experience extreme hardship if you were not reinstated. For example, if you became so ill that you were incapable of attending class or advising your DSO of your condition, this could be considered a circumstance beyond your control. An example of extreme hardship might be that you had already finished three years of a four-year program not offered in your home country—thus destroying your career plans if you were to stop studying now.

Your visa is also invalid if you overstayed your I-20. If your violation was an overstay of your I-20 expiration date, applying for reinstatement may not be all you need. The next time you take a trip outside the United States (before the end of your studies), you will have to apply for a new visa through the consulate in your home country in order to return. Consult with your DSO or an attorney before you go.

D. How to Get Back (Reinstate) Your Student Status

The process of applying for reinstatement is the same for F-1 and M-1 visa holders. You'll need to work with your DSO to assemble certain forms, attach some supporting paperwork and mail it all to an INS office, as described in this section.

⚠ **Don't let the INS dawdle with your reinstatement application.** When applying to reinstate your student status, you must get an answer before the expected completion date on your Form I-20 has passed. Otherwise, and even though the delay was not your fault, you will have reapply for a student visa the next time you're in your home country. When you send in your application, include a cover letter making clear what date you need a decision by. Write reminder letters to the INS as the weeks go by.

1. The Reinstatement Application Forms

You need to fill out only one form to apply for reinstatement, INS Form I-539 (pictured below), together with a supplemental sheet if you have family members with you in the United States. Your DSO, however, will also need to fill out a new Form I-20, and may decide that a Form I-538 will help your application along. Form I-539 is normally printed out double-sided, head to foot. This form has more than one use—don't be confused by questions that don't seem relevant to your situation.

 You'll find a tear-out version of this form in Appendix D.

When you've got a copy of Form I-539 in hand, follow our line-by-line instructions for filling it out.

First, to avoid confusing the INS, write "REINSTATEMENT" in large letters, preferably in red ink, at the top of the form.

Instructions page 5, box at bottom of page: Make sure to fill your name and address in here; the INS will use this to mail its response to you.

Part 1: Information About You: Mostly self-explanatory. You will probably not have a Social Security number unless you formerly had a visa or status that allowed you to work. If you don't have a number, enter "None." You

will have an A-number (an eight-digit number following the letter "A" for Alien) only if you have been in deportation or removal proceedings or submitted certain immigration applications, particularly for permanent residence. If you were in proceedings or had any applications denied, especially for reasons such as fraud, see a lawyer.

Your **I-94 number** should appear on the small white card that you received at the border.

For **"Current Nonimmigrant status,"** enter "Out of Status Student." Your **"expiration date"** will be on your I-94 card, and may just be "Duration of Status" (D/S). (For an explanation of D/S, see the Glossary and Chapter 9, Section B.)

Part 2: Application Type:
Question 1: Check box **1c** and write "reinstatement" on the line next to it.
Question 2: This is where you make sure your family members get included in your application. If you want them to have visa status after your reinstatement, check box **2b**. The number you should enter is the total number of family members plus you.

Part 3: Processing Information:
Question 1: Answer this question even though it seems to mention only extensions. Enter the same date as your latest I-20 shows for the completion of your program.
Questions 2 to 4: Answer No.

Part 4: Additional Information:
Questions 1 and 2: Self-explanatory questions based on the information in your passport and calling for your overseas address.

⚠ **When does your passport expire?** If the expiration date in your passport is within the next six months or less, you should have it renewed. You can usually do this at a consulate of your home country in the United States. If there isn't a consulate in the city where you're living, you can locate one in the phone books for Washington, D.C., Los Angeles, San Francisco or Chicago, or by looking on the Web at http://www.embassy.org/embassies/index.html or http://www.embpage.org.

Question 3: These questions are designed to see whether you are inadmissible. Think carefully before entering your answers, and keep reading for details. If there isn't a good solution below, you'll need to see a lawyer.

Question 3a: If you (or any members of your family) have submitted an application for an immigrant visa, which shows that you're seeking a green card, the INS will probably conclude that you have no intention of returning home after your student stay. Your application may therefore be denied. There isn't a solution for this, and hiding the other application is impossible.

Question 3b: This is similar to the question above except that instead of referring to an application that you filed yourself, it asks whether someone else has filed a petition to start the process for you to permanently immigrate to the United States. Some petitions will only place you on a waiting list that will last many years before you see an immigrant visa. Nevertheless, the INS will likely deny your application if your answer to this question is Yes.

Question 3c: See advice for question 3a. Form I-485 is simply the U.S. version of a green card application.

Question 3d: If you were simply arrested and not charged (for example, the police picked up the wrong person), you are safe entering "Yes" here and attaching a written explanation and a copy of the police report. But for more serious arrests, you must consult a lawyer before going any farther. Most convictions will make you inadmissible to the United States.

Question 3e: See Section B, above, for a reminder of what actions would be violations of your student status. This is the place to mention the violations that led to your request to be reinstated as a student.

Question 3f: If you are now in **"removal proceedings"** (formerly known as exclusion or deportation proceedings), speak to an attorney before submitting this application. Chances are, your immigration situation is now completely in the hands of the Immigration Court. If so, filing this application will get you nowhere unless and until the INS agrees to terminate the court proceedings.

Question 3g: If you have been employed, this is no problem so long as it was within the conditions of your student status and, if required, specifically authorized by the INS. (See Chapter 12 for information on working while you're a student.) Look at the paragraph below the question to see what additional information you'll need to supply (add this information on a separate piece of paper and don't forget to put your name at the top in case it gets separated from the main application). Attach a photocopy of both sides of your INS work permit (EAD) if you had one. But take note that even if you answer "No" to this question, you have to supply additional information. As the next paragraph under the question explains, you'll have to attach a separate sheet assuring or reassuring the INS that you are able to support yourself financially.

Part 5: Signature: Self-explanatory.

Part 6: Signature of person preparing form if other than above: This is where a lawyer or legal assistant will sign. If you simply had some typing help, the person helping you does not need to sign.

2. Line-by-Line Instructions for Form I-539 Supplement

Form I-539 Supp. is a one-page, single-sided form. You'll only need to use it if you have a foreign-born spouse and/or children staying with you with F-2 or M-2 visas or status. As you'll see, it has repeating blocks for information about your spouse and children. Most of it is self-explanatory.

 You'll find a tear-out version of this form in Appendix D.

Under **Date of Arrival**, put the person's most recent arrival into the United States (many people mistakenly put their first arrival). The spouse or children's **Current nonimmigrant status** is either F-2 overstay or M-2 overstay. **Expires on** refers to the date *your* status expires, which will be on your I-20.

Form I-539, Application to Extend/Change Nonimmigrant Status—Page 1

U.S. Department of Justice
Immigration and Naturalization Service

OMB No. 1115-0093; Expires 7/31/04

Application to Extend/Change Nonimmigrant Status

START HERE - Please Type or Print.

FOR INS USE ONLY

Part 1.   Information about you.

Family Name		Given Name		Middle Initial

Address -
In care of -

Street Number and Name			Apt. #

City	State	Zip Code	Daytime Phone #

Country of Birth		Country of Citizenship

Date of Birth (MM/DD/YYYY)	Social Security # (if any)	A # (if any)

Date of Last Arrival Into the U.S.	I-94 #

Current Nonimmigrant Status	Expires on (MM/DD/YYYY)

For INS Use Only:
Returned — Receipt
Date
Resubmitted
Date
Reloc Sent
Date
Reloc Rec'd
Date

Part 2.   Application type. *(See instructions for fee.)*

1. I am applying for: *(Check one.)*
   a. ☐ An extension of stay in my current status.
   b. ☐ A change of status. The new status I am requesting is: _____
   c. ☐ Other: *(Describe grounds of eligibility.)* _____
2. Number of people included in this application: *(Check one.)*
   a. ☐ I am the only applicant.
   b. ☐ Members of my family are filing this application with me.
      The total number of people (including me) in the application is: _____
      (Complete the supplement for each co-applicant.)

☐ Applicant Interviewed on

Date

☐ *Extension Granted to (Date):* _____

Change of Status/Extension Granted
New Class: From *(Date):* _____
                    To *(Date):* _____

Part 3.   Processing information.

1. I/We request that my/our current or requested status be extended until (MM/DD/YYYY): _____
2. Is this application based on an extension or change of status already granted to your spouse, child or parent?
   ☐ No ☐ Yes, Receipt # _____
3. Is this application based on a separate petition or application to give your spouse, child or parent an extension or change of status? ☐ No ☐ Yes, filed with this I-539.
   ☐ Yes, filed previously and pending with INS. INS receipt number: _____
4. If you answered "Yes" to Question 3, give the name of the petitioner or applicant:

_____

If the petition or application is pending with INS, also give the following information:

Office filed at _____	Filed on (MM/DD/YYYY) _____

If Denied:
☐ Still within period of stay
☐ S/D to: _____
☐ Place under docket control

Remarks:

Action Block

Part 4.   Additional information.

1. For applicant #1, provide passport information: | Valid to: (MM/DD/YYYY)
   Country of Issuance

2. Foreign Address: Street Number and Name		Apt. #

City or Town	State or Province

Country	Zip/Postal Code

To be Completed by
Attorney or Representative, **if any**

☐ Fill in box if G-28 is attached to represent the applicant

ATTY State License

Additional pages not shown.

Form I-539 Supplement-1, Page 1

Supplement -1
Attach to Form I-539 when more than one person is included in the petition or application.
(List each person separately. Do not include the person named in the form.)

Family Name	Given Name	Middle Name	Date of Birth (MM/DD/YYYY)
County of Birth	County of Citizenship	Social Security # (if any)	A # (if any)
Date of Arrival (MM/DD/YYYY)		I-94 #	
Current Nonimmigrant Status:		Expires On (MM/DD/YYYY)	
Country Where Passport Issued		Expiration Date (MM/DD/YYYY)	
Family Name	Given Name	Middle Name	Date of Birth (MM/DD/YYYY)
County of Birth	County of Citizenship	Social Security # (if any)	A # (if any)
Date of Arrival (MM/DD/YYYY)		I-94 #	
Current Nonimmigrant Status:		Expires On (MM/DD/YYYY)	
Country Where Passport Issued		Expiration Date (MM/DD/YYYY)	
Family	Given		Date of Birth

When you enter the expiration date of the family member's passport, make sure that it is at least six months into the future. If not, get the passport renewed. However, if waiting for the renewal will cause problems for this application, simply submit this application, write in the existing passport expiration date and then add "renewal pending."

3. Documents You'll Need for Reinstatement Application

In addition to the forms described above, you'll need to submit some documents and other items with your reinstatement application. Two of these items are rather straightforward and need no further explanation. These include

- your I-94 card (original, for you and any family members), and
- a fee (currently $120, but double-check this on the INS website at http://www.ins.gov). Pay in check or money order, payable to the US INS —do not send cash.

In addition, you may want to submit proof of your continued ability to pay your tuition, fees and living expenses. This information is recommended, not required. It would consist of the same type of financial information that you provided to get your visa in the first place.

The most challenging document you'll need for your reinstatement application is your statement explaining why you need and deserve to be reinstated. You'll need to explain:

- what circumstances caused you to fall out of status
- exactly how those circumstances were beyond your control or why not being reinstated would cause you extreme hardship
- that you are not deportable for any reason other than your violation of student status
- that you haven't been employed without authorization, and
- how you will now be able to comply with all the terms in your visa (pursuing a full course of study, not engaging in unauthorized employment, and or whatever else your visa requires).

There is no form or standard way to present the information called for in the above list. Clearly and honestly explain the circumstances that resulted in your losing status. The most important thing is to give enough detail to make the INS understand the problem that led to your falling out of status. Also, use plain English and avoid fancy legal language. For example, in the sample below, Jamal could have just said that his neighbor was "crazy"—but this wouldn't have been as convincing as describing the neighbor's specific actions. Many people think they have to write like lawyers and say things like "I was in a legal situation with an individual who was making false accusations and thereby disturbing my peace." This will only confuse the INS and make them wonder who was really at fault.

Below you'll find a sample Reinstatement Request Statement. Don't just copy this statement and fill in your name. The situation described in this letter is not a typical one—but then, there is no typical situation.

To make your statement appear more official, take it to a notary public and sign it in front of the notary. For a reminder of what notaries do, see Chapter 4, Section C. There should be a notary public at your school's financial aid or housing office. Otherwise you will be able to find one in the Yellow Pages of a local phone book. The notary shouldn't charge more than $15 for this service.

Amherst College
Amherst, Massachusetts

5. Submitting Your Reinstatement Application

When you've put your reinstatement application together, submit it to your local INS District Office. Your DSO will be able to tell you whether your local office requires submissions by mail, or whether it's better to walk the application in. If that office doesn't decide on your application within a few weeks, see Chapter 13, Dealing With Bureaucrats, Delays and Denials.

6. Using the Checklist for Reinstatement Application

The Checklist below summarizes the forms and documents you'll need to apply for reinstatement of your student status. By checking off each box as you've prepared or found the item, you'll ensure that nothing gets forgotten. You don't want to be the cause of delay at a time like this, when your unlawful time in the United States may be adding up day by day.

 You'll find a tear-out version of this Checklist in Appendix E.

Checklist for Reinstatement Application

Here's what you'll need to apply for reinstatement:

- ☐ Form I-539
- ☐ Form I-538 (optional, but it may speed up your application)
- ☐ new Form I-20, with your DSO's signature
- ☐ your I-94 card (original, for you and any family members)
- ☐ your written request for reinstatement
- ☐ proof of your continued ability to pay your tuition, fees and living expenses (recommended, not required)
- ☐ fee (currently $120)

Sample Reinstatement Request Statement

I, Jamal G, hereby declare as follows:

My full and complete name is Jamal G. My admittance number is 123456789. I am an M-1 student visa holder from Sudan.

This statement explains why I fell out of student status and why I qualify for reinstatement to continue my studies.

I entered the United States on [exact date], and began my vocational studies soon after. Everything seemed to be going well: I found a nice apartment, I liked my teachers, and I was having no trouble keeping up with my classes.

Toward the end of September, however, a crazy neighbor of mine began harassing me, with the result that I had to spend all my time dealing with this, including going to court to protect myself and moving apartments.

Apparently this neighbor has a true psychological problem, including delusions. She has, in fact, driven other tenants out of this building, but because she is a relation of the landlord, she hasn't been kicked out. Anyway, she began to believe that I was spying on her. She would call me, bang on my wall, and knock on my door at all hours of the day or night, and yell things like "I know what you're up to, and you're going to pay for this!" At first I just tried to ignore it, though I was losing a great deal of sleep. But after a couple of weeks I began to see that this was only going to get worse—she was leaving bags of disgusting things in my mailbox and tacking strange notes to my front door. Once, she even followed me part way to school.

I talked to my DSO, who referred me to the school's legal clinic. He also referred me to the counseling clinic, to help me with the stress that I was feeling. After many days of work, I got a temporary restraining order against this woman and started to feel a bit better about things. But it was silly of me to believe that a delusional person would follow a TRO. Within a few days, she was up to her old tricks. I called the police so many times that they stopped coming. It was clear that I would have to move apartments, which I did in late October.

The result was I missed so many classes through the months of September and October that I was, in effect, no longer attending school. I missed too much to make up by the end of the semester. As you can see, these circumstances were completely beyond my control. I came to the United States ready to study, and but for this woman, I would be studying now.

Other than having fallen out of student status, I have done nothing else to make myself deportable from the United States. I have not been employed without authorization; I stopped my on-campus job even before I stopped attending classes. With the help of my DSO and certain professors who will work with me individually to make up some of what I missed, I have arranged to take a full course of study next term.

Enclosed please find copies of the following documents: the TRO and other court documents showing the dates when I had to appear in court, a copy of my lawyer's bill showing our many meetings, a letter from my counselor confirming our meeting dates and the stress I experienced, a letter from another tenant in our building describing the crazy woman tenant's behavior, and a letter from the cafeteria supervisor confirming the date I stopped work.

I swear, under penalty of perjury, that the foregoing is true and correct to the best of my knowledge.

Dated: _____   Signed:

7. Approval or Denial of Your Reinstatement

When your reinstatement is approved, the INS will return your Form I-20 with written entries ("endorsements") to show your reinstatement. The INS will also send word to your school.

Your pre-violation student time still counts to your benefit. If you will be applying for any benefits that require you to add up how much time you've been a student—such as a practical training work permit that requires nine months of F-1 student status—you can count the months before you violated your status as well as the months after you were reinstated. The months in between, however, don't count.

If your reinstatement is denied, you have no right to appeal the denial. However, if you acquire some new evidence showing why you shouldn't have been denied, you can ask the INS to reopen the decision—but get the help of a lawyer for this, and act quickly. After a denial, you will probably receive a Notice to Appear in court (NTA) placing you in removal proceedings. At the conclusion of these proceedings the judge could order you deported.

E. How to Transfer Schools

No matter how much research and planning you did before choosing a school, you may find that it isn't right for you. Perhaps the program isn't what you expected, you don't enjoy your fellow students or the school's geographic location is too cold—or too hot. You may be able to transfer to another school, depending on the type of visa you are on.

1. F Visa Holders and School Transfers

F visa holders must start out at the school listed on their I-20. However, if you become dissatisfied with that school, you can change at any time and for any reason. You must, however, have maintained your student status at your original school—if, for example,

your dissatisfaction got to the point that you dropped out of classes, you will not be allowed to transfer schools until you've applied for and been granted reinstatement (see Section D, above).

The procedures for transferring schools are simple. A transfer does not require the INS's approval. All the paperwork will be handled by the DSO at your current school and the DSO at your new school.

Your first step toward a school transfer will be to get accepted by a new school (school application procedures vary from school to school and are not covered in this book). After you're accepted by a new school, it will send you a new Form I-20. Tell the DSO at your present school of your intent to transfer. (You might want to talk to your DSO even before this, to see if she can be of any assistance—but this is the point at which you must tell her.) Then you can transfer to your new school and start classes. No later than 15 days after beginning classes at your new school, you must sign and give your new I-20 to the DSO at your new school. The new DSO then has 30 days in which to take care of advising your old DSO as well as the INS that you have indeed transferred. The new DSO will send you your new I-20 ID copy.

If you had a work permit at your first school, it will automatically be cancelled by your transfer. You'll need to apply for a new work permit if you become eligible to work again.

2. M Visas and School Transfers

If you begin your program and decide that this is not the school for you, act quickly. You can freely transfer only during your first six months of study. After that, you may be able to transfer if you can show all of the following:

- you have maintained your student status for the past six months
- you are unable to continue at this school due to circumstances beyond your control
- you are still capable of supporting yourself financially, and
- you plan to be a full-time student at the new school.

For example, if the professors teaching in your subject area have left for another school, this might be a "circumstance beyond your control" that the INS might recognize. You can transfer only to another vocational program, not to an academic program that requires an F visa.

If you are eligible for a transfer, your first step is to apply to and be accepted by a new school. They must send you a new Form I-20 upon acceptance. Then you'll need to fill out an application form and assemble certain documents, as described next.

a. Application Form for M-1 Student Transfer

You'll need to deal with only one form to request a school transfer, INS Form I-538 (pictured below). Most of Form I-538 will be filled out by your DSO, who will also know how to tailor it for a transfer application (it's usually used to apply for employment authorization). To get the process started quickly, fill out your portion and take it to your DSO, so that you can turn your attention to assembling your supporting documents. If you choose to print out Form I-538 from the INS website, it is normally single-sided.

 You'll find a tear-out copy of this form in Appendix D.

When you've got a copy of Form I-538 in hand, follow these line-by-line instructions.

Section A:
This is the section that you fill out. Most of it is self-explanatory.
Question 3: Your Student Admission Number should be on your I-20 ID.
Question 4: Enter the date that either the consulate or the INS first approved your student status.
Question 5: Your "Level of education being sought" refers to your degree, diploma or certificate.
Question 6: Your major field of study should match the information on your I-20.
Questions 7 and 8: Leave these blank for now—they concern only applications for work permits.

Don't forget to sign at the bottom of Section A.
Section B: Your DSO fills this out, but look it over to make sure that the information is accurate. If anything that the DSO says is new to the INS—for example, you've dropped your study hours to less than full time—make sure your DSO attaches documentation to show that he or she approved it.

b. Documents for M-1 Student Transfer Application

In addition to your application form, your transfer application will need to include the following:
- fee (currently $70, but double-check for changes with your DSO). Pay in check or money order, payable to the US INS; do not send cash
- your I-20 ID copy
- your I-94 (original preferred, but keep a copy for yourself—or send a copy if you no longer have the original)
- the new I-20, and
- if your transfer is after six months of study, a written statement by you showing that your reasons for needing to transfer are beyond your control, that you have maintained valid student status for the previous six months and that you can still support yourself financially. Include any proof, such as a letter from a professor or school official confirming any changes in program offerings. For more information on how to write this statement, see Section D, above, which pertains to F visas and reinstatement—but many of the issues are similar.

c. Using the Checklist for M-1 Student Transfer Application

The following Checklist summarizes everything you'll need for your transfer application. By checking off the boxes as you have prepared or located things, you'll ensure that nothing is forgotten.

Form I-538, Certification by Designated School Official—Page 1

OMB Approval No. 1115-0060

U.S. Department of Justice
Immigration and Naturalization Service

Certification by Designated School Official

SECTION A. This section must be completed by student as appropriate (Please print or type) :

1. Name:	*(Family in CAPS)*	*(First)*	*(Middle)*	2. Date of birth:

3. Student admission number:	4. Date first granted F-1 or M-1 status:

5. Level of education being sought:	6. Student's major field of study:

7. Describe the proposed employment for practical training:

Beginning date :   Ending date: Number of hours per week:

8. List all periods of previously authorized employment for practical training:

A. Curricular or work/study:	B. Post completion of studies

Signature of student: _____ Date: _____

SECTION B. This Section must be completed by the designated school official of the school the student is attending or was last authorized to attend:

9. I hereby certify that:

The student named above:

☐ Is taking a full course of study at this school, and the expected date of completion is: _____

☐ Is taking less than a full course of study at this school because: _____

☐ Completed the course of study at this school on (date): _____

☐ Did not complete the course of study. Terminated attendance on (date): _____

Check one:

☐ A. The employment is for practical training in the student's field of study. The student has been in the educational program for at least 9 months and is eligible for the requested practical training in accordance with INS regulations at 8CFR 214.2(f) (10).

☐ B. The endorsement for off-campus employment is based on the wage-and-labor attestation filed by the employer in accordance with the requirements set forth by the Secretary of Labor. The student has been in F-1 status for at least one year and is in good academic standing. Copy of the employer's attestation is attached.

☐ C. The employment is for an internship with a recognized international organization and is within the scope of the organization's sponsorship. The student has been in F-1 status for at least 9 months and is in good academic standing.

10. Name and title of DSO.	Signature:	Date:

11. Name of school:	School file number:	Telephone no

For Off
Microfilm Index Nu

(See instructions on reverse)

Additional pages not shown.

You'll find a tear-out version of this Checklist in Appendix E.

Checklist for M-1 Student Transfer Application

☐ Form I-538
☐ fee (currently $70)
☐ your I-20 ID copy
☐ your I-94 card
☐ new I-20
☐ if your transfer is after six months of study, your written statement of explanation and any accompanying evidence

---

d. Where to Send the Transfer Application

When you've assembled your application for a transfer, submit it to the INS Service Center which serves your school. The addresses are in Appendix B or on the INS website at http://www.ins.gov.

e. What Happens After You Send the Transfer Application

After sending your application, you should get a receipt notice from the Service Center within three to six weeks. The receipt will tell you when you can expect a decision. If you don't get a receipt notice, or if the INS doesn't make a decision within the time that they predicted on the receipt notice, see Chapter 13, Dealing with Bureaucrats, Delays and Denials.

If the INS doesn't send you a decision on your transfer within 60 days, you are permitted to take your chances and transfer schools anyway—but this involves some risk. If the INS ultimately says "no" to your transfer, you will automatically fall out of status and either have to apply for reinstatement or face the possibility of being sent to Immigration Court for removal proceedings.

Once you are approved, you will receive your Form I-20 ID with an entry showing your new school's name, and your Form I-20N with an entry showing that a school transfer has been authorized.

F. How to Extend Your Student Stay

If you need more time than predicted on your Form I-20 to complete your program, you will have to request an extension of your F-1 or M-1 student status. This is not normally a problem, but it has its limits. To qualify, you must still be keeping up with all the requirements of your student visa, namely attending classes and not working without authorization or committing other violations. Extensions are not meant to be available to students who "drag their feet," but only to those whose medical or academic circumstances have unexpectedly changed. For example, students who have had to change research topics, those who have experienced research problems, or students who become ill could qualify for an extension.

⚠ **Once you've passed your I-20 date, it's too late.** Extensions are not available to students who have already stayed past the completion date on their I-20; they must first apply for reinstatement. If you return to your home country before your studies are over, you will also have to apply for a new student visa. Don't leave at all until your studies are over if you were out of status for six months or more, because you could be found inadmissible and kept out for three or ten years (see Chapter 2, Section B, Dealing With Unlawful Time in the United States).

1. Extension Application Procedures for F-1 students

Procedures for extending F-1 student status have simplified greatly in recent years. Now, instead of submitting an application to the INS, you simply visit your DSO 30 days before the expiration date and ask her for a new I-20. Your DSO will ask you to fill out part of Form I-538 and take care of the rest, including notifying the INS.

2. Extension Application Procedures for M-1 Students

M-1 students who need to extend their stay must apply as follows. First, make sure that you have not waited too long; your application must be turned in at least 15 days before the end of your authorized stay. (However, you cannot submit it more than 60 days before the end of your authorized stay.) Then, assemble the forms and documents described in this section.

a. Application Form for M-1 Extension

Your extension application requires you to fill out only one form, INS Form I-539 (pictured below). Your DSO will also have to fill out a new Form I-20 for you. Include a supplementary sheet (subsection b, below) if you have a foreign-born spouse and/or children staying with you with M-2 visas or status.

 You'll find a tear-out copy of Form I-539 in Appendix D.

If you choose to print out Form I-539 from the INS website, it's normally printed double-sided, head to foot. Once you have a copy of this form in hand, follow these instructions for filling it out.

First, fill in your name and address on page 5 below the instructions.

Part 1. Information About You: Mostly self-explanatory. You will probably not have a Social Security number unless you formerly had a visa or status that allowed you to work. If you don't have a number, enter "None."
You will have an **A-number** (an eight-digit number following the letter "A" for Alien) only if you have been in deportation or removal proceedings or submitted certain immigration applications, particularly for permanent residence. If you were in proceedings

or had any applications denied, especially for reasons such as fraud, see a lawyer.
Your **I-94 number** should appear on the small white card that you received at the border.
For **"Current Nonimmigrant status,"** enter "M-1 Student." Your **"expiration date"** will be on your I-94 card.

Part 2. Application Type:
Question 1: Check box **1a**.
Question 2: This is where you make sure your family members get included in your application. If you want them to have visa status after your extension, check box **2b**, and write in the total number of them plus you.

Part 3. Processing Information:
Question 1: Enter the same date as your latest (new) I-20 shows for the completion of your program.
Questions 2 to 4: Answer **No.**

Part 4. Additional Information:
Questions 1 and 2: Self-explanatory questions based on the information in your passport and calling for your overseas address.

⚠️ **When does your passport expire?** If the expiration date in your passport is within the next six months or less, you should have it renewed. You can usually do this at a consulate of your home country in the United States. If there isn't a consulate in the city where you're living, you can locate one in the phone books for Washington, D.C., Los Angeles, San Francisco or Chicago, or by looking on the Web at http://www.embassy.org/embassies/index.html or http://www.embpage.org.

Question 3: These questions are designed to see whether you are inadmissible. Think carefully before entering your answers, and keep reading for details. If there isn't a good solution below, you'll need to see a lawyer.
Question 3a: If you (or any members of your family) have submitted an application for an immigrant visa, which shows that you're seeking a green card, the INS will probably conclude that you have no intention of returning home after your

Form I-539, Application to Extend/Change Nonimmigrant Status—Page 1

U.S. Department of Justice
Immigration and Naturalization Service

OMB No. 1115-0093; Expires 7/31/04

Application to Extend/Change Nonimmigrant Status

START HERE - Please Type or Print.	FOR INS USE ONLY

Part 1.   Information about you.

Family Name	Given Name	Middle Initial

Address -
In care of -

Street Number and Name		Apt. #

City	State	Zip Code	Daytime Phone #

Country of Birth	Country of Citizenship

Date of Birth (MM/DD/YYYY)	Social Security # (if any)	A # (if any)

Date of Last Arrival Into the U.S.	I-94 #

Current Nonimmigrant Status	Expires on (MM/DD/YYYY)

FOR INS USE ONLY

Returned	Receipt
Date	
Resubmitted	
Date	
Reloc Sent	
Date	
Reloc Rec'd	
Date	

Part 2. Application type. *(See instructions for fee.)*

1. I am applying for: *(Check one.)*
   a. ☐ An extension of stay in my current status.
   b. ☐ A change of status. The new status I am requesting is: _____
   c. ☐ Other: *(Describe grounds of eligibility.)* _____
2. Number of people included in this application: *(Check one.)*
   a. ☐ I am the only applicant.
   b. ☐ Members of my family are filing this application with me.
      The total number of people (including me) in the application is: _____
      (Complete the supplement for each co-applicant.)

☐ Applicant Interviewed on

_____
Date

☐ *Extension Granted to (Date):*
_____

Change of Status/Extension Granted
New Class: From *(Date):* _____
_____   To *(Date):* _____

Part 3. Processing information.

1. I/We request that my/our current or requested status be extended until (MM/DD/YYYY): _____
2. Is this application based on an extension or change of status already granted to your spouse, child or parent?
   ☐ No ☐ Yes, Receipt # _____
3. Is this application based on a separate petition or application to give your spouse, child or parent an extension or change of status? ☐ No ☐ Yes, filed with this I-539.
   ☐ Yes, filed previously and pending with INS. INS receipt number: _____
4. If you answered "Yes" to Question 3, give the name of the petitioner or applicant:

   _____

   If the petition or application is pending with INS, also give the following information:

   Office filed at _____ Filed on (MM/DD/YYYY) _____

If Denied:
☐ Still within period of stay
☐ S/D to: _____
☐ Place under docket control

Remarks:

Action Block

Part 4. Additional information.

1. For applicant #1, provide passport information: | Valid to: (MM/DD/YYYY)
   Country of Issuance

2. Foreign Address: Street Number and Name	Apt. #

City or Town	State or Province

Country	Zip/Postal Code

To be Completed by
Attorney or Representative, if any

☐ Fill in box if G-28 is attached to represent the applicant

ATTY State License

Additional pages not shown.

student stay. Your application may therefore be denied. There isn't a solution for this, and hiding the other application is impossible.

Question 3b: This is similar to the question above except that instead of referring to an application that you filed yourself, it asks whether someone else has filed a petition to start the process of you permanently immigrating to the United States. Some petitions will only place you on a waiting list that will last many years before you see an immigrant visa. Nevertheless, the INS will likely deny your application if your answer to this question is Yes.

Question 3c: See advice for question 3a. Form I-485 is simply the U.S. version of a green card application.

Question 3d: If you were simply arrested and not charged (for example, the police picked up the wrong person), you are safe entering "Yes" here and attaching a written explanation and a copy of the police report. But for more serious arrests, you must consult a lawyer before going any farther. Most convictions will make you inadmissible to the United States.

Question 3e: See Section B, above, for a reminder of what actions would be violations of your student status. If you have violated your status you will have to apply for reinstatement along with applying for an extension (see Section D, above, for instructions on the reinstatement application).

Question 3f: If you are now in removal proceedings (formerly known as exclusion or deportation proceedings), see a lawyer. It's likely that your immigration status is completely in the hands of the court, which would mean the INS administrative office will have no power to act on your application.

Question 3g: As an M-1 student, you should not have been employed in the U.S. during your studies.

Part 5. Signature: Self-explanatory.

Part 6. Signature of person preparing form if other than above: This is where a lawyer or legal assistant would sign. If you simply had some typing help, the person does not need to sign.

b. Line-by-Line Instructions for Form I-539 Supplement-1

The Form I-539 Supplement-1 is a one-page, single-sided form (pictured below). You'll only need to use it if you have a foreign-born spouse and/or children staying with you with M-2 visas or status. As you'll see, it has repeating blocks for information about your spouse and children. Most of it is self-explanatory.

 You'll find a tear-out version of this form in Appendix D.

Under **"Date of Arrival,"** put the person's most recent arrival into the United States (watch out: many people mistakenly put their first arrival). Their **"Current nonimmigrant status"** is either F-2 or M-2 overstay. **"Expires on"** refers to the date your status expires, which will be on your I-20. When you enter the expiration date of the family member's passport, make sure that it is at least six months into the future (an INS requirement, which helps them ensure that you have a right to return to your home country). If not, get it renewed. However, if waiting for the renewal will cause problems for this application, simply submit this application, write in the existing passport expiration date and then add "renewal pending."

c. Documents You'll Need for M-1 Extension Application

In addition to Forms I-539 and I-20, you'll need to assemble the following documents:

- your I-94 card (and those of your spouse and children, if they are here with you). The INS prefers to receive the originals of this card, but keep a copy for yourself—or send a copy if you no longer have the original, and
- a fee (currently $120). If you are mailing your application, pay in check or money order, payable to the USINS. Do not send cash.

Form I-539 Supplement-1, Page 1

Supplement -1
Attach to Form I-539 when more than one person is included in the petition or application.
(List each person separately. Do not include the person named in the form.)

Family Name	Given Name	Middle Name	Date of Birth (MM/DD/YYYY)
County of Birth	County of Citizenship	Social Security # (if any)	A # (if any)
Date of Arrival (MM/DD/YYYY)		I-94 #	
Current Nonimmigrant Status:		Expires On (MM/DD/YYYY)	
Country Where Passport Issued		Expiration Date (MM/DD/YYYY)	
Family Name	Given Name	Middle Name	Date of Birth (MM/DD/YYYY)
County of Birth	County of Citizenship	Social Security # (if any)	A # (if any)
Date of Arrival (MM/DD/YYYY)		I-94 #	
Current Nonimmigrant Status:		Expires On (MM/DD/YYYY)	
Country Where Passport Issued		Expiration Date (MM/DD/YYYY)	

d. Using the Checklist for M-1 Student Extension Application

The following Checklist summarizes everything you'll need for your extension application. By checking off the boxes as you have prepared or located things, you'll ensure that nothing is forgotten.

 You'll find a tear-out version of this Checklist in Appendix 5.

Checklist for M-1 Student Extension Application

☐ Form I-539, signed by DSO
☐ your form I-20 ID
☐ your I-94 card and those of any spouse and children
☐ fee (currently $120)

---

e. Where to Submit Your M-1 Extension Application

Ask your DSO where to submit the application. These applications usually go to an INS Service Center, but a few District Offices accept them. (If your local District Office does accept such applications, take advantage of this—the Service Centers tend are more prone to delays and mishandling of paperwork.)

f. What Happens After You Apply for an M-1 Extension

Since your DSO had to review and sign off on your application, chances are your extension will be approved by the INS. Once it is approved, you will receive a maximum of one year's extension—less if the DSO states that you need less time to complete your studies. You'll also get an additional 30 days' "grace period" in which to prepare to depart the United States.

If your application is denied, you will have to leave the United States by your original departure date or whatever alternate date the INS tells you. Talk to your DSO or an attorney to discuss your options at this point.

G. How to Change or Advance Programs Within Your School

If you're happy with your school but not happy with the program you've signed up for within that school, you may wish to change programs. Unfortunately, the INS wants to know about and control your program changes. In fact, you can apply to change programs only if you have F-1 status, as described in Section 1, below. M-1 students are stuck continuing with the program for which they came to the United States. Similarly, if you want to stay at the same school and pursue an additional degree, you'll have an easier time if you have F-1 status rather than M-1 status, as described in Section 1—but M-1 visa holders should read about their options in Section 2, below.

1. F-1 Status and Program Changes or Advancement

There are many reasons why you might want to change directions after beginning school. Perhaps you planned to get a B.S. in computer science but realized that a B.A. in Art History is your heart's desire. Or, perhaps you've finished your B.A. and want to move on to an M.A. In either situation, you'll need to follow certain procedures to let the INS know of your new plans.

💡 **If you're only changing your major, don't worry.** The INS doesn't need to know about it—for now. For a change in major, don't worry about notifying anyone until and unless you plan to take a trip out of the United States. At that time you'll have to get your I-20 updated.

The procedures for a program change are much like those for a transfer. You will need to get a new I-20, sign it and return it to your DSO within 15 days of starting the new program. The DSO will take care of notifying the INS (within 30 days). If you have a work permit, it will remain valid even after the program change.

2. M-1 Status and Program Changes

As an M-1 visa or status holder, you cannot change educational objectives at all. You must continue in and complete the program you came to the United States to attend.

Similarly, you cannot advance to a higher level or a new program at the same school under your M-1 visa. If, however, after finishing your original program, you want to apply for a different nonimmigrant visa (such as an H-1B temporary work visa), you can do so, with one important exception: You cannot switch from an M-1 to an F-1 visa from within the United States. If you want to enter an academic program you will have to leave the United States first and apply for an F-1 visa from there. As with any visa application, it will be important to show that during previous U.S. visits you always maintained your visa status and didn't stay past the expiration of your permitted stay.

Yale University
New Haven, Connecticut

H. Travel In and Out of the U.S. on Your Student Visa

As long as the completion date on your I-20 has not passed, your student visa has not expired and you haven't done anything to fall out of student status, you are free to travel in and out of the United States. (In fact, Canadian students don't need a formal student visa at all, only an I-20.) Your trip must be limited in length, however. You cannot be away for more than five months without applying for a new visa with which to return. Also, depending on the requirements of your program, taking a long trip might cause you to drop out of student status.

Before you leave the United States, take care of a few important things. First, take your I-20 to your DSO. Review it together to see if there have been any changes in the information it contains (such as your college major or your expected completion date). If there have been changes, you'll need to have your DSO issue a new I-20 document in order to return. Even if there haven't been changes, the DSO should sign the I-20 to confirm this. There are spaces on the form for such signatures.

Next, photocopy your I-94 card. Take both the original and a copy or two with you. Also, make sure the student visa stamped in your passport (if you got one in the first place) has not expired. If it has, don't panic; this doesn't mean you have violated your status. However, plan on making a trip to your local U.S. consulate before returning, to obtain a new visa for readmission to the United States. See subsection 1 below, for details on how to do this. If you never got a visa, but became a student through a Change of Status in the United States, you will also have to visit the U.S. consulate in your home country to obtain a visa, as described in subsection 1.

When you leave the United States, the airlines may take your I-94 card away from you (though they often don't). That's okay—you'll get a new one on your return entry. But don't offer it up if they don't ask for it. Also, keep the photocopy that we already instructed you to make—it will be helpful to show when you return to the United States. Make sure not to stay out of the United States too long, of course, or the border officer will wonder how (unless it's a school vacation) you could be completing your course of study.

To return to the United States, the items you'll present at the U.S. port or border should include your:

- passport (valid for at least another six months)
- most recent I-94 (original or copy)
- student visa (F-1 or M-1)
- Form I-20
- work permit, if you have one, and
- proof of continuing financial support (not always requested).

If your passport has expired but it contains your still-valid student visa, bring your old passport along with a new one. And if you've forgotten something, ask to be admitted anyway—the border officer can give you 30 days to give the INS whatever is missing.

⚠ **You can't leave and come back during your "grace period."** At the very end of your studies, your I-20 will probably still have some time left on it. That time is meant as a "grace period," during which you are expected to be packing your bags and getting ready to leave the United States. If you leave before the end of that period, you will not be able to use the same visa and I-20 to come back in, even if the date on your I-20 hasn't yet passed.

1. Visa Renewals

If the visa stamped in your passport has run out but your I-20 is still valid, you don't have to stop studying or leave the United States. However, if you do take a trip outside the United States, you will need to renew the visa in order to return. This application cannot be made within the United States.

Don't worry about the renewal until your next trip home. At that time, you will need to go to the your local U.S. consulate with your passport, your I-94 (original or copy), your I-20, two photos, a visa fee and a Form OF-156 that you'll fill out in accordance with the instructions in Chapter 7. These items are summarized on the Checklist in Section 2, below. Some consulates may also ask you to submit a certified copy of your grades from the school you are attending and documents much like you submitted with your initial application. These include financial documents showing that you are still able to cover your tuition and other expenses and evidence of your ongoing ties to your home country.

In theory, you could also renew your visa in a third country such as Canada or Mexico—however, you'll need a visa to enter their country, as covered below in subsection 3. In addition, you'll need an appointment with the appropriate U.S. consulate at least three weeks before you leave the United States. The State Department has established an appointment and information telephone line for this purpose: 900-443-3131. There is a service charge for the call (on top of the usual long distance charge), of $1.65 per minute. For more information, see the State Department website at http://www.nvars.com.

2. Using the Checklist for Visa Renewals

The following Checklist summarizes the forms and documents you'll need to present to an overseas U.S. consulate in order to renew your student visa. By checking off the boxes as you've prepared or collected things, you'll ensure that you exit the country without leaving anything behind.

 You'll find a tear-out version of this Checklist in Appendix E.

Checklist for Visa Renewals

- ☐ Form OF-156
- ☐ fee (currently $45 plus any reciprocity fee)
- ☐ passport good for at least six months
- ☐ two passport-style photos
- ☐ Form I-94 (original or copy)
- ☐ Form I-20 endorsed for reentry by your DSO
- ☐ transcripts and school records of your attendance
- ☐ documents showing that you can pay your tuition, fees and living expenses
- ☐ documents showing that you will return to your home country

---

3. Visits to Canada and Mexico

The United States shares borders with Canada and Mexico, making them attractive travel destinations for students. Your fellow students who are U.S. citizens are accustomed to being able to drive across the border without any advance preparation. You, however, will need to talk to a Canadian or Mexican consulate before you leave. Depending on what country you originally come from, you may be required to obtain an entry visa. Also, have handy all of the paperwork that you will use to reenter the United States when you enter Canada or Mexico. Their border officials may want to make sure that the United States will not refuse to let you back in, leaving you stranded on their territory.

I. What Rights Do Your Family Members Get in the U.S.?

Your family members may be spending a lot of time in the United States with you, uprooted from family and friends and without the distraction of classes. You and your school can help connect them to activities they might enjoy—but within the limits of their visa or status.

As already discussed, your family members cannot work in the United States. They can, however, study full-time or part-time. Some colleges and universities make courses available to the family members of F-1 or M-1 students. Some also arrange special social groups and learning programs for international students' family members. Local community centers or adult schools may be a resource as well, offering low-cost classes, including in the English language.

Your younger children can actually enroll in U.S. public schools—unlike you. That's because their study is considered incidental to their visa status, not their entire reason for their entering the United States. You might, however, encounter some confusion at the local public schools, if they don't realize that the law only prohibits F-1 visa holders, not F-2 visa holders, from studying for free. Talk to a lawyer or a local immigrants' rights organization for help.

In any big U.S. city, there are almost guaranteed to be groups of immigrants from your own country —your family members can probably find someone to speak to in their own language if they're still learning English. Ask your DSO or other students for advice.

1. Family Travel In and Out of the U.S.

If your family members need to travel to their home country while you are in school (whether or not you are travelling with them), they should carry the following items with them in order to return to the United States:

- passport good for at least six months
- their F-2 or M-2 visa, and
- proof that you are still in valid student status— a copy of your I-20 will be best.

It is especially important that your family members bring proof that you are still in valid student status if you yourself will not be traveling with them and able to answer INS questions. The INS can't just take a chance and let them enter, knowing that it's possible that you have already finished your program and moved on. Your family members' eligibility for their visas depends entirely on you. If your F-1 or M-1 visa is no longer good, your family members are no longer eligible to use their F-2 or M-2 visas. By simply showing evidence that you are still busy studying, however, your family members' entry to the United States should be granted.

2. Family Members' Visa Renewals

Like you, your family members should not leave the United States unless they already have, or are prepared to get, their own visa with which to return. If your family members don't already have an F-2 or M-2 visa (because all of you applied for changes of status while in the United States), or if their visas have expired, they will need to apply for new visas at a U.S. consulate before returning. In that case, they will need to assemble the following items before they go to the consulate:

- Form OF-156 (filled out by the family member; not a copy of your form)
- family member's passport, good for at least six months
- two passport-style photos
- family member's I-94 card (original or copy)
- copy of your I-20
- proof that you, the student, have sufficient financial resources to support them in the United States without working (particularly if this is their first application overseas)
- documents showing that they plan to return home at the end of your studies
- if you applied to change status while in the United States, a copy of the Change of Status application and the INS approval notice, and
- fee (currently $45).

Not all consulates require the documentation of financial resources and intent to return home on time. They know that your family already had to provide such evidence in order to get the original visa or Change of Status. However, your family members are better off bringing such evidence whether the consulate requires it or not—it can only strengthen the application.

Once your family members have assembled these items, they should contact the consulate to find out when and how they can submit them. It's best not to leave this until a day before their plane is due to return to the United States—some consulates require advance appointments or may be too busy with applicants to see them immediately. ■

12

Can You Work While You Are in School?

A. F Visas and Employment 12/2

    1. On-Campus Work 12/2

    2. Off-Campus Work Due to Severe Economic Hardship 12/3

    3. Curricular Practical Training.. 12/10

    4. Optional Practical Training 12/12

    5. International Organization Internships 12/16

    6. Transition to H-1B Visa Employment.. 12/17

B. M Visas and Employment 12/18

    1. Application Forms for Practical Training Work Permit 12/18

    2. Other Items for Practical Training Work Permit Application 12/19

    3. Using the Checklist for Practical Training Work Permit Application 12/20

    4. Mailing Application and Receiving Your Work Permit 12/20

Foreign students in the United States are expected to cover all their expenses without needing to work. However, both F-1 and M-1 students have limited rights to do paid work. This Chapter guides you through the application requirements and processes, including:

- what kind of work you may do
- where you can work
- how to obtain any needed permits, and
- how long you can work.

⚠ If you apply to the INS for a work permit, don't leave the U.S. until it is approved. Many of the employment possibilities for students require you to apply to the INS for a work permit. The INS may take weeks or even months to reply. During this time, you may be tempted to leave the United States—to take a vacation or return home for a visit—especially if it's summertime. Don't leave! Leaving the United States will automatically cancel your work permit application. (In fact, leaving the United States is almost always considered an abandonment of applications filed with the INS.)

 If you are an M-1 visa holder, skip ahead to Section B.

A. F Visas and Employment

F-1 visa holders (but not their spouses or children) can work at almost any job on their school's campus without needing to obtain INS authorization (see subsection 1, below). If you want to work off campus, however, you'll need to request INS authorization. The INS will authorize only limited types of off-campus work, including:

- off-campus employment due to severe economic hardship (see subsection 2, below)
- curricular practical training (see subsection 3, below)
- optional practical training (either during or after completing the study program; see subsection 4, below), and
- international organization internships (see subsection 5, below).

"Special Student Relief" for F-1 Students From Indonesia, South Korea, Malaysia, Thailand or the Philippines

In 1998, Congress passed special but temporary rules to help students undergoing economic hardship as a result of the rapid devaluation of their currencies against the U.S. dollar. Graduate and undergraduate students who had already been in valid F-1 status for more than a year and whose means of financial support came from Indonesia, South Korea, Malaysia, Thailand or the Philippines got greater rights to work both on and off campus, and were allowed to reduce their course loads without violating their F-1 status. For details, see the *Federal Register*, June 10, 1998 (Volume 63, Number 111), or view the rules on the Web at www.shusterman.com/fregasia.html. These rules do not apply to people just now getting student visas, and the rules will be ended when the economic situation of these countries improves.

1. On-Campus Work

You may work on the campus of your school for up to 20 hours a week while school is in session and up to full-time during school vacations. However, there's an important requirement: Before you start work, the DSO must certify that the job you are offered will not displace nonstudent U.S. workers. In other words, the job you would like must be a job that is typically filled only by students. A job in the cafeteria, library or bookstore; or maybe with a professor or a campus science laboratory as a teaching or research assistant would likely satisfy this requirement. A job as secretary to the dean or as janitor would probably not.

On-campus employment is also allowed if it is part of a scholarship or fellowship and is part of your academic program. In fact, sometimes such work can be done off campus if the workplace is still "educationally related" to or "affiliated" with the school. An example would be working with a professor at an off-campus research facility.

Once your studies are over, you must stop working at your on-campus job. You may, however, be able to obtain authorization to stay in the United States and do paid practical training (described in subsections 3 and 4, below).

2. Off-Campus Work Due to Severe Economic Hardship

Despite all your plans to be self-supporting, something could go wrong. Perhaps your parent loses his or her job, the foundation that supplied your scholarship goes bankrupt, you or your family have new medical bills or your school tuition goes up sky-high. Luckily, the immigration laws provide for such contingencies. If you can show that you are experiencing severe economic hardship because of unforeseen circumstances beyond your control, you may be able to obtain permission to work for an off-campus employer. However, there are risks to submitting this application, as we'll describe below.

If you have been in school for less than one year, you are on your own. You will not be able to obtain this special work authorization, and you will have to

Times Square
New York City, New York

find some other way to cover your expenses. Your only option may be to return home and wait for better times to reapply for a student visa. Of course, you will want to talk to your DSO first—they may be able to help the school arrange a leave of absence, so that you will not have to reapply for school admission when you are ready to return.

Your prospects are better if you've spent at least one year in school. If you have already completed a full academic year of study, are in good academic standing and cannot obtain suitable or available on-campus employment to meet your new need, you can apply to the INS for a permit to work off campus. Even if you already have an on-campus job, you can switch to off-campus work, which you may want to do if it pays more. You can work no more than 20 hours a week while school is in session, but you can work full-time during school holidays or vacations.

To succeed in your application for employment authorization based on economic need you must strike a balance. If you say too little about the novelty and seriousness of this change in your economic circumstances, the INS may conclude that you don't really need the work permission and will deny it. But if you say too much about the extent of your economic difficulty, the INS may think that even the part-time salary you earn with the new work permit will not be enough to help you. Then they'll not only deny the application, but will send you home because you can't pay for your stay in the United States. The solution? Have a chat with your DSO before submitting this application. The DSO will have experience helping students submit such applications, and can work with you to present your financial need convincingly—but not too convincingly—in your application. However, if you fear you are already violating your status (perhaps by having dropped out of school or taken on illegal work), consult with a lawyer rather than your DSO before submitting your application. (The DSO, as you remember, wears two hats. Although the DSO is there to help you, he also has the uncomfortable obligation of reporting your status violations to the INS, whether he wants to or not.) A lawyer can help you determine whether you are indeed violating your status and help you prepare this work permit application, if appropriate (see Chapter 14 for tips on finding a good lawyer).

You'll need to prepare some government forms (see subsection a, below) and assemble certain documents (see subsection b, below) to apply for a work permit based on severe economic hardship. These are summarized in the Checklist in subsection d, below.

a. Application Forms for Work Permit Based on Severe Economic Hardship

If you've decided to apply for a work permit based on severe economic hardship, you'll need to prepare or obtain the following government forms:

- Form I-538 (mostly filled out by your DSO, to certify that the on-campus employment available to you is not enough to meet your economic needs—but see subsection i, below, for help filling out your portion)
- photocopy of your Form I-20 ID
- Form I-765 (see subsection ii, below, for line-by-line instructions)
- Form I-765 Signature Card. This is a small white card that you'll need to sign. You'll need to get this from your local INS office or DSO, or by calling 800-870-3676; it's not something that can be downloaded from the Internet or included in this book (but see the picture of it below). Make sure your signature stays entirely inside the box, or the INS will return the whole application to you.

Form I-765, Signature Card

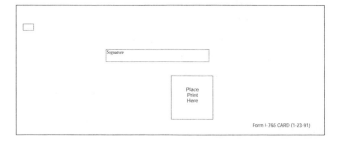

The forms only ask for basic information, but it can be difficult to understand exactly what information they want and whether the answer will reflect negatively on you. To help you, we've included line-by-line instructions in the following sections.

i. Line-by-Line Instructions for Form I-538

Form I-538 (pictured below) is used for a variety of communications between the DSO and the INS. Most of this form will be filled out by your DSO. However, there's no harm in your getting the process started, by filling out your portion and taking it to your DSO. If you choose to print out Form I-538 from the INS website, print it single-sided.

 You'll find a tear-out version of this form in Appendix D.

Section A:

This is the section that you fill out. Most of it is self-explanatory.

Question 3: Your **Student Admission Number** should be on your I-20 ID.

Question 4: Enter the date that either the consulate or the INS first approved your student status.

Question 5: "**Level of education being sought**" refers to your degree (such as B.A., M.A., or J.D.), diploma or certificate.

Question 6: Your major field of study should match the information on your I-20.

Question 7: Speak to your DSO about how best to describe your proposed employment.

Question 8: List the dates of your previous work authorizations and the type of work you did.

Don't forget to sign at the bottom of Section A.

Section B: Your DSO fills this out, but you should look it over afterward to make sure that the information is accurate. If the DSO gives information that conflicts with what the INS has been told in the past, such the fact that you've dropped your study hours to less than full-time, make sure your DSO can attach documentation to show that he or she approved it.

Form I-538, Certification by Designated School Official—Page 1

OMB Approval No. 1115-0060

U.S. Department of Justice
Immigration and Naturalization Service

Certification by Designated School Official

SECTION A.   This section must be completed by student as appropriate (Please print or type) :

1. Name:	(Family in CAPS)	(First)	(Middle)	2. Date of birth:

3. Student admission number:	4. Date first granted F-1 or M-1 status:

5. Level of education being sought:	6. Student's major field of study:

7. Describe the proposed employment for practical training:

Beginning date :   Ending date: Number of hours per week:

8. List all periods of previously authorized employment for practical training:

A. Curricular or work/study:	B. Post completion of studies

Signature of student: _____   Date: _____

**SECTION B.   This Section must be completed by the designated school official of the school the student
is attending or was last authorized to attend:**

9. I hereby certify that:

The student named above:
☐ Is taking a full course of study at this school, and the expected date of completion is: _____

☐ Is taking less than a full course of study at this school because: _____

☐ Completed the course of study at this school on (date): _____

☐ Did not complete the course of study. Terminated attendance on (date): _____

Check one:

☐ A. The employment is for practical training in the student's field of study. The student has been in the
educational program for at least 9 months and is eligible for the requested practical training in accordance
with INS regulations at 8CFR 214.2(f) (10).

☐ B. The endorsement for off-campus employment is based on the wage-and-labor attestation filed by the
employer in accordance with the requirements set forth by the Secretary of Labor. The student has been
in F-1 status for at least one year and is in good academic standing. Copy of the employer's attestation is
attached.

☐ C. The employment is for an internship with a recognized international organization and is within the scope of
the organization's sponsorship. The student has been in F-1 status for at least 9 months and is in good
academic standing.

10. Name and title of DSO.	Signature:	Date:
11. Name of school:	School file number:	Telephone no

For Off
Microfilm Index Nu

(See instructions on reverse)

Additional pages not shown.

ii.   Line-by-Line Instructions for Form I-765

Form I-765 (pictured below) is the main form used by all temporary immigrants applying for work permission. Most of this form is the instructions, which you don't need to send to the INS. If you choose to print this form out yourself from the INS website, print out the last page on a single sheet of paper.

 You'll find a tear-out version of this form in Appendix D.

Once you have a copy of this form in hand, follow these instructions for filling it in.

Under **"I am applying for,"** check "Permission to Accept Employment." However, if you had a previous EAD under another program, check the box for renewals.

Questions 1-8: Self-explanatory.

Question 9: You will probably not have a Social Security number unless you are changing from a visa or status that allowed you to work. If you don't have a number, enter "None."

Did you have a Social Security number when you shouldn't have? If you have a Social Security number but haven't been on a visa that allowed you to be employed in the United States, your answer to this question could send the INS a message that you've worked illegally. If there is an explanation for your having a number that dispels any question of illegality, attach a letter giving the details. If not, you may want to consult a lawyer.

Question 10: You will only have an **Alien registration number (A-Number)** if you have been in deportation or removal proceedings or have submitted certain immigration applications, particularly for permanent residence. If you were in proceedings or had any applications denied, especially for reasons such as fraud, see a lawyer. If you don't have an A-number, enter the number from your I-94 (and before the actual number, write "I-94#").

Question 14: List the type of visa on which you last entered the United States. It was probably an F-1 student visa, unless you entered as a visitor or on

I-765, Application for Employment Authorization

U.S. Department of Justice
Immigration and Naturalization Service

OMB No. 1115-0163: Expires - 10/31/01

Application for Employment Authorization

Do Not Write in This Block

Remarks	Action Stamp	Fee Stamp
A#		
Applicant is filing under §274a.12 _____		

☐ Application Approved. Employment Authorized / Extended (Circle One)   until ——————————— (Date).
——————————— (Date).

Subject to the following conditions: _____
☐ Application Denied.
  ☐ Failed to establish eligibility under 8 CFR 274a.12 (a) or (c).
  ☐ Failed to establish economic necessity as required in 8 CFR 274a.12(c) (14), (18) and 8 CFR 214.2(f)

I am applying for:
☐ Permission to accept employment
☐ Replacement (of lost employment authorization document).
☐ Renewal of my permission to accept employment (attach previous employment authorization document).

1. Name (Family Name in CAPS)   (First)   (Middle)

2. Other Names Used (Include Maiden Name)

3. Address in the United States (Number and Street)   (Apt. Number)

(Town or City)   (State/Country)   (ZIP Code)

11. Have you ever before applied for employment authorization from INS?
☐ Yes (if yes, complete below)   ☐ No
Which INS Office?   Date(s)

Results (Granted or Denied - attach all documentation)

12. Date of Last Entry into the U.S. (Month/Day/Year)

another temporary visa and then applied for a Change of Status to become a student.

Question 15: Your current immigration status is "F-1 student."

Question 16: Your eligibility category depends on the basis for your work permit. If you're applying for off-campus employment due to severe economic hardship, your category is (c)(3)(iii).

b. Documents to Accompany Work Permit Application Based on Severe Economic Hardship

To accompany your work permit application, you will need to attach the following:

- a copy of the front and back of any previous work permits that you've received
- two photos, INS style (see Appendix A for photo instructions). Print your name in pencil on the back of the photos
- supporting documents to show economic need. For example, news articles about the economic situation in your home country, a copy of a letter terminating your family or sponsor's employment or copies of medical bills would be appropriate
- your sworn statement summarizing the reasons you need work authorization. See further explanation and the sample in subsection c, below
- a copy of the identity page and visa page from your passport
- a copy of your I-94 card

Cable Car
San Francisco, California

- the fee (currently $100 for the I-765 and $70 for the I-538). Double-check current fees with your DSO or on the INS website at http://www.ins.gov. Pay by check or money order, payable to the USINS. Do not send cash.

c. Sample Statement of Extreme Economic Hardship

Because your eligibility for a work permit depends entirely on your personal circumstances, you'll have to explain these circumstances to the INS. Your statement will most likely be believed if you:

- describe the facts that led to the problem
- present a picture of someone who found himself in a difficulty that could not be avoided and for which he was not at fault, and
- present a reasonable plan that is short-term and designed to get you out of financial and academic trouble.

These tips were put to good use by the author of the "Sample Statement of Economic Hardship," below. You'll notice that this statement describes a person in extreme economic difficulty. Your situation does not necessarily need to be as bad as the one described —but you will need to prove "extreme" economic hardship rather than just "some" hardship. What does "extreme" mean? It's hard to pin down, but the official reading your application should have the same "Oh my!" reaction that you do after reading the statement below.

⚠️ **The following statement outlines a set of facts unique to one person.** Don't copy these facts, but give a similar amount of detail in describing your situation.

💡 **To make this application look more official, sign it in front of a notary public.** For a review of what it means to notarize a document, see Chapter 4, Section C. Your school's financial aid or housing office should have a notary. If not, check the Yellow pages of your phone book. Notaries usually charge about $15 for their services (the notary stamps the document to confirm that it was really you who signed it).

Sample Statement of Economic Hardship

I, Zoltan Shakarian, hereby declare as follows:

My full and complete name is Zoltan Anders Shakarian. My admittance number is [number from your I-20 ID copy]. I presently live at 242 West College Place, Oakford, MA 02000 with my wife and 7-month old child. I am an F-1 student visa-holder from Armenia.

I am asking for employment authorization based on economic need for two reasons: first, my father was unable to work due to illness for eight months, and therefore could not make his usual contributions to my support; and second, I have some debts because our landlord sold our building and kicked out all the tenants. We had to live in a hotel for two months.

My father is normally my main source of support. He runs his own business in Armenia and usually makes a good living. Because we have a large family, however, and because he tends to invest his profits back into the business, he has not saved much. He contracted a severe gastrointestinal infection in [date], and it wasn't long before his payments stopped coming altogether. On top of this, our landlord kicked out all the tenants in our building on [date], and we had to live in a hotel at $80 a night for two months.

Fortunately, my father is recovering fully and getting back to work. We have found a new rental apartment. However, in addition to our monthly expenses, I now owe $6,000 to my credit card company for our hotel stay and a few other expenses, and I owe the school $8,000 for a delayed tuition payment. Even with my father's monthly checks of $3,000, and my on-campus job adding $480 per month, I cannot cover these costs within the foreseeable future.

My normal monthly expenses are as follows:

Tuition:	$2,000
Supplies and Books:	$80
Food and Home Supplies:	$300
Rent:	$800
TOTAL:	$3,180

I will need to earn approximately $1,200 per month in order to pay off this debt within the next year. This will allow me to protect my student standing and to avoid rising credit card debt due to the 15% interest rate. Thanks to my technical skills, I can find an off-campus job that pays the necessary hourly rate ($60 per hour), but nothing on campus

Sample Statement of Economic Hardship (continued)

comes close. I have talked with my DSO and anyone else who might know of on-campus jobs, and all agree that few jobs pay more than $10 an hour, and none of these are currently open.

Enclosed are documents supporting the contents of this statement, including copies of my father's medical bills, a copy of his letter to his employees and customers explaining that he must close his business for a certain time (with English language translation), a copy of a local newspaper article about the temporary closure of his business (with English language translation), a copy of his recent checks to show that he can make payments again, the letter from our landlord evicting us, a copy of unpaid school and credit card bills and a copy of my old and new lease agreements. Finally, I am adding a letter from my school explaining their agreement to my delayed payments of back-tuition and allowing me to continue my studies while I repay. Thank you for your consideration.

I swear, under penalty of perjury, that the contents of this statement are true and correct to the best of my knowledge.

Zoltan Anders Shakarian
Zoltan Anders Shakarian

Date: _____

d. Using the Checklist for Work Permit Based on Economic Hardship

The Checklist below lists all the items you'll need to apply for permission to work based on severe economic hardship. By checking off each box as you've prepared or collected the item, you'll ensure that nothing is forgotten.

 You'll find a tear-out copy of this Checklist in Appendix E.

Checklist for Work Permit Based on Economic Hardship

☐ Form I-538
☐ photocopy of your Form I-20 ID
☐ Form I-765
☐ Form I-765 Signature Card
☐ copy of the front and back of any previous work permits that you've received
☐ two photos, INS style
☐ supporting documents to show economic need
☐ sworn statement by you summarizing the reasons you need work authorization
☐ copy of the identity page and visa page from your passport
☐ copy of your I-94 card
☐ fee (currently $100)

---

e. Mailing and Receiving Your Work Permit

When you've assembled your application for a work permit based on severe economic hardship, send it to the INS Service Center listed in Appendix B or on the INS website at http://www.ins.gov—the address to look for is the one listed as handling Form I-765. Certified mail is the best way to send anything to the INS, preferably with a request for a return receipt. When you mail something with a "return receipt," the Post Office attaches a postcard to the mailing, which the INS will sign and mail back to you when

they receive your application. If the application is lost at the INS, your postcard allows you to prove that it was received.

You should get a receipt notice from the INS within about six weeks. The receipt notice will tell you when you can expect a decision. If you don't receive this notice, or if your decision doesn't come within the time predicted on the receipt notice, see Chapter 13, Dealing With Bureaucrats, Delays and Denials. When your work permit is approved, you will receive a wallet-sized plastic card in the mail with your photo on it. The permit will be good for one year.

3. Curricular Practical Training

Curricular practical training is off-campus work that has been set up by your school as an important part of your curriculum or program. If your course of studies already has such a program, you may take one of these jobs. You may or may not be paid for such work. For example, if you are studying psychology and your program requires you to earn credit or fulfill your graduation requirements by working at a hospital or treatment facility, this would be considered curricular practical training. You will be allowed to work even if the work is not required—if it is "elective" (not a requirement for your degree) but your school lists it in the catalogue, names a faculty member in charge and gives academic credit for it, it will qualify as curricular practical training.

Curricular practical training is open only to students who have already been studying for nine months at the college level or above. The exception is if you are enrolled in a graduate program that requires immediate participation in such training. Practical training is completely closed to students who are in English-language-only programs.

As far as the INS is concerned, you can do your curricular practical training either during or after completion of your academic studies (of course, your school may not give you a choice). However, if you do one year of full-time practical training (curricular or optional, described below) during your studies, you'll lose your eligibility to do more practical training once your studies are completed. That means you'll lose a valuable right to spend some post-study time in the United States. You can avoid this problem by doing less than one year of curricular practical training, or making sure that your curricular practical training is part-time, not full-time.

You do not need INS permission ahead of time to do curricular practical training. The only procedural requirements are that your DSO:

- approves your plan
- endorses your I-20 and I-20 ID to show her approval, and
- sends word to the INS.

The DSO will use Form I-538. You'll have to fill out the top portion—see the line-by-line instructions below. You'll be authorized for 12 months under this procedure, starting when the DSO endorses your I-20. Unlike some other forms of off-campus work, you do not need a work permit card ("employment authorization document" or "EAD").

a. Line-by-Line Instructions for Form I-538

Form I-538 (pictured below) is used for a variety of communications between the DSO and the INS. Most of this form will be filled out by your DSO. However, if you want to help out and get the process started, you can fill out your portion and take it to your DSO. If you choose to print this form out yourself from the INS website, print it out single-sided.

 You'll find a tear-out copy of this form in Appendix D.

When you've got a copy of Form I-538 in hand, follow these line-by-line instructions.

Section A:

This is the section that you fill out. Most of it is self-explanatory.

Question 3: Your **Student Admission Number** should be on your I-20 ID.

Form I-538, Certification by Designated School Official—Page 1

OMB Approval No. 1115-0060

U.S. Department of Justice
Immigration and Naturalization Service

Certification by Designated School Official

SECTION A. This section must be completed by student as appropriate (Please print or type) :

1. Name: *(Family in CAPS)* *(First)* *(Middle)*	2. Date of birth:

3. Student admission number:	4. Date first granted F-1 or M-1 status:

5. Level of education being sought:	6. Student's major field of study:

7. Describe the proposed employment for practical training:

Beginning date :   Ending date: Number of hours per week:

8. List all periods of previously authorized employment for practical training:

A. Curricular or work/study:	B. Post completion of studies

Question 4: Enter the date that the consulate or the INS first approved your student status.

Question 5: "Level of education being sought" refers to your degree (such as B.A., M.A. or J.D.), diploma or certificate.

Question 6: Your major field of study should match the one stated on your I-20.

Question 7: You may want to wait until you've spoken to your DSO to fill in your description of proposed employment. The DSO can help make sure that the wording is appropriate.

Question 8: List the dates of your previous work authorizations and the type of work you did. Figure out the dates carefully, because the INS will examine them to make sure you haven't used up your practical training time.

Don't forget to sign at the bottom of Section A.

Section B: Your DSO fills this out, but look it over afterward to make sure that the information is accurate. If anything the DSO states is new information to the INS, such as your having dropped your study hours to less than full time, make sure your DSO attaches documentation to show that he or she has approved it.

4. Optional Practical Training

Optional practical training (OPT) is another form of off-campus work available to F-1 students. Unlike curricular practical training, it doesn't need to be a specific part of your school's academic offerings. It does, however, need to be related to your studies—working at a coffee shop while you're in a nursing program isn't going to satisfy the INS. The training must be directly related to your major and in accordance with your educational level. Unlike curricular practical training however, you do need a work permit card ("employment authorization document," or EAD).

Optional practical training is open only to students who have already studied for nine months at the college level or above. The maximum you can do is one year of full-time optional practical training. Part-time employment is deducted from your one-year maximum at one-half the rate. This means that if you

continually worked part-time, you could do two years of optional practical training. Optional practical training is not available to elementary or secondary school students or to students who are in school for the purpose of studying the English language. You can change employers during your period of practical training, so long as the new employer also provides work that is related to your studies.

 You don't have to wait until your nine months' study are up to submit your work permit application. It will probably take the INS at least a few months to approve your work permit. For this reason, the INS allows you to submit the permit ahead of your accumulated nine months of study, so long as you're asking that the work permit be valid *after* the nine months are completed.

You can do your optional practical training while school is in session (for 20 hours a week or less); during vacations; after completing your degree requirements; or after graduating or finishing all

Disneyland
Anaheim, California

your requirements, as long as this training period is completed within 14 months of graduation. The work can be full-time or part-time, depending on the recommendation of your DSO. Don't use up your practical training too soon, however. If you do one or more years of full-time practical training (curricular or optional) during your studies, you'll lose your eligibility to do more practical training once your studies are completed. That means you'll lose a valuable right to spend some post-study time in the United States. You can avoid this problem by doing less than one year of curricular practical training, or making sure that your curricular practical training is part-time, not full-time.

If you decide to do your optional practical training after graduating, don't wait too long to apply—your application must be received by the INS within 60 days of your graduation.

⚠ Optional practical training is a one-time offer. After you've finished your year of post-graduation full-time practical training, that's it. You won't be permitted any more practical training periods during this stay in the United States, even if you go back to school and get another degree first. However, if you go home for a "significant" amount of time (at least five months) and then come back and do a different study program, you may be able to do more practical training.

The application process involves both your DSO and the INS. First, the DSO must approve your plan. You and the DSO will each fill out the appropriate portions of Form I-538, and your DSO will endorse your I-20 and I-20 ID to show her approval. You'll assemble and complete some additional forms and documents (discussed in the sections below and summarized in the Checklist in subsection c, below) and mail the completed application to the INS.

a. Application Forms for Optional Practical Training

The INS forms that you or your DSO will need to fill out include:

- a copy of your Form I-20 (by your DSO)

- a copy of your Form I-20 ID with your DSO's recommendation of practical training
- Form I-538 with the DSO's certification that the work is appropriate to your study (see subsection i, below, for line-by-line instructions)
- Form I-765 (see subsection ii, below, for line-by-line instructions)
- Form I-765 Signature Card. This is a small white card (pictured below) that you'll need to sign. To obtain the card, visit your local INS office or DSO, or call 800-870-3676 (the card can't be downloaded from the Internet). Make sure your signature stays entirely inside the box, or the INS will return the whole application to you.

Form I-765, Signature Card

i. Line-by-Line Instructions for Form I-538

Form I-538 (pictured in subsection 3a, above) is used for a variety of communications between the DSO and the INS. Most of this form will be filled out by your DSO. However, you can start the process by filling out your portion and taking it to your DSO. If you choose to print out Form I-538 yourself from the INS website, print it single-sided.

 You'll find a tear-out version of this form in Appendix D.

This is the section that you fill out. Most of it is self-explanatory.

Question 3: Your Student Admission Number should be on your I-20 ID.

Question 4: Enter the date that the consulate or the INS first approved your student status.

Question 5: *"Level of education being sought"* refers to your degree (such as B.A., M.A. or J.D.), diploma or certificate.

Question 6: Your major field of study should match the information on your I-20.

Question 7: You may want to wait until you've spoken to your DSO to fill in your description of proposed employment. The DSO can help make sure that the wording is appropriate.

Question 8: List the dates of your previous work authorizations and the type of work you did. Figure out the dates carefully, because the INS will examine them to make sure you haven't used up your practical training time.

Don't forget to sign at the bottom of Section A.

Section B: Your DSO fills this out, but look it over afterward to make sure that the information is accurate. If anything the DSO states is new information to the INS, such as your having dropped your study hours to less than full time, make sure your DSO attaches documentation to show that he or she approved it.

ii. Line-by-Line Instructions for Form I-765

Form I-765 (pictured below) is the main form used by applicants for work permits. Most of the pages are instructions, which you don't need to give to the INS. If you choose to print this form out yourself from the INS website, make sure the last page, containing the actual application, is printed out on a single, separate sheet of paper.

 You'll find a tear-out version of this form in Appendix D.

When you have a copy of Form I-765 in hand, follow these line-by-line instructions.

Under **"I am applying for,"** check "Permission to Accept Employment," unless you have had a previous EAD under another program, in which case you should check the box for renewals.

Questions 1-8: Self-explanatory.

Question 9: You will probably not have a Social Security number unless you are changing from a

I-765, Application for Employment Authorization

U.S. Department of Justice
Immigration and Naturalization Service

OMB No. 1115-0163: Expires - 10/31/01

Application for Employment Authorization

Do Not Write in This Block

Remarks	Action Stamp	Fee Stamp
A#		

Applicant is filing under §274a.12 _____

☐ Application Approved. Employment Authorized / Extended (Circle One)   until _____ (Date).
_____ (Date).

Subject to the following conditions: _____

☐ Application Denied.
  ☐ Failed to establish eligibility under 8 CFR 274a.12 (a) or (c).
  ☐ Failed to establish economic necessity as required in 8 CFR 274a.12(c) (14), (18) and 8 CFR 214.2(f)

I am applying for:
☐ Permission to accept employment
☐ Replacement (of lost employment authorization document).
☐ Renewal of my permission to accept employment (attach previous employment authorization document).

1. Name (Family Name in CAPS) (First) (Middle)

2. Other Names Used (Include Maiden Name)

3. Address in the United States (Number and Street) (Apt. Number)

(Town or City) (State/Country) (ZIP Code)

11. Have you ever before applied for employment authorization from INS?
☐ Yes (if yes, complete below) ☐ No
Which INS Office? Date(s)

Results (Granted or Denied - attach all documentation)

12. Date of Last Entry into the U.S. (Month/Day/Year)

visa or status that allowed you to work. If you don't have a number, enter "None."

Question 10: You will have an **Alien registration number (A-number)** only if you have been in deportation or removal proceedings or have submitted certain immigration applications, particularly for permanent residence. If you were in proceedings or had any applications denied, especially for reasons such as fraud, see a lawyer. If you don't have an A-number, enter the number from your I-94 (and before the actual number, write "I-94#").

Question 14: List the type of visa on which you last entered the United States, which is probably a student visa, unless you entered as a visitor or on another temporary visa and then applied for a Change of Status to become a student.

Question 15: Your current immigration status is "F-1 student."

Question 16: Your eligibility category depends on the basis for your work permit. As an F visa holder applying for optional practical training, your category is (c)(3)(i).

b. Documents for Optional Practical Training Application

Along with the forms described above, you'll need the following documents to complete your application:

- a copy of the identity page and visa page from your passport
- if you have a job offer, a copy of the offer letter. A job offer is not required, however. Your DSO can certify that you will work in an appropriate job (and usually the school has a career planning office that can help ensure that you find such a job).
- two photos (INS style; see Appendix A for photo instructions); print your full name in pencil on the back of the photos
- the fee (currently $100 for the Form I-765 and $70 for the Form I-538, but double-check with your DSO or on the INS website at http://www.ins.gov). Pay by check or money order, payable to the USINS. Do not send cash.

c. Using the Checklist for Optional Practical Training Application

The Checklist below lists all the items you'll need to apply for permission to work in an optional practical training setting. By checking off each box as you've prepared or collected the item, you'll ensure that nothing is forgotten.

 You'll find a tear-out version of this Checklist in Appendix E.

Checklist for Optional Practical Training Application

- ☐ copy of Form I-20
- ☐ copy of Form I-20 ID
- ☐ Form I-538
- ☐ Form I-765
- ☐ Form I-765 Signature Card
- ☐ original Form I-94
- ☐ copy of the identity page and visa page from your passport
- ☐ if you have a job offer, a copy of the offer letter
- ☐ two photos
- ☐ fee (currently $100 for Form I-765 plus $70 for Form I-538)

---

d. Mailing Optional Practical Application and Receiving Your Work Permit

Once you have prepared all the application materials, make a photocopy for your records. Then mail them (by certified mail with a return receipt requested) to the INS Service Center listed in Appendix B—look for the Post Office box that's set up to handle Form I-765. The INS will send you a receipt notice within about six weeks. The receipt notice will tell you when you can expect an answer (it all depends on how busy the INS is). If you don't get a receipt notice, or if the time predicted on that notice passes with no

INS decision, see Chapter 13, Dealing With Bureaucrats, Delays and Denials.

Once you are approved, the INS will mail you a wallet-sized plastic work permit card with your photo on it. The card will indicate how many months you are allowed to work—usually 12, but this will be reduced if you've logged any previous curricular practical training time. You are not allowed to work until you receive this card.

⚠️ **Your work period may get shortened if the INS delays in approving your work permit.** Students who are doing their optional practical training after finishing their studies have a 14-month time limit to start and finish their 12 months of work. Unfortunately, the INS starts counting those 14 months from the day their receive your application for a work permit. So, for example, if it takes them three months to approve your work permit, your 12 months of optional practical training will go down to 11 months. To avoid this problem, you may apply for your work permit up to 120 days before you are scheduled to start work.

5. International Organization Internships

If you obtain an offer of employment with an international organization that qualifies under the "International Organizations Immunities Act," you may be eligible to work. As a practical matter, these organizations are usually only found in Washington, D.C. Ask your school's DSO or career planning office for more information. To apply, you'll need to prepare certain forms and documents, discussed in the next subsections and summarized on the Checklist in subsection c, below.

a. Application Forms for International Organization Internship Work Permit

To apply for a work permit based on an offer to intern with a qualifying international organization, you'll need to prepare the following forms:

- Form I-20 ID, endorsed by your DSO within the last 30 days

- Form I-538, signed by your DSO (see subsection i, below)
- Form I-765 (see subsection ii, below), and
- Form I-765 Signature Card. This is a small white card (pictured below) that you'll need to sign. Get one by visiting your local INS office or DSO, or by calling 800-870-3676 (it's not something that can be downloaded from the Internet or included in this book). Make sure your signature stays entirely inside the box, or the INS will return the whole application to you.

Form I-765, Signature Card

i. Line-by-Line Instructions for Form I-538

Form I-538 (pictured in Section A2 above) is used for a variety of communications between the DSO and the INS. Most of this form will be filled out by your DSO. However, you can get the process started by filling out your portion and taking it to your DSO. If you choose to print out Form I-538 yourself from the INS website, print it single-sided.

📄 You'll find a tear-out copy of this form in Appendix D and a picture of it in subsection A2, above.

When you have a copy of Form I-538 in hand, follow the line-by-line instructions for how to fill it out in subsection A4, above.

ii. Line-by-Line Instructions for Form I-765

Form I-765 is the main application used by immigrants needing work permits. It looks like a long form when you print it out, but the bulk of the pages are instructions, which you don't need to fill out or return to the INS. Make sure the last page, containing the actual application, is printed out on a single, separate sheet of paper.

 You'll find a tear-out copy of this form in Appendix D and a picture of it in subsection A4, above.

When you have a copy of this form in hand, follow the instructions in subsection 4a, above, for guidance on how to fill it out. When you get to Question 16, however, understand that your eligibility category depends on the basis for your work permit request. For an international organization internship application, your category is (c)(3)(ii).

b. Other Items for International Organization Internship Work Permit

To apply for a work permit based on an offer to intern with an international organization, you'll need to prepare the following two items:

- two photos (INS style; see Appendix A). Print your full name in pencil on the back of the photos, and
- the fee (currently $100 but double-check this with your DSO or on the INS website at http://www.ins.gov). Pay by check or money order, payable to the USINS. Do not send cash.

c. Using the Checklist for International Organization Internship Work Permit Application

The Checklist below lists all the items you'll need to apply for permission to work as an intern in an international organization. By checking off each box as you've prepared or collected the item, you'll ensure that nothing is forgotten.

 You'll find a tear-out copy of this Checklist in Appendix E.

> ### Checklist for International Organization Internship Work Permit Application
>
> ☐ Written certification from the international organization
> ☐ Form I-20 ID
> ☐ Form I-538
> ☐ Form I-765
> ☐ two photos
> ☐ Form I-765 Signature Card
> ☐ fee (currently $100 for Form I-765 plus $70 for Form I-538)

---

d. Mailing Application and Receiving Your Work Permit

Once you've prepared all the application materials for your international organization work permit prepared, mail it (certified mail with a return receipt requested) to the INS Service Center listed in Appendix B or on the INS website at http://www.insgov—look for the Post Office box that's set up to handle Form I-765. The INS will send you a receipt notice within about six weeks. The receipt notice will tell you when you can expect an answer (it all depends on how busy the INS is). If you don't get a receipt notice, or if the time predicted on that notice passes with no INS decision, see Chapter 13, Dealing With Bureaucrats, Delays and Denials.

If you are approved, the INS will mail you a plastic work permit card with your photo on it. The card will indicate how many months you are allowed to work. You are not allowed to work until you receive this card.

6. Transition to H-1B Visa Employment

At the end of their studies or practical training, many students find an employer willing to sponsor them as a temporary specialty worker, on an H-1B visa. This is not the same as sponsorship for a green card, which is much more difficult to obtain. However, the

H-1B visa has many benefits. It is usually good for three years, with the possibility of renewals. A large overall number of H-1B visas are available (unlike many other work-related visas), thanks to recent increases in the allocations by Congress. H-1B visa holders are also treated with more flexibility than other work-related visa holders when it comes to applying for permanent U.S. residency.

This book does not cover applications for H-1B visas. However, because many students apply for them, we mention an important regulation affecting students.

In certain years, the number of H-1B visa applications exceeds the supply of visas, and some applicants end up waiting an extra year for their visa to be approved. However, when the demand exceeds the supply of visas, the INS regulations allow the INS Commissioner to extend the duration of status of any F-1 student whom an employer has applied to sponsor. This allows you to stay in the United States on your F-1 status while you wait. However, this extension isn't automatic—you'll need to apply for it. Also, you must not have violated your F-1 visa status in order to obtain this extension—just another reason to be careful to stay in-status.

For more on qualifying and applying for H-1B visas, talk to your DSO and an attorney. Also see *U.S. Immigration Made Easy*, by Laurence A. Canter and Martha S. Siegel (Nolo).

B. M Visas and Employment

As an M visa holder, you are not allowed to work on or off campus while you are still completing your study program. Your spouses and children are similarly not allowed to work. After you have successfully completed your studies, however, you can be approved for a period of paid (or unpaid) practical training, up to six months. The INS calculates the number of months based on how long you've been studying: You'll get one month of work permission for every four months of full-time study.

Here's how to apply for practical training. First, make sure that you'll be applying at the right time.

You can't apply earlier than 60 days before the end of your studies; but you can't apply later than 30 days after the end of your studies. Then pull together or prepare the items described in the following subsections and summarized on the Checklist in subsection 3, below.

1. Application Forms for Practical Training Work Permit

The forms you'll need to apply for INS permission to do practical training are:

- Form I-20 ID, endorsed by your DSO
- Form I-538 signed and endorsed by your DSO (see subsection a, below)
- Form I-765 (see subsection b, below), and
- Form I-765 Signature Card. This is a small white card (pictured below) that you'll need to sign. Get one by visiting your local INS office or DSO, or by calling 800-870-3676 (the card can't be downloaded from the Internet or included in this book). Make sure your signature stays entirely inside the box, or the INS will return the whole application to you.

Form I-765, Signature Card

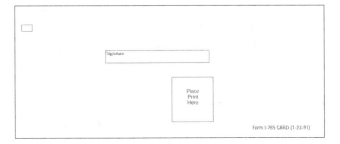

a. Line-by-Line Instructions for Form I-538

Form I-538 is used for a variety of communications between the DSO and the INS. Most of this form will be filled out by your DSO. However, if you want to help out and get the process started, you can fill out your portion and take it to your DSO. If you choose to print out Form I-538 yourself from the INS website, print it single-sided.

You'll find a tear-out copy of this form in Appendix D and a picture of it in subsection A2, above.

When you've got a copy of Form I-538 in hand, follow these line-by-line instructions on how to fill it out.

Section A:

This is the section that you fill out. Most of it is self-explanatory.

Question 3: Your **Student Admission Number** should be on your I-20 ID.

Question 4: Enter the date that the consulate or the INS first approved your student status.

Question 5: **"Level of education being sought"** refers to the type of degree, diploma or certificate you're working toward.

Question 6: Your major field of study should match the one stated on your I-20.

Question 7: You may want to wait until you've spoken to your DSO to fill in your description of proposed employment. The DSO can help make sure that the wording is appropriate.

Question 8: As an M-1 student, you shouldn't have worked before, so your answer should be "N/A." Don't forget to sign your name at the bottom of Section A.

Section B: Your DSO fills this out, but look it over afterward to make sure that the information is accurate.

b. Line-by-Line Instructions for Form I-765

Form I-765 is the main form used by immigrant applicants for work permits. Most of the pages are instructions, which you don't need to fill out or return to the INS. However, if you choose to print out Form I-765 yourself from the INS website, make sure the last page, containing the actual application, is printed out on a single, separate sheet of paper.

 You'll find a tear-out copy of this form in Appendix D and a picture of it in subsection A4, above.

When you have a copy of this form in hand, follow these instructions on how to fill it out.

Under **"I am applying for,"** check "Permission to Accept Employment," unless you have had a previous EAD under another visa, in which case you should check the box for renewals.

Questions 1-8: Self-explanatory.

Question 9: You will probably not have a Social Security number unless you are changing from a visa or status that allowed you to work. If you don't have a number, enter "None."

Question 10: You will have an **Alien registration number (A-number)** only if you have been in deportation or removal proceedings or have submitted certain immigration applications, particularly for permanent residence. If you were in proceedings or had any applications denied, especially for reasons such as fraud, see a lawyer. If you don't have an A-number, enter the number from your I-94 (and before the actual number, write "I-94#").

Question 14: List the type of visa on which you last entered the United States, which is probably an M-1 student visa, unless you entered as a visitor or on another temporary visa and then applied for a Change of Status to become a student.

Question 15: Your current immigration status is "M-1 student."

Question 16: Your eligibility category depends on the basis for your work permit. As an M-1 visa holder applying for practical training, your category is (c)(6).

2. Other Items for Practical Training Work Permit Application

In addition to the application forms described above, you'll need the following in order to complete your application for a practical training work permit:

- two photos (INS-style; see Appendix A). Print your name in pencil on the back of the photos.
- the fee (currently $100 for Form I-765 and $70 for Form I-538), but double-check with your DSO or on the INS website at http://www.ins.gov). Send a check or money order, payable to the USINS. Do not send cash.

3. Using the Checklist for Practical Training Work Permit Application

The Checklist below lists everything you'll need to apply for permission to do practical training. By checking off each box as you've prepared or collected the item, you'll ensure that nothing is forgotten.

 You'll find a tear-out copy of this Checklist in Appendix E.

Checklist for Practical Training Work Permit Application

☐ Form I-20 ID
☐ Form I-538
☐ Form I-765
☐ two photos
☐ Form I-765 Signature Card
☐ fee (currently $100 for Form I-765 plus $70 for Form I-538)

---

4. Mailing Application and Receiving Your Work Permit

When you've prepared all your application materials, mail them (by certified mail with a return receipt requested) to the INS Service Center listed in Appendix B or on the INS website at http://www.ins.gov— look for the Post Office box that's set up to handle Form I-765. The INS will send you a receipt notice within about six weeks. The receipt notice will tell you when you can expect an answer (it all depends on how busy the INS is). If you don't get a receipt notice, or if the time predicted on that notice passes with no INS decision, see Chapter 13, Dealing With Bureaucrats, Delays and Denials.

Once you're approved, you'll receive a plastic work permit card with your photo on it and an expiration date. The card will be good for a maximum of six months' work. You are not allowed to work until you receive this card. ■

Dealing With Bureaucrats, Delays and Denials

If you think your application is taking too long, welcome to the crowd. Although your plans to visit or study in the United States may be the most important thing in your present-day life, to the bureaucrats reviewing your case you are just a number. Thousands of people have applied for visas or other immigration benefits at the same time as you, and delays and frustrations have become an inevitable part of the process. And if you think your application has been unfairly denied, you're not alone in this, either.

If you're coming from overseas, things should start out smoothly: Visa applications at the U.S. consulates are usually decided within days or even minutes. The real slowdowns usually hit after you're in the United States. A Change of Status application filed with the U.S. INS may take months. And even if you use a tourist or student visa to come from overseas, there is a good chance that you will have to file further applications with the INS while you are here. For instance, many people ask for an extension of their stay, and students may want to ask for work permits, school transfers and more. These applications will normally have to be mailed to the INS, rather than hand-delivered and decided in person—adding more possibilities for loss and delay.

Fortunately, there are steps you can take—before, during and after each application process—that will minimize the chances for delay or denial. This chapter discusses:

- how to anticipate and deal with problems during any part of the immigration process (Section A), and
- how to respond to negative decisions (Sections B and C).

A. Anticipating and Dealing With Delays

In view of the number of people applying for visas and status changes, it's almost guaranteed that your application will spend some time in processing limbo. Although you can't prevent delays, you can anticipate them and be ready to deal with them when the time comes.

Behind the Scenes

Reporters for *The Oregonian* newspaper visited the INS Service Center in Burlington, Vermont, and found "crates of files teeter[ing] along the walkways between overstuffed cubicles. Even with new computers, the center relies on time-tested filing techniques. 'I don't know what we'd do without hand trucks and milk crates,' says Paul E. Novak, Jr., director of the INS' Vermont Service Center."

The reporters also described a 1998 case in which "INS officials stored 30,000 files in a storage room where workers later found asbestos. A crew had to seal off the room—but the INS didn't bother to notify the applicants." (See "INS Bureaucracy, Blundering Create 'Agency from Hell,'" by Brent Walth and Kim Christensen, *The Oregonian*, Monday, December 11, 2000.)

1. Plan Ahead for Lost or Wayward Papers

Knowing the likelihood of problems in advance, you can minimize them by keeping a copy of everything you send to the INS. If you're in the United States, take the additional precaution of sending everything by certified mail with a return receipt. This means that you'll go to a U.S. Post Office and fill out a small postcard that will be attached to your envelope. When your application arrives at the INS, they'll have to sign the postcard and mail it back to you. The signed postcard is your proof that your envelope was received.

If you're mailing from your own country, use the safest method available, preferably with some form of tracking. No matter where you are, be aware that many INS addresses are Post Office boxes, where services like Federal Express will not always deliver. (These delivery companies need an actual person at the destination to immediately sign for the article.) For P.O. box addresses, you'll need to use regular mail.

By taking these steps, you'll have the evidence you need in case you must show immigration authorities that it was their fault that a file was delayed or mislaid. In some cases, they'll rely on your own photocopies to proceed with the application.

2. Asking Questions by Mail

If your application drags on too long or some other problem arises, write courteous, clear letters asking for action, as shown in the samples in the subsequent sections. All correspondence should include the processing number on your last INS or consular correspondence and any identification number that you have been assigned. Students should use the admission number found on their Form I-20 ID. Tourists should use the number found on their I-94 card.

If you're dealing with an INS Service Center, you should get a receipt notice within a few weeks of filing your application. Your receipt notice will contain a processing number for that particular application (it's not a number that permanently applies to you). You'll recognize it because it starts with a three-letter abbreviation—either WAC, LIN, EAC, SRC or TSC. These abbreviations refer to the Service Center handling your application: California uses "WAC," Nebraska uses "LIN," Vermont uses "EAC" and Texas uses "SRC" or "TSC." If you haven't been assigned a processing number or haven't even gotten a receipt notice, include copies of previous correspondence and/or certified mail receipts when you write your inquiry letters.

Keep your letters clear and to the point. The people at the other end don't want to read long passages about how you've been checking your mail every day and can't sleep at night for worry. Answers to inquiry letters usually take at least six weeks.

3. Inquiring About Delayed Receipt Notices

Initial receipt notices from INS Service Centers, which simply tell you that the INS got your paperwork, should arrive fairly quickly—six weeks is the longest you should have to wait. If you don't get a receipt notice, send a letter like the one in the Sample below.

Sample Letter About Delayed Receipt Notice

344 Noview Drive
Fremont, CA 90000
(510) 555-1212

June 16, 200x

INS/California Service Center
P.O. Box 10765
Laguna Niguel, CA 92607-0765

[See Appendix B for the address of the Service Center for your geographic region.]

Re: Application for Employment Authorization
Document
I-94#: 002345678
Admission Number: 012345678.90

Dear Sir/Madam:

I filed an application for an Employment Authorization Document on May 1, 200x. It has been over six weeks and I have not gotten a receipt notice or any other communication from you. I did, however, receive the U.S. Postal Service's certified mail receipt, indicating that my application arrived safely in your office. A copy of that receipt is enclosed.

Please advise me of the status of my application at the above address or phone number. I look forward to your response.

Very truly yours,

Josef Renouf

Josef Renouf

Enclosure: Copy of Certified Mail Receipt

4. Emergency Attention

If there is some reason that your application really should be given immediate attention—that is, put ahead of all the other waiting applications—be sure to highlight this in a letter. But limit your cries for help to true emergencies, such as:

- a family member is dying in your home country and you need permission to leave the United States during your application processing to visit them, or
- you have scheduled surgery on the same day as an important INS or consular appointment.

If possible, include proof of any claimed emergency, such as a letter from a doctor.

5. INS Service Center Time Estimates

Sooner or later, you'll get a receipt notice from the INS Service Center, whether in response to your first inquiry or in the normal course of processing. The notice will give you an estimate of how long the INS expects it will take to approve or deny your application. Look at the box in the sample receipt notice below—you'll see that it predicts 90 days for completion.

6. Inquiring About Late Service Center Decisions

The Service Center won't want to hear from you with more inquiries about your application until the number of processing days predicted on your receipt notice has passed. They'll ignore any letters that you send them during this time. But if the predicted number of days passes with no results, it's time to write a letter like the one below.

Sample Letter for Delayed INS Decision

344 Noview Drive
Fremont, CA 90000
(510) 555-1212

September 30, 200x

INS/California Service Center
P.O. Box 10765
Laguna Niguel, CA 92607-0765

[NOTE: See Appendix B for the address of the Service Center for your geographic region.]

Re: Application for Employment Authorization Document
Processing Number: WAC 01-432-12345

Dear Sir/Madam:

I filed an application for an Employment Authorization Document on May 1, 200x. According to your receipt notice, which I received on June 1, 200x, I could expect a decision from you within 90 days. A copy of that notice is enclosed. It has now been approximately 120 days and I have received neither a decision nor any requests for further information.

Please advise me of the status of my application at the above address or phone number. I look forward to your response.

Very truly yours,

Josef Renouf

Josef Renouf

Encl.

If you hear nothing from the INS after four weeks, write another, similar letter. Write another every two weeks until you get an answer. It's best to start with very polite, short letters, and then get more insistent as time goes on. Be careful, however—although eloquent and justified outrage may eventually get the INS's attention, never insult or threaten a government official. This will get you nowhere and, if your

Sample INS Receipt Notice

U.S. Department of Justice
Immigration and Naturalization Service

Notice of Action

THE UNITED STATES OF AMERICA

RECEIPT NUMBER		CASE TYPE I765
WAC-96-223-11111		APPLICATION FOR EMPLOYMENT AUTHORIZATION

RECEIPT DATE	PRIORITY DATE	APPLICANT A11 111 111
August 13, 2001		ASSADI, JALEH M.

NOTICE DATE	PAGE	
August 14, 2001	1 of 1	

ILONA BRAY
950 PARKER STREET
BERKELEY, CA 94710

Notice Type: Receipt Notice

Fee Waived
Representative's Copy
Class requested: A05

The above application for an Employment Authorization Document (EAD), Form I-765, has been received. Processing time is approximately 80 days from the date of this receipt notice.

A Notice of Action, Form I-797, will be sent to you at the address listed above when a decision on this case is made.

If any of the above information is incorrect, or you do not receive a decision on this application within 90 days, please notify us immediately at the number listed below.

Case status information is available 24 hours a day by calling the number below from a touch-tone phone. You will need the receipt number listed on this notice to obtain the information.

If inquiry is written, please attach a copy of this notice.

Please see the additional information on the back. You will be notified separately about any other cases you filed.
IMMIGRATION & NATURALIZATION SERVICE
CALIFORNIA SERVICE CENTER
P. O. BOX 30111
LAGUNA NIGUEL CA 92607-0111
Customer Service Telephone: (714) 360-2769

Form I-797C (Rev. 09/07/93)N

letter is interpreted as a threat, may lead to a criminal prosecution as well as a quick denial.

If several letters have not produced results, consult an attorney or call a U.S. Congressperson's office for help.

7. Telephone Calls

If you're waiting for weeks without a response from the INS or a consulate, you might be tempted to pick up the phone and ask about the progress of your application. Unfortunately, phone calls often produce frustration instead of answers. You might get through to a consulate after many tries. But the INS almost never gives out phone numbers, except those to its main information line, which is far removed from where your personal file is stored.

INS Service Centers are a special case. If your application is pending at an INS Service Center, your receipt notice will show the appropriate phone number to call for inquiries. However, you'll find that after hours trying to get through, the person who picks up the phone has no access to your actual file. Usually, the most they will do is read

Totem Poles
Saxman Village, Alaska

from a computer screen, telling you that your case is pending. However, if the computer shows that the Service Center sent you a request for more documents or actually denied your case, the phone call will be worth the effort—but count on many hours of effort.

8. Incomplete or Lost Portions of Your Application

If the INS or consulate needs something to complete your application, such as photos or a missing document, they will usually mail you a request. If you receive a request for more documentation, try to gather whatever the immigration authorities have asked for and get it in the mail as soon as possible. Don't forget to include the notification form as a cover sheet—but make a copy for yourself first. A sample of the kind of notice a Service Center might send is shown below (this sample is from a work permit application).

What should you do if you're asked for something that you know you've already sent? This is a surprisingly common occurrence—in fact, an investigative report by *The Oregonian* newspaper found that, "With 25 million case files in storage, the INS misplaces tens of thousands of files each year—80,000 in 1998 alone—and leaves immigrants to resubmit applications and pay fees all over again." (From "INS Bureaucracy, Blundering Create 'The Agency From Hell,'" by Brent Walth and Kim Christensen, *The Oregonian*, Monday, December 11, 2000.) If the requested item is something inexpensive or easy to come by, don't waste time arguing with the INS or consulate—even if you have photocopies proving that you already sent the item. Just assume it's been lost and send another one.

Lost checks or money orders are a different matter. Don't send the INS another check or money order until you've found out what happened to the first draft. If you sent a check and haven't received information about it with your monthly bank statement, ask your bank to tell you whether your check has been cashed. If so, get the check and send the INS a copy of both sides, so that INS officials can see their

Sample INS Request for Further Evidence—Page 1

U.S. Department of Justice
Immigration and Naturalization Service

Notice of Action

THE UNITED STATES OF AMERICA

RECEIPT NUMBER WAC-01-013-99999		CASE TYPE I765 APPLICATION FOR EMPLOYMENT AUTHORIZATION
RECEIPT DATE	PRIORITY DATE	APPLICANT A99 999 999 IVAN PLATOV
NOTICE DATE October 20, 2000	PAGE 1 of 1	

IVAN PLATOV
2367 BROADWWAY
NEW YORK, NEW YORK 20012

Notice Type: Rejection Notice

Your Application for Employment Authorization, Form I-765, is being rejected for incorrect fee.

To establish the correct fee, you must select one eligibility category and submit the fee according to the directions on the application.

Select one eligibility category from Part 2 on the instruction sheet and write it in Item 16 on the form. Return the completed form I-765 with the correct fee as indicated on Part 5 of the instructions for processing.

Please see the additional information on the back. You will be notified separately about any other cases you filed.
IMMIGRATION & NATURALIZATION SERVICE
CALIFORNIA SERVICE CENTER
P. O. BOX 30111
LAGUNA NIGUEL CA 92607-0111
Customer Service Telephone: (949) 831 8427

Form I-797C (Rev. 09/07/93)N

Sample INS Request for Further Evidence—Page 2

U.S. Department of Justice
Immigration and Naturalization Service
California Service Center
P.O. Box 10765
Laguna Niguel, CA 92607-0765

Ivan Platov
2367 Broadway
New York, New York 20012

Date: *8/13/01*
Form: I-765
"A" #: *12345678*

Dear Applicant:

Your application(s) is/are being returned to you for the following reason(s):

1. ___   You have failed to correctly or properly complete the portion of your application which begins "I AM APPLYING FOR _____". Please check the proper box and return to the above address.

2. ___   You have improperly completed or failed to complete Item #16 of your application. Please read the instruction marked "ELIGIBILITY" on the back of the application. Complete Block #16 and return.

3. ___   Please sign your I-765 application.

4. ✗   The I-765 application fee is $100.00

5. ___   Please go to your local INS office nearest you for assistance

6. ___   You failed to submit the required "Form I-765 signature card" with your application. Attached is the I-765 signature card. Sign this card in the blue box marked "signature". **Your signature must fit within the blue box.**

7. ___   You have indicated one of the following eligibility codes in block 16 of your I-765: (a)(3), (a)(4), (a)(5). (a)(7), (a)(8). These eligibility codes are not processed in the California Service Center. Please forward your I-765 to the **Nebraska Service Center**, P.O. Box 82521, Lincoln, NE 68501-2521.

8. ___   A fee is not required for the application or petition you submitted. Your fee, in the amount of _____ is being returned to you.

9. ___   The Form I-765 you submitted has been revised. You must submit the Form I-765 with a revision dated of **4/11/91 or later** to this office.

10. ___   Please complete Section 1 (NAME) or section 3 (ADDRESS).

11. ___   You may ONLY apply for an employment authorization document under one eligibility classification on the application you are submitting.

12. ___   OTHER _____

**IF YOU WISH TO FILE UNDER THE TEMPORARY PROTECTED STATUS AVAILABLE TO HONDURANS AND NICARAGUANS, PLEASE SUBMIT FORM I-765 UNDER (C)(19) ELIGIBILITY CODE FILED TOGETHER WITH FORM I-821, SUPPORTING EVIDENCE AND CORRECT FEES. CALL 1-888-557-5398 FOR MORE INFORMATION. FOR FORMS, CALL 1-800-870-3676.

IMPORTANT NOTE: Please review the instructions carefully to be sure all required documentation is attached to your application (i.e., copy of INS decision notice, copy of your current I-94 or copy of your current EAD card).

IF YOU NEED ASSISTANCE, PLEASE VISIT THE INS OFFICE NEAREST YOUR PLACE OF RESIDENCE. PLACE THIS NOTICE ON TOP OF THE APPLICATION AFTER COMPLETING THE REQUESTED ACTION(S) AND RETURN IT TO THE SERVICE CENTER AT THE ABOVE ADDRESS.

ID# _____
INS Conc._____
rev 9/27/00 fm I 765

own stamp and processing number on the back. If the check hasn't been cashed, make sure to cancel the old check at the same time that you send a new one.

If you sent a money order and kept the receipt with the tracer number, call the company that issued the money order to find out whether it's been cashed. Ask for a copy of the cashed money order or other evidence, which you can use to prove to the INS that they were the ones who cashed it. If you can't get a copy of the cashed money order, send the INS a copy of your receipt and an explanation. Hopefully, they will stop bugging you for the money.

9. Never Offer or Give Bribes

Although there are countries where the only way to get anything from a government official is to offer cash or other gifts, the United States is not one of them. Personnel at the INS and consulates are proud of the fact that the United States operates strictly according to the rule of law—and they know that they can be fired or imprisoned for many years for taking bribes. Offering a bribe will very likely hurt your chances of getting your visa or other application approved.

If, however, you are asked to pay a bribe or have solid evidence that something like this is going on, write a detailed letter like the sample one below. The sample is tailored for someone applying through a U.S. consulate; we'll give you the address for INS-related complaints below. If you need to write a letter exposing goings-on like this, be sure to substitute the facts of what you experienced or observed in your letter.

The Inspector General's office also has a website, at http://oig.state.gov/main.html and their telephone number is 202-647-9450.

If you encounter corruption at a U.S. INS office, write a similar letter to the Office of Professional Responsibility. Their website is http://www.usdoj.gov/opr/index.html, and their address is H. Marshall Jarrett, Counsel, Office of Professional Responsibility, U.S. Department of Justice, Room 3355, 950 Pennsylvania Avenue, NW, Washington, DC 20530. A copy of the letter should also be sent to the appropriate U.S. Attorney's Office in the INS district where the act occurred, and to the Attorney General of the United States, Main Justice, 950 Pennsylvania Avenue, NW, Washington, DC 20530.

Riverboat
Mississippi River

Corruption Complaint Letter

202 Main Street
Centreburg, New Largedonia

July 27, 200x

Inspector General
U.S. Department of State
HOTLINE
P.O. Box 9778
Arlington, Virginia 22219

Dear Inspector General:

I am writing to inform you of a recent experience of concern to you. I recently applied for an F-1 student visa at the consular section of the U.S. Embassy in Centreburg, New Largedonia. I know that it is against the law for government officials or for employees of the U.S. government to either take money or try to get money from people who are applying for visas.

On July 15, I went to the Consular section to wait in line for a visa interview. I believe there were several hundred people waiting in line. We were told that our wait could be for as long as four or five hours. There was a man in uniform who walked up and down the line looking at our papers and asked us questions. After he looked at my papers, he said something was missing. I told him that everything that was needed was in the envelope. He told me that I would not be able to get to see the Consul today and that I should come back the next day. I insisted that I had all of the papers that were required. He looked at me and said "I see that you do not understand, I can make sure that you get in today and that you receive your visa but I will need a little help." I understood this to mean that I should pay him. I asked him how much and he said, "You must decide and we will see." I knew that this was not right so I did not pay him, but I did see other people who paid him money.

When I got to the Consular section, I noticed that the same man who had pressured me for money was inside talking to a man that I later learned was the Vice Consul. They seemed to be very friendly since they were laughing and talking a lot. When I finally saw the Consul he asked me if I had spoken with the man who I had seen in line and that I should make sure that I have all of my documents ready at the time of the interview for the visa. He then made another appointment for me to come in the following week.

I am hoping that something can be done about this situation. I am writing to your office because I know that you are separate from the Consulate and the Embassy and that part of your job is to prevent this kind of corruption.

Sincerely,

Carl White

Carl White

B. Reapply If Your Application Is Denied

Despite all your careful preparation, your application for a visa or other benefit may ultimately receive a firm "no," with no openings for further discussion or submission of information. In most cases described in this book, there is nothing you can do if your application is denied. Where possibilities for follow-up after a denial do exist, we've given you specific information in the chapters dealing with application procedures. The general rule, however, particularly with the initial tourist or student visa application, is that it's easier to start fresh with the consulates and INS than to convince them that they were wrong.

In preparation for reapplying, pay close attention to the reasons that you were denied, especially if they're given to you in person. You may pick up some clues for improving your next application. For example, if the consular officer says, "How can I give you a visa with all those family members living in the United States?" assume that you need to beef up your documents showing that you are likely to return home after your stay.

Don't assume, however, that your chances will be better the second time around simply because you're going to be dealing with a different government official—consular and INS officers are all trained in the same way and follow the same rules. The way one officer perceives your application is a good indicator of how the next one will respond. Even if you think the first officer was completely off-base, take the time to look for more documents or ways to deal with the issues he or she raised.

If you're already in the United States, the denial of an application is a good time to call a lawyer. If you're here as a student, talk to your DSO as well. The lawyer can give you the final word on whether there is any possible appeal or other follow-up in your situation. Perhaps more importantly, the lawyer can help you prevent the denial from mushrooming into a larger problem for your immigration status or record. See Chapter 14 for tips on finding a good lawyer.

⚠ Never ignore a notice to appear in Immigration Court. Attorneys regularly receive questions from immigrants who were scheduled for a hearing in Immigration Court and either forgot, couldn't make it or just hoped the problem would go away. Failing to appear for a court date is the worst thing you can do. It will earn you an automatic order of deportation, which means that the INS can pick you up and put you on a plane home anytime, with no more hearings. You'll also be hit with a ten-year prohibition on returning to the United States and further punishments if you return illegally.

C. When All Else Fails, Call Your U.S. Congressperson

If your case turns into a true bureaucratic nightmare or a genuine miscarriage of justice, ask a U.S. Congressperson in the state where you are living for help. Some of them have a staff person dedicated to helping constituents who have immigration problems. Although their main concern is to help their U.S. citizen constituents (their voting public), they also understand the need to act as a representative of the U.S. government and to help maintain good relations with foreign governments. You could also call the consulate of your own country and ask them to get involved.

A simple inquiry by a U.S. Congressperson can end months of INS or consular stonewalling or inaction. In rare cases, the Congressperson's office might be willing to put some actual pressure on the INS or consular office.

EXAMPLE: Yana, a pre-med student at Brown University, applies for a work permit to do practical training at an HIV clinic during her summer break. The INS Service Center receipt estimates that the INS decision will take three months. After five months she has still heard nothing, even after writing three inquiry letters. She writes a letter to the U.S. Congressperson for the school's district, outlining the problem. She includes a letter from the clinic stating that they are anxiously waiting for her help. The Congressperson contacts the Service Center, and the case is approved within two weeks.

Your Congressperson probably won't be surprised to hear from you. Illinois Congresswoman Janice Schakowsky reports that eight out of ten calls from her constituents are complaints about the INS. (See "Unchecked Power of the INS Shatters American Dream," by Kim Christensen, Richard Read, Julie Sullivan and Brent Walth, *The Oregonian*, Sunday December 20, 2000.) ■

Legal Help Beyond This Book

ourist and student visa applicants rarely need a lawyer at the beginning of the process, when they're getting their visa or status. This is particularly true for overseas applicants—even if a lawyer were willing, he wouldn't be allowed into your consular interview. The most the lawyer might do is consult with you on a ground of inadmissibility or advise you on preparation of your application.

But as you know by now, your dealings with the consulates or INS may not end when you enter the United States. You may need to apply for work permits, extensions or even reinstatement of your status. If these or other issues get to be too much for you to handle, you'll need good legal help, and fast. In this chapter, we'll explain:

- when applicants typically need to consult an attorney (Section A)
- how to find suitable counsel (Sections B, C and D)
- hiring, paying and (if necessary) firing your lawyer (Sections E, F and G), and
- how to do some legal research on your own (Section H).

⚠ If you are or have ever been in removal (formerly called deportation or exclusion) proceedings, you must see a lawyer. If the proceedings aren't yet over or are on appeal, your entire immigration situation is probably in the power of the courts—and you are not allowed to use the procedures described in this book. Even if the proceedings are over, you should ask a lawyer whether the outcome affects your current application.

A. When Do You Need a Lawyer?

The most common legal problem encountered by would-be tourist or student visa applicants is the claim by the INS or consulate that they are inadmissible for one or more of the reasons listed in Chapter 2. If you know that any of these grounds apply to you, or if you have ever been refused admission by an INS officer at a U.S. border, air or seaport it makes sense to get legal help before you begin the applica-

tion process. Similarly, if you have ever been in immigration court proceedings either after arrival or when you were trying to come into the U.S. you should consult with a lawyer about your options.

Another circumstance that often drives people to lawyers is the failure of the INS or consulate to act on or approve their application, for reasons that have more to do with bureaucracy than law. For example, Change of Status applicants may put their whole life on hold as months go by while they wait for approval of their application.

Lawyers don't have much power when it comes to simple but lengthy delays. In some cases, lawyers may have access to inside "fax inquiry" lines, where they (and only they) can fax in questions about delayed or problematic cases—but even lawyers have trouble getting answers to such inquiries. Experienced lawyers may have contacts inside the INS or consulate who can give them information or locate a lost file. But these lawyers can't use this privilege on an everyday basis, and long delays are an everyday occurrence. The bottom line is that a lawyer has no magic words that will force the INS into taking action. So you'll have to decide whether it's worth it to pay a lawyer for this limited help. After all, the lawyer will basically be doing what you can probably do yourself—repeatedly calling or writing to the INS or consulate until they come up with an answer.

You will definitely need a lawyer to represent you, however, if you are suspected of committing a crime or violating your status and are placed in removal proceedings. If you are a student and believe you have violated your status but no one knows it yet, it's safer to talk to a lawyer than to your DSO—after all, as explained at the opening of Chapter 11, the DSO is obligated to advise the INS of your status violation.

⚠ Don't rely on advice by INS officers. Would you want the receptionist in your doctor's office to tell you whether to get brain surgery? Asking INS information officers for advice about your case (beyond asking basic procedural information such as where to file an application and what the fees are) is equally unsafe. The people who staff INS phone and information services are not experts. The INS takes no responsibility if their advice is wrong. Even following the advice of officials higher up in the agency (who know more, but may not give close attention to your case) may not protect you if they're wrong—always get a second opinion.

B. Where to Get the Names of Good Immigration Lawyers

Finding a good lawyer can involve a fair amount of work—as well it should. Many people spend more time choosing a car to buy than choosing a lawyer to hire—yet the lawyer will probably have more responsibility for your life and future than the car.

First of all, you only want to consult with a lawyer who is licensed to practice in the United States—lawyers from your own country are not helpful, or authorized to advise you about U.S. immigration law. But even among U.S. lawyers, immigration law is a specialized area—in fact it has many subspecialties within it—so you don't want to consult the lawyer who wrote your friend's will. And whatever you do, don't open the telephone book and pick the immigration lawyer with the biggest advertisement. Even bar association referral panels (lawyer listing services run by groups of lawyers) are often not very helpful. Such services tend to place lawyer-members on their lists without screening them as to whether they're qualified to handle cases such as yours.

It is far better to ask a trusted person for a referral. You probably know someone in the United States who is sophisticated in practical affairs and has been through an immigration process. Perhaps this person can recommend his or her lawyer, or can ask that lawyer to recommend another. Students can also ask their DSO for lawyer recommendations.

Local nonprofit organizations serving immigrants can also be excellent sources for referrals. A nonprofit organization is a charity that seeks funding from foundations and individuals to help people in need. Since they exist to serve others rather than to make a profit, they charge less and are usually staffed by people whose hearts and minds are in the right places.

Sources of Lawyer Referrals

Most nonprofits keep lists of lawyers whom they know do honest immigration work for a fair price. In the immigrant services field, examples of nonprofits include the Albuquerque Border City Project (New Mexico); Northwest Immigrant Rights Project (Seattle), El Rescate Legal Services (Los Angeles), Public Advocates (Los Angeles), the International Institutes (nationwide) and Catholic Charities (nationwide). For a list of INS-approved nonprofits, ask your local INS office or Immigration Court or check the INS website at http://www.ins. usdoj.gov/graphics/lawsregs/advice.htm. You don't need to use a nonprofit from the INS list, but it may be safer to do—supposed nonprofit organizations can be unscrupulous too, or may actually be for-profit businesses.

Yet another good resource is the American Immigration Lawyer's Association (AILA), at 800-954-0254 or on the Internet at http://www. aila.org. AILA offers a lawyer referral service. Their membership is limited to lawyers who have passed a screening process, which helps keep out the less scrupulous practitioners. But not all good immigration lawyers have joined AILA (membership is a bit pricey).

Try to get a list of a few lawyers whom you've heard do good work, then meet or talk to each and choose one. We'll talk more about lawyers' fees below.

C. How to Avoid Sleazy Lawyers

There are good and bad immigration lawyers looking for your business. Some of the good ones are candidates for sainthood—they put in long hours dealing with a difficult bureaucracy on behalf of a clientele that typically can't pay high fees.

The bad ones are a nightmare—and there are more than a few of them. They typically try to do a high-volume business, churning out the same forms for every client regardless of the client's situation. Such lawyers can get clients into deep trouble by overlooking critical issues in their cases or failing to submit applications or court materials on time. But the one thing they never seem to forget is to send you a huge bill for their supposed help. Some signs to watch for are:

- **The lawyer approaches you in an INS office or other public location and tries to solicit your business.** This is not only against the lawyers' rules of professional ethics, but a sure sign that you're dealing with a loser. No competent lawyer ever needs to find clients this way.
- **The lawyer makes big promises, such as "I guarantee I'll win your case" or "I've got a special contact that will put your application at the front of the line."** The INS is in ultimate control of your application, and lawyers who imply they have special powers are either lying or may be involved in something you don't want to be a part of.
- **The lawyer has a very fancy office and wears a lot of flashy gold jewelry.** A fancy office or a $2,000 outfit aren't necessarily signs of a lawyer's success at winning cases. These trappings may instead be signs that the lawyer charges high fees and counts on impressing his clients with clothing rather than results.
- **The lawyer encourages you to lie on your application.** This is a tricky area. On the one hand, a good lawyer can assist you in learning what information you don't want to needlessly offer up, and can help you present the truth in the best light possible. But a lawyer who coaches you to lie—for example, by telling you to pretend you injured yourself in order to qualify for an extension—isn't ethical. There's every chance that the INS knows the lawyer's reputation and will scrutinize your application harder because of it.

You might think that the really bad lawyers would be out of business by now, but that isn't the case. Sad to say, neither the attorney bar associations nor the courts nor even the police take much interest in going after people who prey on immigrants. Occasionally, nonprofits devoted to immigrants' rights will attempt to get the enforcement community interested in taking action. Unfortunately, this threat of official scrutiny isn't much of a deterrent.

If you are the victim of an unscrupulous lawyer, complain! Law enforcement won't go after lawyers who prey on immigrants until there is enough community pressure. If a lawyer pulls something unethical on you, report it to the state and local bar association and the local District Attorney's office. Ask your local nonprofits if anyone else in your area is collecting such information.

D. How to Choose Among Lawyers

Once you've got your "short list" of lawyers, it's a good idea to speak to each one. How much a lawyer charges is bound to be a factor in whom you choose (see Section F below). But it shouldn't be the only factor. Here are some other important considerations.

1. Familiarity With Cases Like Yours

As mentioned above, immigration law is a specialized area. And some immigration lawyers spend much of their time in sub-specialties, such as helping people obtain political asylum or secure employment-based visas. To learn how much experience a lawyer has in issues concerning tourists or students, ask some very practical questions, such as the following:

- How long do you expect my application to take?
- What is the reputation of the officers at the INS or consular office that will be handling my case?
- How many cases like mine did you handle this year?

The more experience the lawyer has, and the more detailed his or her answers, the better. Immigration law is one of the hardest areas to learn out of books—the experienced lawyers can anticipate problems that the newer ones may have never heard of. If the lawyer you like best after speaking to a few is new to the profession, it doesn't mean you must completely avoid him or her—but make sure she comes recommended by other immigration lawyers and gives you a price break. You're safest if the new lawyer shares an office with more experienced immigration lawyers who can provide quick advice.

2. Client Rapport

Your first instinct in hiring a lawyer may be to look for a shark—someone you wouldn't want to leave your child with, but who will be a tough fighter for your case. This isn't necessarily the best choice in the immigration context. Since you may need to share some highly confidential issues with your lawyer, you'll want to know that the person is discreet and thoughtful. Also, realize that a lawyer's politeness goes a long way in front of immigration officials—sharks often produce a bureaucratic backlash, whereas the lawyers with good working relations with the INS may have doors opened to them.

Don't expect the lawyer to make all your decisions for you. One of the most common questions clients ask their lawyer is, "What do you think I should do?" There are many situations in which the immigration law doesn't provide clear guidance and you'll have to make a decision about how best to act. For example, if you wanted to come to the U.S. as a tourist using a Visa Waiver, but there was a chance you could be found inadmissible at the border, a lawyer can't tell you whether buying the plane ticket is worth the risk. A good lawyer will describe the pluses and minuses of the paths legally open to you, but will not direct you to one path or another.

3. Access to Your Lawyer

You'll want to know that you can reach your lawyer during the months that your application winds its way through the INS or consular bureaucracy. A lawyer's accessibility may be hard to judge at the beginning, but try listening to the lawyer's recep-

tionist as you wait in the office for the first time. If you get the sense that the receptionist is rude and trying to push people off or give them flimsy excuses about why the lawyer hasn't returned their calls or won't talk to them, don't hire that lawyer.

Many immigration lawyers are sole practitioners and use an answering machine rather than a receptionist. In that case, you'll have to draw your conclusions based on how quickly the lawyer answers your initial calls. In your first meeting, ask the lawyer how quickly he or she will normally get back to you. If the lawyer regularly breaks his or her promise, you'll have grounds on which to complain. Of course, you too have a responsibility not to harass your lawyer with frequent calls. The lawyer should be available for legitimate questions about your case, including inquiries about approaching deadlines.

4. Explaining Services and Costs

Take a good look at any printed materials the lawyer gives you on your first visit. Are they glitzy, glossy pieces that look more like advertising than anything useful? Or are they designed to acquaint you with the process you're getting into and the lawyer's role in it? Think about this issue again before you sign the lawyer's fee agreement, described in the section immediately below. Being a good salesperson doesn't necessarily make someone a good lawyer.

E. Signing Up Your Lawyer

Many good lawyers will ask you to sign an agreement covering their services and the fees you will pay them. This is a good idea for both of you and can help prevent misunderstandings. The contract should be written in a way you can understand; there's no law that says it has to be in confusing legal jargon. The lawyer should go over the contract with you carefully, not just push it under your nose, saying, "Sign here." Some normal contract clauses include:

- **Scope of work.** A description of exactly what the lawyer will do for you.
- **Fees.** Specification of the amount you'll pay, either as a flat fee (a lump sum you pay for a stated task, such as $600 for a Change of Status application) or at an hourly rate, with a payment schedule. If you hire someone at an hourly rate, you can ask to be told as soon as the hours have hit a certain limit.

Don't pay a big flat fee up front. Since the lawyer already has your money, he or she will have little incentive to please you. And if you don't like the lawyer later on, chances are you won't get any of your money back. Instead, pay for a few hours' service —then if you don't like the lawyer's work, end the relationship.

- **Responsibility for expenses.** Most lawyers will ask you to cover the incidental expenses associated with the work that they do, such as phone calls, postage and photocopying. This is fair. After all, if your case requires a one-hour phone call to the consulate in Brunei, that call shouldn't eat up the lawyer's fee. But check carefully to be sure that the lawyer charges you the actual costs of these items. Some lawyers have been known to turn a tidy profit by charging, for example, 20 cents a page for a photocopy job that cost them only three cents a page.

- **Effect of nonpayment.** Many lawyers charge interest if you fail to pay on time. This is normal and probably not worth making a big fuss about. If you have trouble paying on time, call the lawyer and ask for more time—he or she may be willing to forego the interest if it's clear you're taking your obligation seriously.
- **Exclusion of guarantee.** The lawyer may warn you that there's no guarantee they'll win your case. Though this may appear as if they're looking for an excuse to lose, it is actually a responsible way for the lawyer to protect against clients who assume they're guaranteed a win; or who later accuse the lawyer of having made such promises. After all, the INS or consulate is the ultimate decision-maker on your case.
- **Effect of changes in your case.** Most lawyers will warn you that if there is something you didn't tell them about (for example, that you are married to a U.S. citizen) or a significant life change affects your case (for instance, you get arrested), they will charge you additional fees to cover the added work these revelations may cause. This too is normal; but to protect yourself against abuse, make very sure that the contract specifies in detail all the work that is already included. For example, a contract for a lawyer to help you with an extension application within the United States might specify that the lawyer will be responsible for "preparation

A Pueblo
Taos, New Mexico

and submission of application and reasonable follow-up with the INS." If the lawyer agrees to include work on any special documents, make sure these are mentioned in the contract (for example, an Affidavit of Support from a family member).

Watch Out for Nonlawyers Practicing Immigration Law

Because much of immigration law involves filling out forms, people assume it's easy. They're wrong. Be careful about whom you consult with or hand your case over to. Unless you see certification that the person you're dealing with is a lawyer, an "accredited representative" or a paralegal working under the direct supervision of a lawyer, that person is simply a typist. (An accredited representative is a non-lawyer who has received training from a lawyer and been recognized by the INS as qualified to prepare INS applications and represent clients in court.) Don't be fooled by people using fancy titles such as "immigration consultant" or "notary public"—these people do not have a law degree. To check on whether someone is really a lawyer, ask for their Bar Number and call the state bar association.

Hiring a non-lawyer or non-accredited representative is only appropriate if you want help with the form preparation, and no more. But as you know from reading previous portions of this book, the most innocent-seeming questions can have legal consequences. Don't just turn your case over and let the consultant make the decisions.

F. Paying Your Lawyer

You may have to pay an initial consultation fee as well as a fee for the lawyer's services. The initial consultation fee is usually around $50 (in fact, this is the mandatory upper limit for lawyers who receive AILA referrals). Some good lawyers provide free consultations. But many have found that they can't afford to spend a lot of their time this way, since many immigrants have no visa or remedy available to them, which means the lawyer gets no work after the initial consultation. Be ready to pay a reasonable fee for your initial consultation, but do not sign any contracts for further services until you're confident you've found the right lawyer. This usually means consulting with several lawyers first.

1. Flat Rates and Hourly Rates

Many lawyers charge flat rates for their services. That means you can compare prices. If the lawyer quotes an hourly rate instead, expect to pay between $100 and $300 per hour.

A higher rate doesn't necessarily mean a better lawyer. Those who charge less may be keeping their overhead low, still making their name in the business or philosophically opposed to charging high fees. But an extremely low fee may be a sign that the person isn't really a lawyer, as covered in "Watch Out for Nonlawyers Practicing Immigration Law," above.

2. If All the Rates Are Too High

If the prices you are being quoted are beyond your reach but you definitely need legal help, you have a couple of options. One is to ask the lawyer to split the work with you. With this arrangement, the lawyer consults with you solely about the issue causing you difficulty, reviews a document or performs some other key task, at the hourly rate; while you do the follow-up work, such as filling out the application forms and translating or writing documents, statements, letters or more.

Be forewarned, though, that while many lawyers will sell you advice on an hourly basis, most won't want to get into a mixed arrangement unless they are sure they won't end up cleaning up anything you might do wrong. For example, a lawyer might not agree to represent you in an INS interview if they weren't hired to review your forms and documents before you submitted them to the INS.

Another option is to look for a nonprofit orga- nization that serves individual immigrants. A few provide free services, while most charge reduced rates. Also check with local law schools, some of which run immigration law clinics where law students take on immigrant cases under the supervision of a professor. But don't get your hopes too high. The U.S. government does not fund organizations that provide services to immigrants (except for very limited types of services), which means that most nonprofits depend on private sources of income and are chronically underfunded. Meanwhile, the demand for such services is very high. The result is that many nonprofits as well as law school clinics have long backlogs of cases and may not be able to take your case at all.

G. Firing Your Lawyer

You have the right to fire your lawyer at any time. But before you take this step, make sure that your disagreement is about something that is truly the lawyer's fault. Many people blame their lawyer for delays that are actually caused by the INS or consulates.

You can always consult with another lawyer regarding whether your case has been mishandled. Ask your lawyer for a complete copy of your file first (you have a right to have it any time). If it appears that your case was mishandled or if relations with your lawyer have deteriorated badly, firing the lawyer may be the healthiest thing for you and your immigration case.

You will have to pay the fired lawyer for any work that has already been done on your case. If you originally paid a flat fee, the lawyer is permitted to keep enough of the fee to cover the work already done, at the hourly rate, limited by the total flat fee amount. Ask for a complete list of hours worked and how those hours were spent. Don't count on getting any money back, however—flat fees are often artifi- cially low, and it's very easy for lawyers to show that they used up your fee on the work that was done.

Firing your lawyer will not affect the progress of your applications with the INS or consulate. However,

send a letter to the last INS or consular office you heard from, directing them to send all future cor- respondence directly to you (or to your new law- yer).

H. Do-It-Yourself Legal Research

With or without a lawyer, you may at some point wish to look at the immigration laws yourself. If so, we applaud your self-empowerment instinct—but need to give you a few warnings. An INS spokesper- son recently called the immigration laws a "mystery, and a mastery of obfuscation." (INS spokeswoman Karen Kraushaar, quoted in *The Washington Post*, April 24, 2001.) She couldn't have said it better. One is tempted to think that the members of the U.S. Congress who write and amend the immigration laws deliberately make them unreadable, perhaps to confuse the rest of the representatives so they won't understand what they're voting on.

The result is that researching the immigration laws is something even the experts find difficult— which means you may be wading into treacherous waters if you try it on your own. Figuring out local INS office procedures and policies can be even more difficult. Lawyers learn a great deal through trial and error, or by attending meetings and reading articles written by other lawyers who tried some- thing first or who learned important information from INS or State Department cables, memos or other instructions. Unfortunately, you won't have access to these sources.

Does all this mean that you shouldn't ever look farther than this book? Certainly not. And some research inquiries are quite safe—for instance, if we've cited a section of the law and you want to read the exact language or see whether that section has changed, there's no magic in looking up the law and reading it. But in general, be cautious when researching and look at several sources to confirm your findings.

Immigration laws are federal, meaning they are written by the U.S. Congress and do not vary from one state to another (though procedures and priorities for carrying out the laws may vary among INS offices in different cities or states). Below we give you a rundown on the most accessible research tools—and not coincidentally, the ones that immigration lawyers most often use.

Law libraries aren't just for lawyers. Many law libraries, particularly those connected with public law schools, are state-funded "federal depository" libraries. That means that federal statutes and regulations are regularly sent to the library and the library is responsible for making these materials available to the public. Don't be shy about using such libraries as a resource.

1. The Federal Code

The federal immigration law is found in Title 8 of the United States Code. Any law library (such as the one at your local courthouse or law school) should have a complete set of the U.S. Code (traditionally abbreviated as U.S.C.). The library may also have a separate volume containing exactly the same material, but called the Immigration and Nationality Act, or I.N.A.

Unfortunately, the two sets of laws are numbered a bit differently, and not all volumes of the I.N.A. cross-reference to the U.S. Code, and vice versa. For this reason, when code citations are mentioned in this book, we include both the U.S.C. and I.N.A. numbers. You can also access the U.S. Code via Nolo's website, at http://www.nolo.com. On the home page, click on Legal Research Center, then choose U.S. Laws and Regulations. If you already know the title (which is 8) and section, you can enter them and pull up the text immediately. If you don't have the section number, use Nolo's site to link you to a search engine.

2. INS and State Department Regulations and Guidance

Another important source of immigration law is the Code of Federal Regulations, or C.F.R. Federal regulations are written by the agencies responsible for carrying out federal law. The regulations are meant to explain in greater detail just how the federal agency is going to carry out the law. You'll find the INS regulations at Title 8 of the C.F.R., and the Department of State regulations (relevant to anyone whose application is being decided at a U.S. consulate) at Title 22 of the C.F.R. The INS and Department of State regulations are helpful, but certainly don't have all the answers. Again, your local law library will have the C.F.R.s, as does Nolo's Legal Research Center at http://www.nolo.com.

If you are applying from overseas, you may also wish to look at the State Department's *Foreign Affairs Manual*. This is primarily meant to be an internal government document, containing instructions to the consulates on handling immigrant and nonimmigrant visa cases. However, it is available for public researching as well; your local law library may be able to find you a copy, or see the State Department's website, at http://www.foia.state.gov/fam/fam.asp.

3. Information on the Internet

If you have Internet access, you will want to familiarize yourself with the INS and State Department websites. The addresses are http://www.ins.gov and http://www.state.gov. The INS website offers advice on various immigration benefits and applications (though the advice is so brief as to sometimes be misleading), downloads of most immigration forms and current fees. On the State Department website, most of the useful information is found under "visas," including links to U.S. embassies and consulates overseas and downloads of a few consular forms.

The Internet is full of sites put up by immigration lawyers as well as immigrants. Because the quality of these sites varies widely, we don't even attempt to review them here. Many of the lawyers' sites are blatant attempts to give out only enough information to bring in business. The sites by other immigrants are well-meaning and can be good for finding out about people's experiences, but they're not reliable when it comes to hard legal or procedural facts. That said, a couple of lawyer sites that contain useful information include http://www.shusterman.com (with current processing times at the INS Service

Centers); http://www.visalaw.com (run by the firm of Siskind, Susser, Haas & Devine, which includes regular updates on immigration law matters); and http://www.ilw.com (a privately run website called the "immigration portal", which includes various chat room opportunities).

4. Court Decisions

Immigrants who have been denied visas or green cards often appeal these decisions to the federal courts. The courts' decisions in these cases are supposed to govern the future behavior of the INS and consulates. However, your case should never get to the point where you're discussing court decisions with an INS or State Department official, arguing that your case should (or should not) fit within a particular court decision. For one thing, the officials are not likely to listen until they get a specific directive from their superiors or the court decision is incorporated into their agency's regulations (the C.F.R.). For another thing, such discussions probably mean that your case has become complicated enough to need a lawyer. We do not attempt to teach you how to research federal court decisions here.

5. Legal Publications

Two high-quality and popular resources used by immigration lawyers are *Interpreter Releases*, a weekly update published by Federal Publications Inc. (a West Group company); and *Immigration Law and Procedure*, a multi-volume, continually updated looseleaf set by Charles Gordon, Stanley Mailman and Stephen Yale-Loehr (LEXIS Publishing). Again, you should be able to find both at your local law library. Both are very well indexed. They are written for lawyers, so you'll have to wade through some technical terminology.

Internet Resources

This list summarizes the useful Internet sites that have been mentioned in this book.

- The U.S. Immigration and Naturalization Service (INS): http://www.ins.usdoj.gov
- The U.S. Department of State: http://www.state.gov
- U.S. consulates and embassies abroad: http://www.travel.state.gov/links.html
- INS Offices in the U.S. and abroad: http://www.ins.usdoj.gov/graphics/fieldoffices/index.htm
- List of nonprofit agencies approved by the INS: http://www.ins.usdoj.gov/graphics/lawsregs/advice.htm
- Attorney Carl Shusterman: http://www.shusterman.com
- Siskind, Susser, Haas & Devine: http://www.visalaw.com
- The "Immigration Portal": http://www.ilw.com
- U.S. Customs Service: http://www.customs.gov/travel/travel.htm
- Study in the USA, Inc.: http://www.studyusa.com
- The "Embark" network for students and universities: http://www.embark.com
- The International Education Service: http://www.ies-ed.com
- The Institute for International Education: www.iie.org
- National Association of Foreign Student Advisors: http://www.nafsa.org/students/funding.html
- The International Student Organization: http://www.isoa.org
- U.S. Federal Trade Commission: www.ftc.gov
- Lists of overseas embassies in the U.S.: http://www.embassy.org/embassies/index.html or http://www.embpage.org.

Glossary

Words You Will Need to Know

A-Number: An eight-digit number following the letter A (for Alien) that the INS assigns to people who apply for a green card or certain other immigration benefits, or who have been placed in removal proceedings. If you are assigned this number, the INS will use it to track your file.

Admission Number: A number given to students by the INS when they enter the United States, indicated on their Form I-20 ID.

Alien: The INS uses this term to refer to "a foreign-born person who is not a citizen or national of the United States." I.N.A. Section 101(a)(3), 8 U.S.C. Section 1101(a)(3). In other words, the word covers everyone from illegal aliens to green card holders. We don't use the term very much in this book, but you'll need to get used to the word if you do additional research.

B-1 Visa: The State Department's code name for a business visitor visa, not covered in this book. The name is derived from the section of the federal statute which authorizes this visa: I.N.A. § 101(a)(15)(B); 8 U.S.C. § 1101(a)(15)(B).

B-2 Visa: The State Department's code name for a visitor for pleasure visa, commonly known as a tourist visa, covered in this book. The name is derived from the section of the federal statute which authorizes this visa: I.N.A. 101(a)(15)(B); 8 U.S.C. 1101(a)(15)(B).

Citizen (U.S.): A person who owes allegiance to the U.S. government, is entitled to its protection and enjoys the highest level of rights due to members of U.S. society. People become U.S. citizens through their birth in the United States or its territories, through their parents or through naturalization (applying for citizenship and passing a citizenship exam). Citizens cannot have their status taken away except for certain extra-ordinary reasons. See the immigration section of Nolo's legal encyclopedia at http://www.nolo.com for more information.

Consulate: An office of the U.S. Department of State located overseas and affiliated with a U.S. embassy in that country's capital city. The consulate's many responsibilities usually include issuing visas to foreigners wishing to travel or immigrate to the United States. When there are several U.S. consulates within one country, each serves a designated territory or area.

Department of Justice: An agency of the United States federal government that oversees the Immigration and Naturalization Service (INS) and controls the U.S. borders. These are within its broader responsibilities for federal law enforcement.

Department of State: An agency of the United States federal government that oversees U.S. embassies and consulates as part of its broader responsibility to implement U.S. foreign policy. The head of the department is the Secretary of State.

Deport/Deportation: See Removal, below.

Deportable: An immigrant who falls into one of the grounds listed at I.N.A. §237, 8 U.S.C. §1227, is said to be deportable, and can be removed from the United States by the INS after a hearing in Immigration Court. Even a permanent resident can be deported—the only people who cannot be deported are U.S. citizens.

Designated School Official (DSO): An employee of the school to which you are applying or have been admitted, who helps you with the paperwork to become and successfully continue as an international student. The DSO serves as your link with the INS, but must report your status violations to the INS as well.

District Office: One of 33 INS offices in the United States that serves the public in a specified geographical area. District offices are where most INS field staff are located. District offices usually have an information desk, provide INS forms and accept and make decisions on some—but not all—applications for immigration benefits. For a list of locations, see Appendix C or the INS website at http://www.ins.gov.

D/S: See Duration of Status, below.

DSO: See Designated School Official, above.

Duration of Status (D/S): Upon arriving or being approved for a Change of Status in the United States, most F-1 students are given a notation in their I-94 card saying that they may stay for the "Duration of [their] status" or simply "D/S." This is different from the actual expiration date that most other visitors to the United States receive. It indicates that the student doesn't have to leave until his or her studies are completed. It's not open-ended, however—the student's school will attach a firm date to it. Students must leave by the expected completion date shown on the Form I-20 that they receive from their school.

EAD: See Employment Authorization Document, below.

Embassy: The chief U.S. consulate within a given country, usually located in the capital city and headed by the U.S. ambassador. Most of the embassies handle applications for visas to the United States. The embassy also serves many other functions, such as economic and political reporting, facilitating international trade, distributing foreign aid and more.

Employment Authorization Document (EAD): More commonly called a work permit, this is a card with the holder's photo indicating that the card holder has the right to work in the United States.

Executive Office for Immigration Review: See Immigration Court, below.

Expedited Removal: This refers to the all-too-short and not-so-sweet procedures by which immigration officers at U.S. borders and ports of entry may decide that a person cannot enter the United States. See I.N.A. Section 235(b), 8 U.S.C. Section 1225(b). The officers can refuse entry when they believe the person has used fraud in obtaining their travel document or is carrying false documents or no documents. People removed this way are barred from reentering the United States for five years.

Green Card: No longer green, this slang term refers to the identification card carried by lawful permanent residents of the United States. The INS name for the green card is an "I-551" or "Alien Registration Receipt Card." Don't confuse it with the other card often carried by noncitizens, the work permit or Employment Authorization Document (see definition above).

I-94: A small green or white card that is placed in all nonimmigrants' passports when they enter the United States (it's about twice the size of a U.S. driver's license or a U.S. green card). The I-94 is the official arrival-departure record for people coming to the United States. Most of it is filled out by the traveler while on the plane or at the U.S. border. The border patrol will add the date when the person's authorized stay expires. Many people wrongly believe that they can stay until the expiration date in their original visa. Unfortunately, it's the date in the I-94 that controls (although if the visa remains valid, the person may reenter the United States).

Illegal Alien: Illegal alien is more of a slang term than a legal term, usually referring to people who have no permission to live in the United States. The preferred legal term is "undocumented person."

Immigrant: Though the general public usually calls any foreign-born newcomer to the United States an immigrant, the INS prefers to think of immigrants as including only those persons who have attained "permanent residency" or a green card—or intend to. People who are here on temporary visas, however, are called nonimmigrants, even though they're in the United States.

Immigration Court: A special court for immigration proceedings. It's part of the Department of Justice's "Executive Office for Immigration Review" or "EOIR" (a handy name to know if you ever need to look it up in the phone book). This is the first court that will hear your case if you are placed in removal proceedings. Cases are heard by an "Immigration Judge," who is not part of the INS and doesn't hear any other type of case. The INS has its own crew of trial attorneys who represent the agency in court.

Immigration and Nationality Act (I.N.A.): A portion of the federal code containing all the immigration laws. The I.N.A. is also contained in the United States Code (U.S.C.) at Title 8, which you can find via the Legal Research Center of Nolo's website at http://www.nolo.com.

Immigration and Naturalization Service (INS): A branch of the United States Department of Justice, responsible for controlling the United States borders, enforcing the immigration laws and processing and judging the cases of immigrants living in the United States.

Inadmissible: A person to whom the U.S. government will deny a visa or admission to the United States because he or she falls into one of the categories listed at I.N.A. Section 212, 8 U.S.C. Section 1182. Broadly speaking, these categories of inadmissibility cover people who might be a burden on or risk to the U.S. government or public for health, security or financial reasons. Replaces the formerly used term "excludible."

Nonimmigrant: A broad term meant to cover everyone who comes to the United States temporarily. Most nonimmigrants have a specific expiration date attached to their stay. Some others may stay for the "duration of status," such as F-1 students, most of whom who can stay until they complete their study program.

Out of Status: When a person has a visa or status, but stays past its expiration date or does something else to violate its terms, that person is said to have "fallen out of status" (sometimes abbreviated "OOS"). That usually means that the person is at risk of removal from the United States. For students, it's sometimes possible to apply for reinstatement of status (see Reinstatement).

Public Charge: The immigration law term for an immigrant who has insufficient financial support and goes on welfare.

Reinstatement: Students who violate the rules concerning their visa or status will need to apply to the INS for reinstatement. The application process is discussed in Chapter 11.

Removal: A relatively new legal term combining the former terms "exclusion" and "deportation." Removal now means the process of sending an alien back to his or her home country because he or she is (or has become) inadmissible or deportable. (Before the laws changed in the 1990s, "exclusion" meant sending a person back before they'd entered the United States, and "deportation" meant sending someone away who was already in the United States.)

Service Center: An INS office responsible for accepting and making decisions on particular applications from people in specified geographical areas. Unlike the INS District Offices, the Service Centers are not open to the public; all communication must be by letter, with limited telephone access. Though inconvenient to work with, you may have no choice—an application that must be decided by a Service Center will not be accepted or decided by a District Office. For information on Service Centers locations, call the INS information line at 800-375-5283 or see the INS website at http://www.ins.usdoj.gov/graphics/fieldoffices/statemap.htm.

Sponsor (noun): Someone who is sponsoring an immigrant or nonimmigrant financially, by signing an Affidavit of Support on the person's behalf.

Status: In the INS's vocabulary, to have "status" means to have a legal right (temporary or permanent) to remain in the United States. For example, people on student visas are in student status.

Time Bars: The common name for the three or ten years that a person may have to spend outside the United States as a penalty for having previously lived here illegally for six months or more. See Chapter 2, Section B, for details.

Tourist Visa: The non-technical term for a B-2 visitor visa, covered in this book.

United States Code: See Immigration and Nationality Act.

Unlawful Time: "Unlawful" is a legal term referring to time spent in the United States without a valid visa or other legal right to be here. How much time a person has spent in the United States unlawfully has become extremely significant, for reasons explained in Chapter 2, Section B.

Visa: A right to enter the United States. Physically, the visa usually appears as a stamp in the applicant's passport, given by a United States consulate overseas. Different types of visas have different names, usually with letter codes. For example, a "B" visa is a visitor visa and an "F" visa is a student visa.

Visa Waiver Program: A program that allows citizens of certain countries to enter the United States as tourists without a visa and stay for up to 90 days. For details and a list of countries, see Chapter 1, Section A, and the State Department website at http://www.travel.state.gov/vwp.html. This used to be called the Visa Waiver Pilot Program, when it was a temporary, test program. But in the year 2000, Congress made this program a permanent part of the law.

Visitor Visa: The more technical term for a B-2 tourist visa, covered in this book. There is also a visitor visa for business visitors, called a B-1.

Waiver: An application filed in combination with an application for a visa or other immigration benefit, asking the INS or consulate to overlook, or forgive, something that would normally make that person ineligible for an immigration benefit or for entry to the United States. Only certain problems can be waived.

Work Permit: See Employment Authorization Document (EAD), above. ■

INS Photo Instructions

Form M-378, U.S. Immigration & Naturalization Service

U. S. IMMIGRATION & NATURALIZATION SERVICE

COLOR PHOTOGRAPH SPECIFICATIONS

IDEAL PHOTOGRAPH
◄

IMAGE MUST FIT INSIDE THIS
BOX ►

THE PICTURE AT LEFT IS IDEAL SIZE, COLOR, BACKGROUND, AND POSE. THE IMAGE SHOULD BE 30MM (1 3/16IN) FROM THE HAIR TO JUST BELOW THE CHIN, AND 26MM (1 IN) FROM LEFT CHEEK TO RIGHT EAR. THE IMAGE MUST FIT IN THE BOX AT RIGHT.

THE PHOTOGRAPH

* THE OVERALL SIZE OF THE PICTURE, INCLUDING THE BACKGROUND, MUST BE AT LEAST 40MM (1 9/16 INCHES) IN HEIGHT BY 35MM (1 3/8IN) IN WIDTH.

* PHOTOS MUST BE FREE OF SHADOWS AND CONTAIN NO MARKS, SPLOTCHES, OR DISCOLORATIONS.

* PHOTOS SHOULD BE HIGH QUALITY, WITH GOOD BACK LIGHTING OR WRAP AROUND LIGHTING, AND MUST HAVE A WHITE OR OFF-WHITE BACKGROUND.

* PHOTOS MUST BE A GLOSSY OR MATTE FINISH AND UN-RETOUCHED.

* POLAROID FILM HYBRID #5 IS ACCEPTABLE; HOWEVER SX-70 TYPE FILM OR ANY OTHER INSTANT PROCESSING TYPE FILM IS UNACCEPTABLE. NON-PEEL APART FILMS ARE EASILY RECOGNIZED BECAUSE THE BACK OF THE FILM IS BLACK. ACCEPTABLE INSTANT COLOR FILM HAS A GRAY-TONED BACKING.

THE IMAGE OF THE PERSON

* THE DIMENSIONS OF THE IMAGE SHOULD BE 30MM (1 3/16 INCHES) FROM THE HAIR TO THE NECK JUST BELOW THE CHIN, AND 26MM (1 INCH) FROM THE RIGHT EAR TO THE LEFT CHEEK. IMAGE CANNOT EXCEED 32MM BY 28MM (1 1/4IN X 1 1/16IN).

* IF THE IMAGE AREA ON THE PHOTOGRAPH IS TOO LARGE OR TOO SMALL, THE PHOTO CANNOT BE USED.

* PHOTOGRAPHS MUST SHOW THE ENTIRE FACE OF THE PERSON IN A 3/4 VIEW SHOWING THE RIGHT EAR AND LEFT EYE.

* FACIAL FEATURES **MUST BE IDENTIFIABLE.**

* CONTRAST BETWEEN THE IMAGE AND BACKGROUND IS ESSENTIAL. PHOTOS FOR VERY LIGHT SKINNED PEOPLE SHOULD BE SLIGHTLY UNDER-EXPOSED. PHOTOS FOR VERY DARK SKINNED PEOPLE SHOULD BE SLIGHTLY OVER-EXPOSED.

SAMPLES OF UNACCEPTABLE PHOTOGRAPHS

INCORRECT POSE

IMAGE TOO LARGE

IMAGE TOO SMALL

IMAGE TOO DARK UNDER-EXPOSED

IMAGE TOO LIGHT

DARK BACKGROUND

OVER-EXPOSED

SHADOWS ON PIC

B

Addresses of INS Service Centers

The following is a list of the INS Service Center addresses to which you may need to send certain INS forms, including Forms I-539 (for a Change of Status, extension of stay or reinstatement of student status) and I-765 (for a work permit). Most of the Service Centers designate different Post Office boxes for receipt of the different forms, so always check this list before sending a new form. (In the future, if you need to submit forms not covered by this book, you'll need to see the INS website at http://www.ins.usdoj.gov/graphics/fieldoffices/statemap.htm for the appropriate address. If you do not have Internet access, call the INS information line at 800-375-5283.)

If you're in the United States as a tourist, choose the INS Service Center that covers the region where you are staying. If you're here as a student, choose the Service Center that covers the region where your school is located.

Alabama	Louisiana	South Carolina
Arkansas	Mississippi	Oklahoma
Florida	New Mexico	Tennessee
Georgia	North Carolina	Texas
Kentucky		

For Form I-539:
USINS Texas Service Center
P.O. Box 851182
Mesquite, TX 75185-1182

For Form I-765:
USINS Texas Service Center
P.O. Box 851041
Mesquite, TX 75185-1041

Arizona	California	Guam
Hawaii	Nevada	

For Form I-539:
INS/California Service Center
P.O. Box 10539
Laguna Niguel, CA 92607-1053

For Form I-765:
INS/California Service Center
P.O. Box 10765
Laguna Niguel, CA 92607-0765

Connecticut	New Jersey	Virginia
Delaware	New York	Virgin Islands
Maine	Pennsylvania	West Virginia
Maryland	Puerto Rico	District
Massachusetts	Rhode Island	of Columbia
New Hampshire	Vermont	

This Service Center does not have separate Post Office boxes for different applications.

USINS Vermont Service Center
75 Lower Welden St.
Saint Albans, VT 05479-0001

Alaska	Michigan	Oregon
Colorado	Minnesota	South Dakota
Idaho	Missouri	Utah
Illinois	Montana	Washington
Indiana	Nebraska	Wisconsin
Iowa	North Dakota	Wyoming
Kansas	Ohio	

For Form I-539:
INS/Nebraska Service Center
P.O. Box 87539
Lincoln, NE 68501-7539

For Form I-765:
USINS Nebraska Service Center
P.O. Box 87765
Lincoln, NE 68501-7765

INS District Offices

Anchorage, Alaska
620 E. 10th Avenue, Suite 102
Anchorage, AK 99501

Atlanta, Georgia
Martin Luther King Jr. Federal Bldg.
77 Forsythe Street, SW
Room G-85
Atlanta, GA 30303-3427

Baltimore, Maryland
Fallon Federal Bldg.
31 Hopkins Plaza
Baltimore, MD 21201

Boston, Massachusetts
John F. Kennedy Federal Bldg.
Government Center, Room 1700
Boston, MA 02203-0701

Buffalo, New York
Federal Center
130 Delaware Ave.
Buffalo, NY 14202-2404

Chicago, Illinois
10 W. Jackson Blvd., Room 610
Chicago, IL 60604

Cleveland, Ohio
A.J.C. Federal Bldg.
1240 E. 9th St., Room 1917
Cleveland, OH 44199-2085

Dallas, Texas
8101 N. Stemmons Freeway
Dallas, TX 75247

Denver, Colorado
4730 Paris Street
Denver, CO 80239

Detroit, Michigan
333 Mount Elliott St.
Detroit, MI 48207-4381
313-259-8560

El Paso, Texas
1545 Hawkins Blvd.
El Paso, TX 79925

Harlingen, Texas
2102 Teege Avenue
Harlingen, TX 78550

Helena, Montana
2800 Skyway Drive
Helena, MT 59602

Honolulu, Hawaii
595 Ala Moana Blvd.
Honolulu, HI 96813

Houston, Texas
126 Northpoint
Houston, TX 77060

Kansas City, Missouri
9747 Northwest Conant Ave.
Kansas City, MO 64153

Los Angeles, California
300 N. Los Angeles Street
Room 1001
Los Angeles, CA 90012
213-894-6249

Miami, Florida
7880 Biscayne Blvd.
Miami, FL 33138-4797

New Orleans, Louisiana
701 Loyola Avenue
Room T-8011
New Orleans, LA 70113-1912
504-589-6326

New York, New York
Jacob K. Javits Federal Building
26 Federal Plaza
New York, NY 10278-0127

Newark, New Jersey
Federal Building
970 Broad Street
Newark, NJ 07102-2506

Omaha, Nebraska
3736 S. 132nd Street
Omaha, NE 68144

Philadelphia, Pennsylvania
1600 Callowhill St.
Philadelphia, PA 19130-4106

Phoenix, Arizona
2035 N. Central Ave.
Phoenix, AZ 85004

Portland, Maine
176 Gannett Dr.
So. Portland, ME 04106-6909

Portland, Oregon
Federal Building
511 NW Broadway
Portland, OR 97209

St. Paul, Minnesota
2901 Metro Drive, Suite 100
Bloomington, MN 55425
612-313-9001

San Antonio, Texas
8940 Four Winds
San Antonio, TX 78239

San Diego, California
880 Front Street
San Diego, CA 92101

San Francisco, California
Appraisers Building
630 Sansome Street
San Francisco, CA 94111

San Juan, Puerto Rico
San Patricio Office Center
7 Tabonuco St., Suite 100
Guaynabo, PR 00968

Seattle, Washington
815 Airport Way South
Seattle, WA 98134

Washington, D.C.
4420 N. Fairfax Drive
Arlington, VA 22003-1611

Tear-Out INS and Consular Forms

Form No.	Form Name
OF-156	Nonimmigrant Visa Application
I-134	Affidavit of Support
I-538	Certification by Designated School Official
I-539	Application to Extend/Change Nonimmigrant Status
I-539 Supp. 1	Supplement-1 to Application to Extend/Change Nonimmigrant Status
I-765	Application for Employment Authorization

PLEASE TYPE OR PRINT YOUR ANSWERS IN THE SPACE PROVIDED BELOW EACH ITEM.

1. SURNAMES OR FAMILY NAMES (*Exactly as in Passport*)

2. FIRST NAME AND MIDDLE NAME (*Exactly as in Passport*)

3. OTHER NAMES (*Maiden, Religious, Professional, Aliases*)

4. DATE OF BIRTH (*mm-dd-yyyy*)

8. PASSPORT NUMBER

5. PLACE OF BIRTH
City, Province | Country

DATE PASSPORT ISSUED (*mm-dd-yyyy*)

6. NATIONALITY

7. SEX
☐ MALE
☐ FEMALE

DATE PASSPORT EXPIRES (*mm-dd-yyyy*)

9. HOME ADDRESS (*Include apartment no., street, city, province, and postal zone*)

10. NAME AND STREET ADDRESS OF PRESENT EMPLOYER OR SCHOOL (*Postal box number unacceptable*)

11. HOME TELEPHONE NO.

12. BUSINESS TELEPHONE NO.

13. MARITAL STATUS
☐ Married ☐ Single ☐ Widowed ☐ Divorced ☐ Separated
If married, give name and nationality of spouse

14. NAMES AND RELATIONSHIPS OF PERSONS TRAVELING WITH YOU
(NOTE: *A separate application must be made for a visa for each traveler, regardless of age.*)

15. HAVE YOU EVER APPLIED FOR A U.S. NONIMMIGRANT VISA?
☐ NO ☐ YES

HAVE YOU EVER APPLIED FOR A U.S. IMMIGRANT VISA?
☐ NO ☐ YES

WHERE? _____

WHEN? _____

VISA WAS ISSUED ☐   VISA WAS REFUSED ☐

16. HAS YOUR U.S. VISA EVER BEEN CANCELED?
☐ NO ☐ YES

WHERE? _____
WHEN? _____
BY WHOM? _____

17. Bearers of visitor visas may generally not work or study in the U.S.
DO YOU INTEND TO WORK IN THE U.S.? ☐ NO ☐ YES
If YES, explain.

18. DO YOU INTEND TO STUDY IN THE U.S.? ☐ NO ☐ YES
If YES, write name and address of school as it appears on Form I-20.

DO NOT WRITE IN THIS SPACE

B-1/B-2 MAX   B-1 MAX   B-2 MAX

OTHER_____ MAX
Visa Classification

MULT OR_____
Number Applications

MONTHS_____
Validity

L.O. CHECKED

ON_____ BY _____

ISSUED/REFUSED

ON_____ BY _____

UNDER SEC.   214(b)   221(g)

OTHER:_____ INA

REFUSAL REVIEWED BY _____

19. PRESENT OCCUPATION (*If retired, state past occupation*)

20. WHO WILL FURNISH FINANCIAL SUPPORT, INCLUDING TICKETS?

21. AT WHAT ADDRESS WILL YOU STAY IN THE U.S.A.?

22. WHAT IS THE PURPOSE OF YOUR TRIP?

23. WHEN DO YOU INTEND TO ARRIVE IN THE U.S.A.?

24. HOW LONG DO YOU PLAN TO STAY IN THE U.S.A.?

25. HAVE YOU EVER BEEN IN THE U.S.A.?
☐ NO ☐ YES
WHEN? _____
FOR HOW LONG?_____

NONIMMIGRANT VISA APPLICATION

COMPLETE ALL QUESTIONS ON REVERSE OF FORM

4

26. HAVE YOU OR ANYONE ACTING FOR YOU EVER INDICATED TO A U.S. CONSULAR OR IMMIGRATION EMPLOYEE A DESIRE TO IMMIGRATE TO THE U.S., OR HAVE YOU EVER ENTERED A U.S. VISA LOTTERY?

☐ NO   ☐ YES

HAS ANYONE EVER FILED AN IMMIGRANT VISA PETITION ON YOUR BEHALF?

☐ NO   ☐ YES

HAS A LABOR CERTIFICATION FOR EMPLOYMENT IN THE U.S. EVER BEEN REQUESTED BY YOU OR ON YOUR BEHALF?

☐ NO   ☐ YES

27. ARE ANY OF THE FOLLOWING IN THE U.S., RESIDE IN THE U.S., OR HAVE U.S. LEGAL PERMANENT RESIDENCE? (Circle YES or NO and indicate that person's status in the U.S., i.e., studying, working, permanent resident, U.S. citizen, etc.)

YES NO   Husband/Wife _____   YES NO   Fiance/Fiancee _____   YES NO   Brother/Sister _____

YES NO   Father/Mother _____   YES NO   Son/Daughter _____   _____

28. WHERE HAVE YOU LIVED FOR THE PAST FIVE YEARS? DO NOT INCLUDE PLACES YOU HAVE VISITED FOR PERIODS OF SIX MONTHS OR LESS.

Countries	Cities	Approximate Dates *(mm-dd-yyyy)*

29. IMPORTANT: ALL APPLICANTS MUST READ AND CHECK THE APPROPRIATE BOX FOR EACH ITEM.

A visa may not be issued to persons who are within specific categories defined by law as inadmissible to the United States (except when a waiver is obtained in advance). Are any of the following applicable to you?

- Have you ever been afflicted with a communicable disease of public health significance, a dangerous physical or mental disorder, or been a drug abuser or addict? [212(a)(1)]   ☐ YES ☐ NO

- Have you ever been arrested or convicted for any offense or crime, even though subject of a pardon, amnesty or other similar legal action? Have you ever unlawfully distributed or sold a controlled substance (drug), or been a prostitute or procurer for prostitutes? [212(a)(2)]   ☐ YES ☐ NO

- Do you seek to enter the United States to engage in export control violations, subversive or terrorist activities, or any other unlawful purpose? Are you a member or representative of a terrorist organization as currently designated by the U.S. Secretary of State? Have you ever participated in persecutions directed by the Nazi government of Germany; or have you ever participated in genocide? [212(a)(3)]   ☐ YES ☐ NO

- Have you ever been refused admission to the U.S., or the subject of a deportation hearing, or sought to obtain or assist others to obtain a visa, entry into the U.S., or sought to obtain a visa or any U.S. immigration benefit by fraud or willful misrepresentation? Have you attended a U.S. public elementary school on student (F) status, or a public secondary school without reimbursing the school after November 30, 1996? [212(a)(6)]   ☐ YES ☐ NO

- Have you ever departed or remained outside the United States to avoid military service? [212(a)(8)]

- Have you ever violated the terms of a U.S. visa, or been unlawfully present in, or deported from, the United States? [212(a)(9)]   ☐ YES ☐ NO

- Have you ever withheld custody of a U.S. citizen child outside the United States from a person granted legal custody by a U.S. court, voted in the United States in violation of any law or   ☐ YES ☐ NO
- regulation, or renounced U.S. citizenship for the purpose of avoiding taxation? [212(a)(10)]   ☐ YES ☐ NO

A YES answer does not automatically signify ineligibility for a visa, but if you answered YES to any of the above, or if you have any question in this regard, a personal appearance at this office is recommended. If an appearance is not possible at this time, attach a statement of facts in your case to this application.

30. I certify that I have read and understood all the questions set forth in this application and the answers I have furnished on this form are true and correct to the best of my knowledge and belief. I understand that any false or misleading statement may result in the permanent refusal of a visa or denial of entry into the United States. I understand that possession of a visa does not entitle the bearer to enter the United States of America upon arrival at port of entry if he or she is found inadmissible.

DATE OF APPLICATION *(mm-dd-yyyy)* _____

APPLICANT'S SIGNATURE _____

If this application has been prepared by a travel agency or another person on your behalf, the agent should indicate name and address of agency or person with appropriate signature of individual preparing form.

SIGNATURE OF PERSON PREPARING FORM _____
(If other than applicant)

DO NOT WRITE IN THS SPACE

37 mm x 37 mm

PHOTO

Glue photo here

OPTIONAL FORM 156   PAGE 2
10-2000
U.S. Department of State

(Answer All Items: Fill in with Typewriter or Print in Block Letters in Ink.)

I, _____ residing at _____
(Name)   (Street and Number)

(City)	(State)	(Zip Code if in U.S.)	(Country)

BEING DULY SWORN DEPOSE AND SAY:

1. I was born on_____ at _____
(Date)   (City)   (Country)

    If you are **not** a native born United States citizen, answer the following as appropriate:

    a. If a United States citizen through naturalization, give certificate of naturalization number _____

    b. If a United States citizen through parent(s) or marriage, give citizenship certificate number _____

    c. If United States citizenship was derived by some other method, attach a statement of explanation.

    d. If a lawfully admitted permanent resident of the United States, give "A" number _____

2. That I am _____ years of age and have resided in the United States since (date) _____

3. That this affidavit is executed in behalf of the following person:

Name		Gender	Age
Citizen of (Country)	Marital Status	Relationship to Sponsor	
Presently resides at (Street and Number)	(City)	(State)	(Country)

    Name of spouse and children accompanying or following to join person:

Spouse	Gender	Age	Child		Gender	Age
Child	Gender	Age	Child		Gender	Age
Child	Gender	Age	Child		Gender	Age

4. That this affidavit is made by me for the purpose of assuring the United States Government that the person(s) named in item 3 will not become a public charge in the United States.

5. That I am willing and able to receive, maintain and support the person(s) named in item 3. That I am ready and willing to deposit a bond, if necessary, to guarantee that such person(s) will not become a public charge during his or her stay in the United States, or to guarantee that the above named person(s) will maintain his or her nonimmigrant status, if admitted temporarily and will depart prior to the expiration of his or her authorized stay in the United States.

6. That I understand this affidavit will be binding upon me for a period of three (3) years after entry of the person(s) named in item 3 and that the information and documentation provided by me may be made available to the Secretary of Health and Human Services and the Secretary of Agriculture, who may make it available to a public assistance agency.

7. That I am employed as, or engaged in the business of_____ with _____
(Type of Business)   (Name of concern)

    at _____
(Street and Number)   (City)   (State)   (Zip Code)

I derive an annual income of *(if self-employed, I have attached a copy of my last income tax return or report of commercial rating concern which I certify to be true and correct to the best of my knowledge and belief. See instructions for nature of evidence of net worth to be submitted.)* $_____

I have on deposit in savings banks in the United States $_____

I have other personal property, the reasonable value of which is $_____

OVER

I have stocks and bonds with the following market value, as indicated on the attached list, which I certify to be true and correct to the best of my knowledge and belief. $ _____

I have life insurance in the sum of $ _____

With a cash surrender value of $ _____

I own real estate valued at $ _____

With mortgage(s) or other encumbrance(s) thereon amounting to $ _____

Which is located at _____

(Street and Number)   (City)   (State)   (Zip Code)

8. That the following persons are dependent upon me for support: *(Place an "x" in the appropriate column to indicate whether the person named is wholly or partially dependent upon you for support.)*

Name of Person	Wholly Dependent	Partially Dependent	Age	Relationship to Me

9. That I have previously submitted affidavit(s) of support for the following person(s). If none, state *"None."*

Name _____ Date submitted _____

10. That I have submitted visa petition(s) to the Immigration and Naturalization Service on behalf of the following person(s). If none, state none.

Name _____ Relationship _____ Date submitted _____

11. *(Complete this block only if the person named in the item 3 will be in the United States temporarily.)*

That I ☐ intend ☐ do not intend, to make specific contributions to the support of the person named in item 3. *(If you check "intend," indicate the exact nature and duration of the contributions. For example, if you intend to furnish room and board, state for how long and, if money, state the amount in United States dollars and state whether it is to be given in a lump sum, weekly or monthly, or for how long.)*

_____

_____

_____

Oath or Affirmation of Sponsor

I acknowledge at that I have read Part III of the Instructions, *Sponsor and Alien Liability,* and am aware of my responsibilities as an immigrant sponsor under the *Social Security Act, as amended,* and the *Food Stamp Act, as amended.*

I swear (affirm) that I know the contents of this affidavit signed by me and the statements are true and correct.

Signature of sponsor _____

Subscribed and sworn to (affirmed) before me this _____ day of _____, _____,

at _____ . My commission expires on _____

Signature of Officer Administering Oath _____ Title _____

If affidavit prepared by other than sponsor, please complete the following: I declare that this document was prepared by me at the request of the sponsor and is based on all information of which I have knowledge.

_____ (Signature)   _____ (Address)   _____ (Date)

U.S. Department of Justice
Immigration and Naturalization Service

Affidavit of Support

INSTRUCTIONS

I. Execution of Affidavit.

A separate affidavit must be submitted for each person. You, as the sponsor, must sign the affidavit in your full, true and correct name and affirm or make it under oath. If you are in the United States, the affidavit may be sworn to or affirmed before an immigration officer without the payment of fee, or before a notary public or other officer authorized to administer oaths for general purposes, in which case the official seal or certificate of authority to administer oaths must be affixed. If you are **outside the United States** the affidavit must be sworn to or affirmed before a United States consular or immigration officer.

II. Supporting Evidence.

The sponsor must submit, in duplicate, evidence of income and resources, as appropriate.

A . Statement from an officer of the bank or other financial institution in which you have deposits giving the following details regarding your account:

1. date account opened
2. total amount deposited for the past year
3. present balance

B. Statement of your employer on business stationery, showing:

1. date and nature of employment
2. salary paid
3. whether position is temporary or permanent

C. If self-employed:

1. copy of last income tax return filed, or
2. report of commercial rating concern

D. List containing serial numbers and denominations of bonds and name of record owner(s).

III. Sponsor and Alien Liability.

Effective October 1, 1980, amendments to section 1614(f) of the Social Security Act and Part A of Title XVI of the Social Security Act establish certain requirements for determining the eligibility of aliens who apply for the first time for Supplemental Security Income (SSI) benefits. Effective October 1, 1981, amendments to section 415 of the Social Security Act establish similar requirements for determining the eligibility of aliens who apply for the first time for Aid to Families with Dependent Children (AFDC) benefits. Effective December 22, 1981, amendments to the Food Stamp Act of 1977 affect the eligibility of alien participation in the Food Stamp Program. These amendments require that the income and resources of any person, who as the sponsor of an alien's entry into the United States, executes an affidavit of support or similar agreement on behalf of the alien, and the income and resources of the sponsor's spouse *(if living with the sponsor)* shall be deemed to be the income and resources of the alien under formulas for determining eligibility for SSI, AFDC and Food Stamp benefits during the three years following the alien's entry into the United States.

An alien applying for SSI must make available to the Social Security Administration documentation concerning his or her income and resources and those of the sponsor, including information that was provided in support of the application for an immigrant visa or adjustment of status. An alien applying for AFDC or Food Stamps must make similar information available to the State public assistance agency. The Secretary of Health and Human Services and the Secretary of Agriculture are authorized to obtain copies of any such documentation submitted to INS or the Department of State and to release such documentation to a State public assistance agency.

Sections 1621(e) and 415(d) of the Social Security Act and subsection 5(i) of the Food Stamp Act also provide that an alien and his or her sponsor shall be jointly and severably liable to repay any SSI, AFDC or Food Stamp benefits that are incorrectly paid because of misinformation provided by a sponsor or because of a sponsor's failure to provide information. Incorrect payments that are not repaid will be withheld from any subsequent payments for which the alien or sponsor are otherwise eligible under the Social Security Act or Food Stamp Act, except that the sponsor was without fault or where good cause existed.

These provisions do not apply to the SSI, AFDC or Food Stamp eligibility of aliens admitted as refugees, granted political asylum by the Attorney General, or Cuban/ Haitian entrants as defined in section 501(e) of P.L. 96-422 and of dependent children of the sponsor or sponsor's spouse. The provisions also do not apply to the SSI or Food Stamp eligibility of an alien who becomes blind or disabled after admission to the United States for permanent residency.

IV. Authority/ Use/ Penalties.

Authority for the collection of the information requested on this form is contained in 8 USC 1182(a)(15),1184(a) and 1258. The information will be used principally by INS, or by any consular officer to whom it may be furnished, to support an alien's application for benefits under the Immigration and Nationality Act and specifically the assertion that he or she has adequate means of financial support and will not become a public charge. Submission of the information is voluntary. It may also, as a matter of routine use, be disclosed to other federal, state, local and foreign law enforcement and regulatory agencies, including the Department of Health and Human Services, Department of Agriculture, Department of State, Department of Defense and any component thereof (if the deponent has served or is serving in the armed forces of the United States), Central Intelligence Agency, and individuals and organizations during the course of any investigation to elicit further information required to carry out Service functions. Failure to provide the information may result in the denial of the alien's application for a visa or his or her removal from the United States.

Privacy Act Notice.

We ask for the information on this form, and associated evidence, to determine if you have established eligibility for the immigration benefit you are seeking. Our legal right to ask for this information is in 8 USC 1203 and 1225. We may provide this information to other government agencies. Failure to provide this information and any requested evidence may delay a final decision or result in denial of your request.

Paperwork Reduction Act Notice.

We try to create forms and instructions that are accurate, can be easily understood and which impose the least possible burden on you to provide us with information. Often this is difficult because some immigration laws are very complex. The estimated average time to complete and file this application is 20 minutes per application. If you have comments regarding the accuracy of this estimate or suggestions for making this form simpler, you can write to the Immigration and Naturalization Service, HQPDI, 425 I Street, N.W., Room 4034, Washington, D.C. 20536; OMB No. 1115-0005. **DO NOT MAIL YOUR COMPLETED APPLICATION TO THIS ADDRESS.**

U.S. Department of Justice
Immigration and Naturalization Service

Certification by Designated School Official

SECTION A. This section must be completed by student as appropriate (Please print or type) :

1. Name: *(Family in CAPS)*   *(First)*   *(Middle)*   2. Date of birth:

3. Student admission number: 4. Date first granted F-1 or M-1 status:

5. Level of education being sought: 6. Student's major field of study:

7. Describe the proposed employment for practical training:

Beginning date :   Ending date: Number of hours per week:

8. List all periods of previously authorized employment for practical training:

A. Curricular or work/study:	B. Post completion of studies

Signature of student: _____ Date: _____

SECTION B. This Section must be completed by the designated school official of the school the student is attending or was last authorized to attend:

9. I hereby certify that:

    The student named above:

    ☐ Is taking a full course of study at this school, and the expected date of completion is: _____

    ☐ Is taking less than a full course of study at this school because: _____

    ☐ Completed the course of study at this school on (date): _____

    ☐ Did not complete the course of study. Terminated attendance on (date): _____

    Check one:

☐ A. The employment is for practical training in the student's field of study. The student has been in the educational program for at least 9 months and is eligible for the requested practical training in accordance with INS regulations at 8CFR 214.2(f) (10).

☐ B. The endorsement for off-campus employment is based on the wage-and-labor attestation filed by the employer in accordance with the requirements set forth by the Secretary of Labor. The student has been in F-1 status for at least one year and is in good academic standing. Copy of the employer's attestation is attached.

☐ C. The employment is for an internship with a recognized international organization and is within the scope of the organization's sponsorship. The student has been in F-1 status for at least 9 months and is in good academic standing.

10. Name and title of DSO.	Signature:	Date:
11. Name of school:	School file number:	Telephone no.:

For Official Use only
Microfilm Index Number:

(See instructions on reverse)

Form I-538 (Rev. 09/18/00)Y

Instructions

A student seeking authorization for off-campus employment (F-1 only) or practical training (F-1 and M-1) must submit as supporting documentation to Form I-765, Application for Employment Authorization, a certification by the designated school official (DSO) of the school the student was last authorized to attend. Certification by the DSO is required of all students (F-1 and M-1) seeking authorization for employment of campus or practical training, including required or optional curricular practical training. The DSO must certify on Form I-538 that the proposed employment is directly related to the student's field of study. A copy of the DSO's certification must be mailed to the STSC date processing center, P.O. Box 140, Highway 25 South, London, KY. 40741.

All students requesting school certification must complete questions 1 through 6. Students requesting recommendation for practical training must complete questions 7 and 8. Answers to questions 7 through 9 may be continued on this page if needed.

M-1 students seeking extensions of stay must submit a completed Form I-539, Application to Extend time of Temporary Stay, supported by a current Form I-20M-N as appropriate.

Reporting Burden

Public reporting burden for this collection of information is estimated to average 4 minutes per response, including the time for reviewing instructions, searching existing data sources, gathering and maintaining the data needed, and completing and reviewing the collection of information. Send comments regarding this burden estimate or any other aspect of this collection of information, including suggestions for reducing this burden, to: U.S. Department of Justice, Immigration and Naturalization Service, HQPDI, 425 I Street N.W., Room 4034, Washington, DC 20536; OMB No. 1115-0060. **DO NOT MAIL YOUR COMPLETED APPLICATION TO THIS ADDRESS.**

Comments: _____

_____

_____

_____

_____

_____

_____

_____

_____

_____

_____

_____

_____

Purpose of This Form.

You should use this form if you are one of the nonimmigrants listed below and wish to apply to the Immigration and Naturalization Service (INS) for an extension of stay or a change to another nonimmigrant status. In certain situations, you may be able to use this form to apply for an initial nonimmigrant status.

You may also use this form if you are a nonimmigrant F-1 or M-1 student applying for reinstatement.

Who May File/Initial Evidence.

Extension of Stay or Change of Status:

Nonimmigrants in the United States may apply for an extension of stay or a change of status on this form, except as noted in these instructions under the heading, "Who May Not File."

Multiple Applicants.

You may include your spouse and your unmarried children under age 21 years as co-applicants in your application for the same extension or change of status, if you are all now in the same status or they are all in derivative status.

Required Documentation - Form I-94, Nonimmigrant Arrival/Departure Record.

You are required to submit with your Form I-539 application the original or copy, front and back, of Form I-94 of each person included in your application. If the original Form I-94 or required copy cannot be submitted with this application, include a Form I-102, Application for Replacement/Initial Nonimmigrant Arrival/Departure Document, with the required fee.

Valid Passport.

If you were required to have a passport to be admitted into the United States, you must maintain the validity of your passport during your nonimmigrant stay. If a required passport is not valid when you file the Form I-539 application, submit an explanation with your form.

Additional Evidence.

You may be required to submit additional evidence noted in these instructions.

Nonimmigrant Categories.

This form may be used by the following nonimmigrants listed in alphabetical order:

- **An A, Ambassador, Public Minister, or Career Diplomatic or Consular Officer** and their immediate family members.

  You must submit a copy, front and back, of the Form I-94 of each person included in the application and a Form I-566, Interagency Record of Individual Requesting Change, Adjustment to, or from, A to G Status; or Requesting A, G or NATO Dependent Employment Authorization, certified by the Department of State to indicate your accredited status.

NOTE: An A-1 or A-2 nonimmigrant is not required to pay a fee with the I-539 application.

- **An A-3, Attendant or Servant of an A nonimmigrant** and the A-3's immediate family members.

  You must submit a copy, front and back, of the Form I-94 of each person included in the application.

  The application must be filed with:

  -- a copy of your employer's Form I-94 or approval notice demonstrating A status;

  -- an original letter from your employer describing your duties and stating that he or she intends to personally employ you; and arrangements you have made to depart the U.S.; and

  -- an original Form I-566, certified by the Department of State, indicating your employer's continuing accredited status.

- **A B-1, Visitor for Business or B-2, Visitor for Pleasure.**

  If you are filing for an extension/change, you must file your application with the original Form I-94 of each person included in your application. In addition, you must submit a written statement explaining in detail:

  -- the reasons for your request;

  -- why your extended stay would be temporary, including what arrangements you have made to depart the United States; and

  -- any effect the extended stay may have on your foreign employment or residency.

- **Dependents of an E, Treaty Trader or Investor.**

  If you are filing for an extension/change of status as the dependent of an E, this application must be submitted with:

  -- the Form I-129, Petition for Alien Worker, filed for that E or a copy of the filing receipt noting that the petition is pending with INS;

  -- a copy of the E's Form I-94 or approval notice showing that he or she has already been granted status to the period requested on your application; and

  -- evidence of relationship (example: birth or marriage certificate).

NOTE: An employer or investor should file Form I-129 to request an extension/change to E status for an employee, prospective employee, or the investor. Dependents of E employees should file for an extension/change of status on this form, not Form I-129.

- **An F-1, Academic Student.**

  To request a change to F-1 status or to apply for reinstatement as an F-1 student, you must submit your original Form I-94, as well as the original Form I-94 of each person included in the application.

Your application must include your original Form I-20 (Certificate of Eligibility for Nonimmigrant Student) issued by the school where you will study. To request either a change or reinstatement, you must submit documentation that demonstrates your ability to pay for your studies and support yourself while you are in the United States.

F-1 Extensions:

Do not use this form to request an extension. For information concerning extensions, contact your designated school official at your institution.

F-1 Reinstatement:

You will only be considered for reinstatement as an F-1 student if you establish:

-- that the violation of status was due solely to circumstances beyond your control or that failure to reinstate you would result in extreme hardship;

-- you are pursuing or will pursue a full course of study;

-- you have not been employed without authorization; and

-- you are not in removal proceedings.

- **A G, Designated Principal Resident Representative of a Foreign Government** and his or her immediate family members.

You must submit a copy, front and back, of the Form I-94, of each person included in the application, and a Form I-566, certified by the Department of State to indicate your accredited status.

NOTE: A G-1 through G-4 nonimmigrant is not required to pay a fee with the I-539 application.

- **A G-5, Attendant or Servant of a G nonimmigrant** and the G-5's immediate family members.

You must submit a copy, front and back, of the Form I-94 of each person included in the application.

The application must also be filed with:

-- a copy of your employer's Form I-94 or approval notice demonstrating G status;

-- an original letter from your employer describing your duties and stating that he or she intends to personally employ you; and arrangements you have made to depart the U.S.; and

-- an original Form I-566, certified by the Department of State, indicating your employer's continuing accredited status.

- **Dependents of an H, Temporary Worker.**

If you are filing for an extension/change of status as the dependent of an employee who is an H temporary worker, this application must be submitted with:

-- the Form I-129 filed for that employee or a copy of the filing receipt noting that the petition is pending with INS;

-- a copy of the employee's Form I-94 or approval notice showing that he or she has already been granted status to the period requested on your application; and

-- evidence of relationship (example: birth or marriage certificate).

NOTE: An employer should file Form I-129 to request an extension/change to H status for an employee or prospective employee. Dependents of such employees should file for an extension/change of status on this form, not on Form I-129.

- **A J-1, Exchange Visitor.**

If you are requesting a change of status to J-1, your application must be filed with an original Form IAP-66, Certificate of Eligibility for Exchange Visitor Status, issued by your program sponsor. You must also submit your original Form I-94, as well as the original Form I-94 of each person included in the application.

NOTE: A J-1 exchange visitor whose status is for the purpose of receiving graduate medical education or training, who has not received the appropriate waiver, is ineligible for any change of status. Also, a J-1 subject to the foreign residence requirement, who has not received a waiver of that requirement, is only eligible for a change of status to A or G.

J-1 Extensions:

If you are seeking an extension, contact the responsible officer of your program for information about this procedure.

J-1 Reinstatement:

If you are a J-1 exchange visitor seeking reinstatement, you may need to apply for such approval by the Department of State's Office of Education and Cultural Affairs. Contact the responsible officer at your sponsoring program for information on the reinstatement filing procedure.

- **Dependents of an L, Intracompany Transferee.**

If you are filing for an extension/change of status as the dependent of an employee who is an L intracompany transferee, this application must be submitted with:

-- the Form I-129 filed for that employee or a copy of the filing receipt noting that the petition is pending with INS;

-- a copy of the employee's Form I-94 or approval notice showing that he or she has already been granted status to the period requested on your application; and

-- evidence of relationship (example: birth or marriage certificate).

NOTE: An employer should file Form I-129 to request an extension/change to L status for an employee or prospective employee. Dependents of such employees should file for an extension/change of status on this form, not on Form I-129.

- **An M-1, Vocational or Non-Academic Student.**

To request a change to or extension of M-1 status, or apply for reinstatement as an M-1 student, you must submit your original Form I-94, as well as the original Form I-94 of each person included in the application.

Your application must include your original Form I-20 issued by the school where you will study. To request either extension/change or reinstatement, you must submit documentation that demonstrates your ability to pay for your studies and support yourself while you are in the United States.

M-1 Reinstatement:

You will only be considered for reinstatement as an M-1 student if you establish:

-- that the violation of status was due solely to circumstances beyond your control or that failure to reinstate you would result in extreme hardship;

-- you are pursuing or will pursue a full course of study;

-- you have not been employed without authorization; and

-- you are not in removal proceedings.

NOTE: If you are an M-1 student, you are not eligible for a change to F-1 status and you are not eligible for a change to any H status, if the training you received as an M-1 helps you qualify for the H status. Also, you may not be granted a change to M-1 status for training to qualify for H status.

- **An N-1 or N-2, Parent or Child of an Alien Admitted as a Special Immigrant** under section 101(a)(27)(I) of the Immigration and Nationality Act (I&NA).

  You must file the application with a copy, front and back, of your Form I-94 and a copy of the special immigrant's permanent resident card and proof of the relationship (example: birth or marriage certificate).

- **Dependents of an O, Alien of Extraordinary Ability or Achievement.**

  If you are filing for an extension/change of status as the dependent of an employee who is classified as an O nonimmigrant, this application must be submitted with:

  -- the Form I-129 filed for that employee or a copy of the filing receipt noting that the petition is pending with INS;

  -- a copy of the employee's Form I-94 or approval notice showing that he or she has already been granted status to the period requested on your application; and

  -- evidence of relationship (example: birth or marriage certificate).

  NOTE: An employer should file Form I-129 to request an extension/change to an O status for an employee or prospective employee. Dependents of such employees should file for an extension/change of status on this form, not on Form I-129.

- **Dependents of a P, Artists, Athletes and Entertainers.**

  If you are filing for an extension/change of status as the dependent of an employee who is classified as a P nonimmigrant, this application must be submitted with:

  -- the Form I-129 filed for that employee or a copy of the filing receipt noting that the petition is pending with INS;

  -- a copy of the employee's Form I-94 or approval notice showing that he or she has already been granted status to the period requested on your application; and

  -- evidence of relationship (example: birth or marriage certificate).

  NOTE: An employer should file Form I-129 to request an extension/change to P status for an employee or prospective employee. Dependents of such employees should file for an extension/change of status on this form, not on Form I-129.

- **Dependents of an R, Religious Worker.**

  If you are filing for an extension/change of status as the dependent of an employee who is classified as an R nonimmigrant, this application must be submitted with:

  -- the Form I-129 filed for that employee or a copy of the filing receipt noting that the petition is pending with INS;

  -- a copy of the employee's Form I-94 or approval notice showing that he or she has already been granted status to the period requested on your application; and

  -- evidence of relationship (example: birth or marriage certificate).

- **TD Dependents of TN Nonimmigrants.**

  TN nonimmigrants are citizens of Canada or Mexico who are coming as business persons to the United States to engage in business activities at a professional level, pursuant to the North American Free Trade Agreement (NAFTA). The dependents (spouse or unmarried minor children) of a TN nonimmigrant are designated as TD nonimmigrants. A TD nonimmigrant may accompany or follow to join the TN professional. TD nonimmigrants may not work in the United States.

  The Form I-539 shall be used by a TD nonimmigrant to request an extension of stay or by an applicant to request a change of nonimmigrant status to TD classification.

  -- If applying for an extension of stay at the same time as the TN professional, the TD dependent shall file Form I-539 along with the Form I-129, for the TN professional. This filing procedure is also followed if the applicant is applying for a change of nonimmigrant status to TD at the same time that the professional is applying for a change of nonimmigrant status to TN.

  -- If the applicant is not applying for an extension of stay at the same time that the TN professional is applying for an extension, or applying for a change of nonimmigrant status to TD after the nonimmigrant obtains status, the applicant must present a copy of the TN's Form I-94 to establish that the TN is maintaining valid nonimmigrant status.

- **A V, Spouse or Child of a Lawful Permanent Resident.**
  Use this Form I-539 if you are physically present in the United States and wish to request initial status or change status to a V nonimmigrant, or to request an extension of your current V nonimmigrant status.

  Applicants should follow the instructions on this form and the attached instructions to Supplement A to Form I-539, Filing Instructions for V Nonimmigrants. The supplement contains additional information and the location where V applicants must file their applications.

  Notice to V Nonimmigrants.
  The Legal Immigration Family Equity Act (LIFE), signed into law on December 21, 2000, created a new V visa. This nonimmigrant status allows certain persons to reside legally in the United States and to travel to and from the United States while they wait to obtain lawful permanent residence.

In order to be eligible for a V visa, all of the following conditions must be met:

- you must be the spouse or the unmarried child of a lawful permanent resident:
- a Form I-130, Petition for Alien Relative, must have been filed for you by your permanent resident spouse on or before December 21, 2000; and
- you must have been waiting for at least three years after the Form I-130 was filed for you:

Or you must be the unmarried child (under 21 years of age) of a person who meets the three requirements listed above.

V visa holders will be eligible to adjust to lawful permanent resident status once an immigrant visa becomes available to them. While they are waiting, V visa holders may be authorized to work following their submission and INS approval of their Form I-765, Application for Employment Authorization.

WARNING: Be advised that persons in V status who have been in the United States illegally for more than 180 days may trigger the grounds of inadmissibility regarding unlawful presence (for the applicable 3-year or 10-year bar to admission) if they leave the United States. Their departure may prevent them from adjusting status as a permanent resident.

Who May Not File.

You may not be granted an extension or change of status if you were admitted under the Visa Waiver Program or if your current status is:

- an alien in transit (C) or in transit without a visa (TWOV);
- a crewman (D); or
- a fiancé(e) or dependent of a fiancé(e) (K)(1) or (K)(2).

A spouse (K-3) of a U.S. citizen and their children (K-4), accorded such status pursuant to the LIFE Act, may not change to another nonimmigrant status.

EXCEPTION: A K-3 and K-4 are eligible to apply for an extension of status. They should file for an extension during the processing of the Form I-130 filed on their behalf and up to completion of their adjustment of status application.

NOTE: Any nonimmigrant (A to V) may not change their status to K-3 or K-4.

General Filing Instructions.

Please answer all questions by typing or clearly printing in black ink. Indicate that an item is not applicable with "N/A." If the answer is "none," please so state. If you need extra space to answer any item, attach a sheet of paper with your name and your alien registration number (A#), if any, and indicate the number of the item to which the answer refers. Your application must be filed with the required initial evidence. Your application must be properly signed and filed with the correct fee. If you are under 14 years of age, your parent or guardian may sign your application.

Copies.

If these instructions state that a copy of a document may be filed with this application and you choose to send us the original, we will keep that original document in our records.

Translations.

Any foreign language document must be accompanied by a full English translation that the translator has certified as complete and correct, and by the translator's certification that he or she is competent to translate the foreign language into English.

When and Where to File.

You must submit an application for extension of stay or change of status before your current authorized stay expires. We suggest you file at least 45 days before your stay expires, or as soon as you determine your need to change status. Failure to file before the expiration date may be excused if you demonstrate when you file the application that:

- the delay was due to extraordinary circumstances beyond your control;
- the length of the delay was reasonable;
- you have not otherwise violated your status;
- you are still a bona fide nonimmigrant; and
- you are not in removal proceedings.

If you are filing as a V applicant, follow the instructions on the Supplement A to Form I-539, Filing Instructions for V Nonimmigrants, on where to file your application.

If you are filing for reinstatement as an F-1 or M-1 student, submit this application at your local INS office.

If you are a TD filing for an extension of stay or requesting a change to a nonimmigrant TD status, mail your application to: USINS Nebraska Service Center, P.O. Box 87539, Lincoln, NE 68501-7539.

If you are an E dependent filing for an extension of stay and you live in Alabama, Arkansas, Connecticut, Delaware, District of Columbia, Florida, Georgia, Kentucky, Louisiana, Maine, Maryland, Massachusetts, Mississippi, New Hampshire, New Jersey, New Mexico, New York, North Carolina, Oklahoma, Pennsylvania, Puerto Rico, Rhode Island, South Carolina, Tennessee, Texas, the U.S. Virgin Islands, Vermont, Virginia or West Virginia, mail your application to: USINS Texas Service Center, Box 85182, Mesquite, TX 75185-1182.

If you are an E dependent filing for an extension of stay and you live anywhere else in the United States, mail your application to: USINS California Service Center, P.O. Box 10539, Laguna Niguel, CA 92607-1053.

In all other instances, mail your application to the INS Service Center having jurisdiction over where you live in the United States.

If you live in Connecticut, Delaware, District of Columbia, Maine, Maryland, Massachusetts, New Hampshire, New Jersey, New York, Pennsylvania, Puerto Rico, Rhode Island, the U.S. Virgin Islands, Vermont, Virginia or West Virginia, mail your application to: USINS Vermont Service Center, 75 Lower Welden Street, St. Albans, VT 05479-0001.

If you live in Alabama, Arkansas, Florida, Georgia, Kentucky, Louisiana, Mississippi, New Mexico, North Carolina, Oklahoma, South Carolina, Tennessee or Texas, mail your application to: USINS Texas Service Center, Box 85182, Mesquite, TX 75185-1182.

If you live in Arizona, California, Guam, Hawaii or Nevada, mail your application to: USINS California Service Center, P.O. Box 10539, Laguna Niguel, CA 92607-1053.

If you live elsewhere in the United States, mail your application to: **USINS Nebraska Service Center, P.O. Box 87539, Lincoln, NE 68501-7539.**

Fee.

The fee for this application is $120.00, except for certain A and G nonimmigrants who are not required to pay a fee, as noted in these instructions. The fee must be submitted in the exact amount. It cannot be refunded. **DO NOT MAIL CASH.**

All checks and money orders must be drawn on a bank or other institution located in the United States and must be payable in U.S. currency.

The check or money order should be made payable to the Immigration and Naturalization Service, except that:

-- if you live in Guam and are filing this application in Guam, make your check or money order payable to the "Treasurer, Guam."

-- if you live in the U.S. Virgin Islands and are filing this application in the U.S. Virgin Islands, make your check or money order payable to the "Commissioner of Finance of the Virgin Islands."

Checks are accepted subject to collection. An uncollected check will render the application and any document issued invalid. A charge of $30.00 will be imposed if a check in payment of a fee is not honored by the bank on which it is drawn.

Processing Information.

Acceptance.

Any application that is not signed or is not accompanied by the correct fee will be rejected with a notice that the application is deficient. You may correct the deficiency and resubmit the application. An application is not considered properly filed until accepted by INS.

Initial Processing.

Once the application has been accepted, it will be checked for completeness. If you do not completely fill out the form, or file it without the required initial evidence, you will not establish a basis for eligibility and we may deny your application.

Requests for More Information or Interview.

We may request more information or evidence or we may request that you appear at an INS office for an interview. We may also request that you submit the originals of any copy. We will return these originals when they are no longer required.

Decision.

An application for extension of stay, change of status, initial status or reinstatement, may be approved at the discretion of INS. You will be notified in writing of the decision on your application.

Penalties.

If you knowingly and willfully falsify or conceal a material fact or submit a false document with this application, we will deny the benefit you are seeking and may deny any other immigration benefit. In addition, you will face severe penalties provided by law and may be subject to criminal prosecution.

Privacy Act Notice.

We ask for the information on this form and associated evidence to determine if you have established eligibility for the immigration benefit you are seeking. Our legal right to ask for this information is in 8 U.S.C. 1184 and 1258. We may provide this information to other government agencies. Failure to provide this information and any requested evidence may delay a final decision or result in denial of your request.

Information and Forms.

For information on immigration laws, regulations and procedures and to order INS forms, call our **National Customer Service Center** toll-free at **1-800-375-5283** or visit the INS internet web site at **www.ins.gov.**

Paperwork Reduction Act Notice.

An agency may not conduct or sponsor an information collection and a person is not required to respond to a collection of information unless it displays a currently valid OMB control number. We try to create forms and instructions that are accurate, can easily be understood and which impose the least possible burden on you to provide us with information. Often this is difficult because some immigration laws are very complex. The estimate average time to complete and file this application is as follows: (1) 10 minutes to learn about the law and form; (2) 10 minutes to complete the form; and (3) 25 minutes to assemble and file the application; for a total estimated average of 45 minutes per application. If you have comments regarding the accuracy of this estimate, or suggestions for making this form simpler, you can write to Immigration and Naturalization Service, HQPDI, 425 I Street, N.W., Room 4034, Washington, D.C. 20536; OMB No. 1115-0093. **DO NOT MAIL YOUR COMPLETED APPLICATION TO THIS ADDRESS.**

Mailing Label - Complete the following mailing label and submit this page with your application if you are required to submit your original Form I-94.

Name and address of applicant.

Name

Street Number and Name

City, State, and Zip Code

Your Form I-94, Arrival/Departure Record is attached. It has been amended to show the extension of stay/change of status granted.

U.S. Department of Justice
Immigration and Naturalization Service

OMB No. 1115-0093; Expires 7/31/04

Application to Extend/Change Nonimmigrant Status

START HERE - Please Type or Print.

	FOR INS USE ONLY	

Part 1.   Information about you.

Family Name	Given Name	Middle Initial

Address -
In care of -

Street Number and Name		Apt. #

City	State	Zip Code	Daytime Phone #

Country of Birth	Country of Citizenship

Date of Birth (MM/DD/YYYY)	Social Security # (if any)	A # (if any)

Date of Last Arrival Into the U.S.	I-94 #

Current Nonimmigrant Status	Expires on (MM/DD/YYYY)

FOR INS USE ONLY

Returned	Receipt
Date	
Resubmitted	
Date	
Reloc Sent	
Date	
Reloc Rec'd	
Date	

Part 2.   Application type. *(See instructions for fee.)*

1. I am applying for: *(Check one.)*
   a. ☐ An extension of stay in my current status.
   b. ☐ A change of status. The new status I am requesting is: _____
   c. ☐ Other: *(Describe grounds of eligibility.)* _____
2. Number of people included in this application: *(Check one.)*
   a. ☐ I am the only applicant.
   b. ☐ Members of my family are filing this application with me.
      The total number of people (including me) in the application is: _____
      (Complete the supplement for each co-applicant.)

☐ Applicant Interviewed on
_____
Date

☐ *Extension Granted to (Date):*
_____

Change of Status/Extension Granted
New Class: From *(Date)*: _____
_____   To *(Date)*: _____

Part 3.   Processing information.

1. I/We request that my/our current or requested status be extended until (MM/DD/YYYY): _____
2. Is this application based on an extension or change of status already granted to your spouse, child or parent?
   ☐ No ☐ Yes, Receipt # _____
3. Is this application based on a separate petition or application to give your spouse, child or parent an extension or change of status?   ☐ No ☐ Yes, filed with this I-539.
   ☐ Yes, filed previously and pending with INS. INS receipt number: _____
4. If you answered "Yes" to Question 3, give the name of the petitioner or applicant:

   If the petition or application is pending with INS, also give the following information:

Office filed at _____   Filed on (MM/DD/YYYY) _____

If Denied:
☐ Still within period of stay
☐ S/D to: _____
☐ Place under docket control

Remarks:

Action Block

Part 4.   Additional information.

1. For applicant #1, provide passport information: Valid to: (MM/DD/YYYY)
   Country of Issuance

2. Foreign Address: Street Number and Name	Apt. #

City or Town	State or Province

Country	Zip/Postal Code

To be Completed by *Attorney or Representative*, if any

☐ Fill in box if G-28 is attached to represent the applicant.

ATTY State License #

Form I-539 (Rev. 09/04/01)Y

Part 4. Additional information.

3. **Answer the following questions. If you answer "Yes" to any question, explain on separate sheet of paper.**

		Yes	No
a.	Are you, or any other person included on the application, an applicant for an immigrant visa?		
b.	Has an immigrant petition ever been filed for you or for any other person included in this application?		
c.	Has a Form I-485, Application to Register Permanent Residence or Adjust Status, ever been filed by you or by any other person included in this application?		
d.	Have you, or any other person included in this application, ever been arrested or convicted of any criminal offense since last entering the U.S.?		
e.	Have you, or any other person included in this application, done anything that violated the terms of the nonimmigrant status you now hold?		
f.	Are you, or any other person included in this application, now in removal proceedings?		
g.	Have you, or any other person included in this application, been employed in the U.S. since last admitted or granted an extension or change of status?		

- If you answered "Yes" to Question 3f, give the following information concerning the removal proceedings on the attached page entitled "Part 4. Additional information. Page for answers to 3f and 3g." Include the name of the person in removal proceedings and information on jurisdiction, date proceedings began and status of proceedings.

- If you answered "No" to Question 3g, fully describe how you are supporting yourself on the attached page entitled "Part 4. Additional information. Page for answers to 3f and 3g." Include the source, amount and basis for any income.

- If you answered "Yes" to Question 3g, fully describe the employment on the attached page entitled "Part 4. Additional information. Page for answers to 3f and 3g." Include the name of the person employed, name and address of the employer, weekly income and whether the employment was specifically authorized by INS.

Part 5. Signature. (Read the information on penalties in the instructions before completing this section. You must file this application while in the United States.)

I certify, under penalty of perjury under the laws of the United States of America, that this application and the evidence submitted with it is all true and correct. I authorize the release of any information from my records which the Immigration and Naturalization Service needs to determine eligibility for the benefit I am seeking.

Signature	Print your Name	Date

Please note: If you do not completely fill out this form, or fail to submit required documents listed in the instructions, you may not be found eligible for the requested benefit and this application will have to be denied.

Part 6. Signature of person preparing form, if other than above. (Sign below.)

I declare that I prepared this application at the request of the above person and it is based on all information of which I have knowledge.

Signature	Print your Name	Date

Firm Name and Address	Daytime Phone Number *(Area Code and Number)*
	Fax Number *(Area Code and Number)*

(Please remember to enclose the mailing label with your application.)

Part 4. Additional information. Page for answers to 3f and 3g.

If you answered "Yes" to Question 3f in Part 4 on page 3 of this form, give the following information concerning the removal proceedings. Include the name of the person in removal proceedings and information on jurisdiction, date proceedings began and status of proceedings.

If you answered "No" to Question 3g in Part 4 on page 3 of this form, fully describe how you are supporting yourself. Include the source, amount and basis for any income.

If you answered "Yes" to Question 3g in Part 4 on page 3 of this form, fully describe the employment. Include the name of the person employed, name and address of the employer, weekly income and whether the employment was specifically authorized by INS.

Supplement -1
Attach to Form I-539 when more than one person is included in the petition or application.
(List each person separately. Do not include the person named in the form.)

Family Name	Given Name	Middle Name	Date of Birth (MM/DD/YYYY)
County of Birth	County of Citizenship	Social Security # (if any)	A # (if any)
Date of Arrival (MM/DD/YYYY)		I-94 #	
Current Nonimmigrant Status:		Expires On (MM/DD/YYYY)	
Country Where Passport Issued		Expiration Date (MM/DD/YYYY)	

Family Name	Given Name	Middle Name	Date of Birth (MM/DD/YYYY)
County of Birth	County of Citizenship	Social Security # (if any)	A # (if any)
Date of Arrival (MM/DD/YYYY)		I-94 #	
Current Nonimmigrant Status:		Expires On (MM/DD/YYYY)	
Country Where Passport Issued		Expiration Date (MM/DD/YYYY)	

Family Name	Given Name	Middle Name	Date of Birth (MM/DD/YYYY)
County of Birth	County of Citizenship	Social Security # (if any)	A # (if any)
Date of Arrival (MM/DD/YYYY)		I-94 #	
Current Nonimmigrant Status:		Expires On (MM/DD/YYYY)	
Country Where Passport Issued		Expiration Date (MM/DD/YYYY)	

Family Name	Given Name	Middle Name	Date of Birth (MM/DD/YYYY)
County of Birth	County of Citizenship	Social Security # (if any)	A # (if any)
Date of Arrival (MM/DD/YYYY)		I-94 #	
Current Nonimmigrant Status:		Expires On (MM/DD/YYYY)	
Country Where Passport Issued		Expiration Date (MM/DD/YYYY)	

Family Name	Given Name	Middle Name	Date of Birth (MM/DD/YYYY)
County of Birth	County of Citizenship	Social Security # (if any)	A # (if any)
Date of Arrival (MM/DD/YYYY)		I-94 #	
Current Nonimmigrant Status:		Expires On (MM/DD/YYYY)	
Country Where Passport Issued		Expiration Date (MM/DD/YYYY)	

If you need additional space, attach a separate sheet(s) of paper.
Place your name, A # if any, date of birth, form number and application date at the top of the sheet(s) of paper.

Application for Employment Authorization

Instructions for
Application for Employment Authorization

The Immigration and Naturalization Service (INS) recommends that you retain a copy of your completed application for your records.

Index

Part 1. General.

Purpose of the Application.　　Certain aliens who are temporarily in the United States may file a Form I-765, Application for Employment Authorization, to request an Employment Authorization Document (EAD). Other aliens who are authorized to work in the United States without restrictions should also use this form to apply to the INS for a document evidencing such authorization. Please review Part 2 ELIGIBILITY CATEGORIES to determine whether you should use this form.

If you are a Lawful Permanent Resident, a Conditional Resident, or a nonimmigrant authorized to be employed with a specific employer under 8 CFR 274a.12(b), please do **NOT** use this form.

Definitions.

Employment Authorization Document (EAD): Form I-688; Form I-688A; Form I-688B; or any successor document issued by the INS as evidence that the holder is authorized to work in the United States.

Renewal EAD: an EAD issued to an eligible applicant at or after the expiration of a previous EAD issued under the same category.

Replacement EAD: an EAD issued to an eligible applicant when the previously issued EAD has been lost, stolen, mutilated, or contains erroneous information, such as a misspelled name.

Interim EAD: an EAD issued to an eligible applicant when the INS has failed to adjudicate an application within 90 days of receipt of a properly filed EAD application or within 30 days of a properly filed initial EAD application based on an asylum application filed on or after January 4, 1995. The interim EAD will be granted for a period not to exceed 240 days and is subject to the conditions noted on the document.

Part 2. Eligibility Categories.

The INS adjudicates a request for employment authorization by determining whether an applicant has submitted the required information and documentation, and whether the applicant is eligible. In order to determine your eligibility, you must identify the category in which you are eligible and fill in that category in question 16 on the Form I-765. Enter only **one** of the following category numbers on the application form.

NOTE: **Category (c)(13) is no longer available.** You may not renew or replace your EAD based on (c)(13). If you have an EAD based on that category, please review the categories below to determine if you are eligible under another category.

Asylee, (granted asylum) -- (a)(5). File your EAD application with a copy of the INS letter granting you asylum. It is not necessary to apply for an EAD as an asylee until 90 days before the expiration of your current EAD.

Refugee--(a)(3). File your EAD application with either a copy of your Form I-590, Registration for Classification as Refugee, approval letter or a copy of a Form I-730, Refugee/Asylee Relative Petition, approval notice.

Paroled as a Refugee--(a)(4). File your EAD application with a copy of your Form I-94, Departure Record.

Asylum Applicant (with a pending asylum application) who Filed for Asylum on or after January 4, 1995--(c)(8). If you filed a Form I-589, Request for Asylum and for Withholding of Deportation, on or after January 4, 1995, you must wait at least 150 days before you are eligible to apply for an EAD. If you file your EAD application early, it will be denied and you will have to file a new application. File your EAD application with:

- A copy of the INS acknowledgement mailer which was mailed to you; or
- Other evidence that your Form I-589 was filed with the INS; or
- Evidence that your Form I-589 was filed with an Immigration Judge at the Executive Office for Immigration Review (EOIR); or
- Evidence that your asylum application remains under administrative or judicial review.

Asylum Applicant (with a pending asylum application) who Filed for Asylum and for Withholding of Deportation Prior to January 4, 1995 and is *NOT* in Exclusion or Deportation Proceedings--(c)(8). You may file your EAD application at any time; however, it will only be granted if the INS finds that your asylum application is not frivolous. File your EAD application with:

- A complete copy of your previously filed Form I-589; and
- A copy of your INS receipt notice; or
- A copy of the INS acknowledgement mailer; or
- Evidence that your Form I-589 was filed with EOIR; or
- Evidence that your asylum application remains under administrative or judicial review; or
- Other evidence that you filed an asylum application.

Asylum Applicant (with a pending asylum application) who Filed an Initial Request for Asylum Prior to January 4,1995, and *IS IN* Exclusion or Deportation Proceedings--(c)(8). If you filed your Request for Asylum and Withholding of Deportation (Form I-589) prior to January 4. 1995 and you ARE IN exclusion or deportation proceedings, file your EAD application with:

- A date-stamped copy of your previously filed Form I-589; or
- A copy of Form I-221, Order to Show Cause and Notice of Hearing, or Form I-122, Notice to Applicant for Admission Detained for Hearing Before Immigration Judge; or
- A copy of EOIR-26, Notice of Appeal, date stamped by the Office of the Immigration Judge; or
- A date-stamped copy of a petition for judicial review or for *habeas corpus* issued to the asylum applicant; or
- Other evidence that you filed an asylum application with EOIR.

Asylum Application under the ABC Settlement Agreement--(c)(8)

If you are a Salvadoran or Guatemalan national eligible for benefits under the ABC settlement agreement, American Baptist Churches v. Thornburgh, 760 F. Supp. 976 (N.D. Cal. 1991), please follow the instructions contained in this section when filing your Form I-765.

You must have asylum application (Form I-589) on file either with INS or with an immigration judge in order to receive work authorization. Therefore, please submit evidence that you have previously filed an asylum application when you submit your EAD application. You are not required to submit this evidence when you apply, but it will help INS process your request efficiently.

If you are renewing or replacing your EAD, you must pay the filing fee.

Mark your application as follows:

- Write "ABC" in the top right corner of your EAD application. You must identify yourself as an ABC class member if you are applying for an EAD under the ABC settlement agreement.

- Write "(c)(8)" in Section 16 of the application.

You are entitled to an EAD without regard to the merits of your asylum claim. Your application for an EAD will be decided within 60 days if: (1) you pay the filing fee, (2) you have a complete, pending asylum application on file, and (3) write "ABC" in the top right corner of your EAD application. If you do not pay the filing fee for an initial EAD request, your request may be denied if INS finds that your asylum application is frivolous.

However, if you cannot pay the filing fee for an EAD, you may qualify for a fee waiver under 8 CFR 103.7(c). See instructions in Part 4 regarding eligibility for a fee waiver.

NACARA Section 203 Applicants who are eligible to apply for NACARA relief with INS--(c)(10)

See the instructions to Form I-881, Application for Suspension of Deportation or Special Rule Cancellation of Removal, to determine if you are eligible to apply for NACARA 203 relief with INS.

If you are eligible, follow the instructions below and submit your Form I-765 at the same time you file your Form I-881 application with INS:

- If you are filing a Form I-881 with INS, file your EAD application at the same time and at the same filing location. Your response to question 16 on the Form I-765 should be "(c)(10)."

- If you have already filed your I-881 application at the service center specified on the Form I-881, and now wish to apply for employment authorization, your response to question 16 on Form I-765 should be "(c)(10)." You should file your EAD application at the Service Center designated in Part 5 of these instructions.

- If you are a NACARA Section 203 applicant who previously filed a Form I-881 with the INS, and the application is still pending, you may renew your EAD. Your response to question 16 on Form I-765 should be "(c)(10)." Submit the required fee and the EAD application to the service center designated in Part 5 of these instructions.

Deferred Enforced Departure (DED) / Extended Voluntary Departure--(a)(11). File your EAD application with evidence of your identity and nationality.

F-1 Student Seeking Optional Practical Training in an Occupation Directly Related to Studies--(c)(3)(i). File your EAD application with a Certificate of Eligibility of Nonimmigrant (F-1) Student Status (Form I-20 A-B/I-20 ID) endorsed by a designated school official within the past 30 days.

F-1 Student Offered Off-Campus Employment under the Sponsorship of a Qualifying International Organization--(c)(3)(ii). File your EAD application with the international organization's letter of certification that the proposed employment is within the scope of its sponsorship, and a Certificate of Eligibility of Nonimmigrant (F-1) Student Status--For Academic and Language Students (Form I-20 A-B/I-20 ID) endorsed by the designated school official within the past 30 days.

F-1 Student Seeking Off-Campus Employment Due to Severe Economic Hardship--(c)(3)(iii). File your EAD application with Form 1-20 A-B/I-20 ID, Certificate of Eligibility of Nonimmigrant (F-1) Student Status--For Academic and Language Students; Form I-538, Certification by Designated School Official, and any evidence you wish to submit, such as affidavits, which detail the unforeseen economic circumstances that cause your request, and evidence you have tried to find off-campus employment with an employer who has filed a labor and wage attestation.

J-2 Spouse or Minor Child of an Exchange Visitor--(c)(5). File your EAD application with a copy of your J-1's (principal alien's) Certificate of Eligibility for Exchange Visitor (J-1) Status (Form IAP-66). You must submit a written statement, with any supporting evidence showing, that your employment is not necessary to support the J-1 but is for other purposes.

M-1 Student Seeking Practical Training after Completing Studies--(c)(6). File your EAD application with a completed Form I-538, Application by Nonimmigrant Student for Extension of Stay, School Transfer, or Permission to Accept or Continue Employment, Form I-20 M-N, Certificate of Eligibility for Nonimmigrant (M-1) Status--For Vocational Students endorsed by the designated school official within the past 30 days.

Dependent of CCNAA E-1 Nonimmigrant--(c)(2). File your EAD application with the required certification from the American Institute in Taiwan if you are the spouse, or unmarried child, of an E-1 employee of the Coordination Council for North American Affairs.

Dependent of NATO Personnel--(c)(7). File your EAD application with a letter from the Department of Defense or NATO / SACLANT verifying your principal alien's status, your status, and your relationship to your principal alien.

N-8 or N-9 Nonimmigrant--(a)(7). File your EAD application with the required evidence listed in Part 3.

Family Unity Program--(a)(13). File your EAD application with a copy of the approval notice, if you have been granted status under this program. You may choose to file your EAD application concurrently with your Form I-817, Application for Voluntary Departure under the Family Unity Program. The INS may take up to 90 days from the date upon which you are granted status under the Family Unity Program to adjudicate your EAD application. If you were denied Family Unity status solely because your legalized spouse or parent first applied under the Legalization/SAW programs after May 5, 1988, file your EAD application with a new Form I-817 application and a copy of the original denial. However, if your EAD application is based on continuing eligibility under (c)(12), please refer to **Deportable Alien Granted Voluntary Departure.**

K-1 Nonimmigrant Fiance(e) of US. Citizen or K-2 Dependent--(a)(6). File your EAD application if you are filing within 90 days from the date of entry. This EAD cannot be renewed. Any EAD application other than for a replacement must be based on your pending application for adjustment under (c)(9).

Citizen of Micronesia or the Marshall Islands or Palau--(a)(8). File your EAD application if you were admitted to the United States as a citizen of the Federated States of Micronesia (CFA/FSM) or of the Marshall Islands (CFA/MIS) pursuant to agreements between the United States and the former trust territories.

B-1 Nonimmigrant who is the personal or domestic servant of a nonimmigrant employer--(c)(17)(i). File your EAD application with:

- Evidence from your employer that he or she is a B, E, F, H, I, J, L, M, O, P, R, or TN nonimmigrant and you were employed for at least one year by the employer before the employer entered the United States or your employer regularly employs personal and domestic servants and has done so for a period of years before coming to the United States; and

Evidence that you have either worked for this employer as a personal or domestic servant for at least one year or, evidence that you have at least one year's experience as a personal or domestic servant; and

Evidence establishing that you have a residence abroad which you have no intention of abandoning.

B-1 Nonimmigrant Domestic Servant of a US. Citizen--(c)(17)(ii). File your EAD application with:

- Evidence from your employer that he or she is a U.S. citizen; and

- Evidence that your employer has a permanent home abroad or is stationed outside the United States and is temporarily visiting the United States or the citizen's current assignment in the United States will not be longer than four (4) years; and

- Evidence that he or she has employed you as a domestic servant abroad for at least six (6) months prior to your admission to the United States.

B-1 Nonimmigrant Employed by a Foreign Airline--(c)(17)(iii). File your EAD application with a letter from the airline fully describing your duties and indicating that your position would entitle you to E nonimmigrant status except for the fact that you are not a national of the same country as the airline or because there is no treaty of commerce and navigation in effect between the United States and that country.

Temporary Protected Status (TPS)--(a)(12). File your EAD application with Form I-821, Application for Temporary Protected Status.

- Initial TPS-based application only: include evidence of identity and nationality as required by the Form I-821 instructions.

Temporary treatment benefits --(c)(19) -- For and EAD based on 8 CFR 244.5. Include evidence of nationality and identity as required by the Form I-821 instructions.

- Extension of TPS status: include a copy (front and back) of your last available TPS document: EAD, Form I-94 or approval notice.

- Registration for TPS only without employment authorization: file the Form I-765, Form I-821, and a letter indicating that this form is for registration purposes only. No fee is required for the Form I-765 filed as part of TPS registration. (Form I-821 has separate fee requirements.)

Note-- If you are using this application to register for TPS only and do not want to work in the United States, you must indicate this application is for registration puposes only. No fee is required to register.

Granted Withholding of Deportation--(a)(10). File your EAD application with a copy of the Immigration Judge's order. It is not necessary to apply for a new EAD until 90 days before the expiration of your current EAD.

Dependent of A-1 or A-2 Foreign Government Officials--(c)(1). File your EAD application with a Form I-566, Inter-Agency Record of Individual Requesting Change/Adjustment to or from A or G Status; or Requesting A, G, or NATO Dependent Employment Authorization, with the Department of State endorsement.

Dependent of G-1, G-3 or G-4 Nonimmigrant--(c)(4). File your EAD application with a Form I-566, Inter-Agency Record of Individual Requesting Change/Adjustment to or from A or G Status; or Requesting A, G, or NATO Dependent Employment Authorization with the Department of State endorsement if you are the dependent of a qualifying G-1, G-3 or G-4 officer of, representative to, or employee of an international organization and you hold a valid nonimmigrant status.

Adjustment Applicant--(c)(9). File your EAD application with a copy of the receipt notice or other evidence that your Form I-485, Application for Permanent Residence, is pending. You may file Form I-765 together with your Form I-485.

Applicant for Suspension of Deportation--(c)(10). File your EAD application with evidence that your Form I-256A, Application for Suspension of Deportation, is pending.

Paroled in the Public Interest--(c)(11). File your EAD application if you were paroled into the United States for emergent reasons or reasons strictly in the public interest.

Deportable Alien Granted Voluntary Departure--(c)(12). File your EAD application with a copy of the order or notice granting voluntary departure, and evidence establishing your economic need to work.

Deferred Action--(c)(14). File your EAD application with a copy of the order, notice or document placing you in deferred action and evidence establishing economic necessity for an EAD.

Adjustment Applicant Based on Continuous Residence Since January 1, 1972--(c)(16). File your EAD application with your Form I-485, Application for Permanent Residence; a copy of your receipt notice; or other evidence that the Form I-485 is pending.

Final Order of Deportation--(c)(18). File your EAD application with a copy of the order of supervision and a request for employment authorization which may be based on, but not limited to the following:

- Existence of economic necessity to be employed;

- Existence of a dependent spouse and/or children in the United States who rely on you for support; and

- Anticipated length of time before you can be removed from the United States.

LIFE Legalization applicant -- (c)(24). We encourage you to file your EAD application together with your Form I-485, Application for Permanent Residence to facilitate processing. However, you may file Form I-765 at a later date with evidence that you were a CSS, LULAC, or Zambrano class member applicant before October 1, 2000 and with a copy of the receipt notice or other evidence that your Form I-485 is pending.

Part 3. Required Documentation With Each Application.

All applications must be filed with the documents required below, in addition to the evidence required for the category listed in Part 2 ELIGIBILITY CATEGORIES, with fee, if required.

If you are required to show economic necessity for your category (See Part 2), submit a list of your assets, income and expenses.

Please assemble the documents in the following order:

Your application with the filing fee. See Part 4 FEE for details.

If you are mailing your application to the INS, you must also submit:

- Form I-765 Signature Card. If one is not enclosed with your application, ask your local INS office for one. Sign the card in the blue box marked "signature". Your signature must fit within the blue box. DO NOT fold this card when you mail your application.

- A copy of Form I-94 Departure Record (front and back), if available.

- A copy of your last EAD (front and back).

- 2 photos with a white background taken no earlier than 30 days before submission to the INS. They should be unmounted; printed on thin paper; glossy; and unretouched. The photos should show a three-quarter front profile of the right side of your face, with your

right ear visible. Your head should be bare unless you are wearing a headdress as required by a religious order to which you belong. The photo should not be larger than 1 ½ X 1 ½ inches, with the distance from the top of the head to just below the chin about 1 1/4 inches. Lightly print your name and your A#, if known on the back of each photo with a pencil.

Part 4. Fee.

Applicants must pay a fee of $100 to file this form unless noted below. If a fee is required, it will not be refunded. Pay in the exact amount. Checks and money orders must be payable in U.S. currency. Make check or money order payable to "Immigration and Naturalization Service." If you live in Guam make your check or money order payable to "Treasurer, Guam." If you live in the U.S. Virgin Islands make your check or money order payable to "Commissioner of Finance of the Virgin Islands." A charge of $30.00 will be imposed if a check in payment of a fee is not honored by the bank on which it is drawn. Please do **not** send cash in the mail.

Initial EAD: If this is your initial application and you are applying under one of the following categories, a filing fee is not required:

- (a)(3) Refugee;
- (a)(4) Paroled as Refugee;
- (a)(5) Asylee;
- (a)(7) N-8 or N-9 nonimmigrant;
- (a)(8) Citizen of Micronesia, Marshall Islands or Palau;
- (a)(10) Granted Withholding of Deportation;
- (a)(11) Deferred Enforced Departure;
- (c)(1) or (c)(4) Dependent of certain foreign government or international organization personnel; or
  (c)(8) Applicant for asylum [an applicant filing under the special ABC procedures must pay the fee].

Renewal EAD: If this is a renewal application and you are applying under one of the following categories, a filing fee is not required:

- (a)(8) Citizen of Micronesia, Marshall Islands, or Palau.

- (a)(10) Granted Withholding of Deportation;
- (a)(11) Deferred Enforced Departure; or
- (c)(l) or (c)(4) Dependent of certain foreign government or international organization personnel.

Replacement EAD: If this is your replacement application and you are applying under one of the following categories, a filing fee is not required:

- (c)(1) or (c)(4) Dependent of certain foreign government or international organization personnel.

You may be eligible for a fee waiver under 8 CFR 103.7(c).

The INS will use The Community Service Administration Income Poverty Guidelines ("Poverty Guidelines") found at 45 CFR 1060.2 as the basic criteria in determining the applicant's eligibility when economic necessity is identified as a factor.

The Poverty Guidelines will be used as a guide, but not as a conclusive standard, in adjudicating fee waiver requests for employment authorization applications requiring a fee.

Part 5. Where to File.

If your response to question 16 is:
(a)(3), (a)(4), (a)(5), (a)(7), or (a)(8)

mail your application to:

> INS Service Center
> P.O. Box 87765
> Lincoln, NE 68501-7765

If your response to question 16 is:

(a)(6), (a)(11), (a)(13),
(c)(2), (c)(3)(i), (c)(3)(ii), (c)(3)(iii), (c)(5), (c)(6), (c)(7), (c)(8),
(c)(17)(i), (c)(17)(ii), or (c)(17)(iii)

mail your application based on your address to the appropriate Service Center:

If you live in: Connecticut, Delaware, the District of Columbia, Maine, Maryland, Massachusetts, New Hampshire, New Jersey, New York, Pennsylvania, Puerto Rico, Rhode Island, Vermont, Virginia, West Virginia or the U.S. Virgin Islands, mail your application to:

> INS Service Center
> 75 Lower Welden Street
> St. Albans, VT 05479-0001

If you live in: Arizona, California, Guam, Hawaii or Nevada, mail your application to:

> INS Service Center
> P.O. Box 10765
> Laguna Niguel, CA 92607-0765

If you live in: Alabama, Arkansas, Florida, Georgia, Kentucky, Louisiana, Mississippi, New Mexico, N. Carolina, Oklahoma, S. Carolina, Tennessee or Texas, mail your application to:

> INS Service Center
> P.O. Box 851041
> Mesquite, TX 75185-1041

If you live elsewhere in the U.S., mail your application to:

> INS Service Center
> P.O. Box 87765
> Lincoln, NE 68501-7765

If your response to question 16 is:

> (a)(10), (a)(12),
> (c)(1), (c)(4), (c)(11), (c)(12), (c)(14), (c)(16),
> (c)(18)

apply at the local INS office having jurisdiction over your place of residence.

LIFE Legalization applicants submit your application to:

If your response to question 16 is (c)(24), mail your application to:

> United States Immigration and Naturalization Service
> Post Office Box 7219
> Chicago, IL 60680-7219

NOTE:

If your response to question 16 is (c)(8) under the special ABC filing instructions and you are filing your asylum and EAD applications together, mail your application to the office where you are filing your asylum application.

If your response to question 16 is (c)(9), file your application at the same local INS office or Service Center where you submitted your adjustment application.

If your response to question 16 is (c)(10), and you are a NACARA 203 applicant eligible to apply for relief with the INS, or if your I-881 application is still pending with INS and you wish to renew your EAD, mail your EAD application with the required fee to the appropriate INS service center below:

- If you live in Alabama, Arkansas, Colorado, Connecticut, Delaware, the District of Columbia, Florida, Georgia, Louisiana, Maine, Maryland, Massachusetts, Mississippi, New Hampshire, New Jersey, New Mexico, New York, North Carolina, Oklahoma, Pennsylvania, Puerto Rico, Rhode Island, South Carolina, Tennessee, Texas, Utah, the Unites States Virgin Islands, Vermont, Virginia, West Virginia or Wyoming, mail your application to:

> USINS Vermont Service Center
> 75 Lower Welden St.
> St. Albans, VT 05479-0001

- If you live in Alaska, Arizona, California, the Commonwealth of Guam, Hawaii, Idaho, Illinois, Indiana, Iowa, Kansas, Kentucky, Michigan, Minnesota, Missouri, Montana, Nebraska, Nevada, North Dakota, Oregon, Ohio, South Dakota, Washington, or Wisconsin, mail your application to:

UNINS California Service Center
P.O. Box 10765
Laguna Niguel, CA 92607-0881

You should submit the fee for the EAD application on a separate check or money order. Do not combine your check or money order with the fee for the Form I-881.

If your response to question 16 is (c)(10) **and you are not eligible to apply for NACARA 203 relief with INS,** but you are eligible for other deportation or removal relief, apply at the local INS office having jurisdiction over your place of residence.

Part 6. Processing Information.

Acceptance. An application filed without the required fee, evidence, signature or photographs (if required) will be returned to you as incomplete. You may correct the deficiency and resubmit the application; however, an application is not considered properly filed until the INS accepts it. If your application is complete and filed at an INS Service Center, you will be mailed a Form I-797 receipt notice.

Decision on your application.

- **Approval.** If approved, your EAD will either be mailed to you or you may be required to appear at your local INS office to pick it up.

- **Request for evidence.** If additional information or documentation is required, a written request will be sent to you specifying the information or advising you of an interview.

- **Denial.** If your application cannot be granted, you will receive a written notice explaining the basis of your denial.

No decision

- **Interim EAD.** If you have not received a decision within 90 days of receipt by the INS of a properly filed EAD application or within 30 days of a properly filed initial EAD application based on an asylum application filed on or after January 4, 1995, you may obtain interim work

authorization by appearing in person at your local INS district office. You must bring proof of identity and any notices that you have received from the INS in connection with your application for employment authorization.

Part 7. Other Information.

Penalties for Perjury. All statements contained in response to questions in this application are declared to be true and correct under penalty of perjury. Title 18, United States Code, Section 1546, provides in part:

> . . . Whoever knowingly makes under oath, or as permitted under penalty of perjury under 1746 of Title 28, United States Code, knowingly subscribes as true, any false statement with respect to a material fact in any application, affidavit, or other document required by the immigration laws or regulations prescribed thereunder, or knowingly presents any such application, affidavit, or other document containing any such false statement-shall be fined in accordance with this title or imprisoned not more than five years, or both.

The knowing placement of false information on this application may subject you and/or the preparer of this application to criminal penalties under Title 18 of the United States Code. The knowing placement of false information on this application may also subject you and/or the preparer to civil penalties under Section 274C of the Immigration and Nationality Act (INA), 8 U.S.C. 1324c. Under 8 U.S.C. 1324c, a person subject to a final order for civil document fraud is deportable from the United States and may be subject to fines.

Authority for Collecting this Information. The authority to require you to file Form I-765, Application for Employment Authorization, when applying for employment authorization is found at 8 CFR 274A(b)(1)(C)(iii). Information you provide on your Form I-765 is used to determine whether you are eligible for employment authorization and for the preparation of your Employment Authorization Document if you are found eligible. Failure to provide all information as requested may result in the denial or rejection of this application. The information you provide may also be disclosed to other federal, state, local and foreign law enforcement and regulatory agencies during the course of the INS investigations.

Paperwork Reduction Act. A person is not required to respond to a collection of information unless it displays a currently valid OMB control number. The Immigration and Naturalization Service (INS) tries to create forms and instructions which are accurate and easily understood. Often this is difficult because immigration law can be very complex. The public reporting burden for this form is estimated to average three (3) hours and twenty-five (25) minutes per response, including the time for reviewing instructions, gathering and maintaining the data needed, and completing and reviewing the collection of information. The INS welcomes your comments regarding this burden estimate or any other aspect of this form, including suggestions for reducing this burden to Immigration and Naturalization Service, HQPDI, 425 I Street, N.W., Room 4034, Washington, DC 20536; OMB No. 1115-0163. **DO NOT MAIL YOUR COMPLETED APPLICATION TO THIS ADDRESS.**

U.S. Department of Justice
Immigration and Naturalization Service

OMB No. 1115-0163: Expires - 10/31/01

Application for Employment Authorization

Do Not Write in This Block

Remarks	Action Stamp	Fee Stamp
A#		

Applicant is filing under §274a.12 _____

☐ Application Approved. Employment Authorized / Extended (Circle One)

until ——————————————— (Date).
——————————————— (Date).

Subject to the following conditions: _____

☐ Application Denied.
☐ Failed to establish eligibility under 8 CFR 274a.12 (a) or (c).
☐ Failed to establish economic necessity as required in 8 CFR 274a.12(c) (14), (18) and 8 CFR 214.2(f)

I am applying for:
☐ Permission to accept employment
☐ Replacement (of lost employment authorization document).
☐ Renewal of my permission to accept employment (attach previous employment authorization document).

1. Name (Family Name in CAPS)　(First)　(Middle)

2. Other Names Used (Include Maiden Name)

3. Address in the United States (Number and Street)　(Apt. Number)

(Town or City)　(State/Country)　(ZIP Code)

4. Country of

5. Place of Birth (Town or City)　(State/Province)　(Country)

6. Date of Birth　7. Sex　☐ Male ☐ Female

8. Marital Status　☐ Married ☐ Single ☐ Widowed ☐ Divorced

9. Social Security Number (Include all Numbers you have ever used) (if

10. Alien Registration Number (A-Number) or I-94 Number (if any)

11. Have you ever before applied for employment authorization from INS?
☐ Yes (if yes, complete below)　☐ No
Which INS Office?　Date(s)

Results (Granted or Denied - attach all documentation)

12. Date of Last Entry into the U.S. (Month/Day/Year)

13. Place of Last Entry into the U.S.

14. Manner of Last Entry (Visitor, Student, etc.)

15. Current Immigration Status (Visitor, Student, etc.)

16. Go to Part 2 of the instructions, Eligibility Categories. In the space below, place the letter and number of the category you selected from the instructions (For example, (a)(8), (c)(17)(iii), etc.).

Eligibility under 8 CFR 274a.12

(　) (　) (　)

Certification

Your Certification: I certify, under penalty of perjury under the laws of the United States of America, that the foregoing is true and correct. Furthermore, I authorize the release of any information which the Immigration and Naturalization Service needs to determine eligibility for the benefit I am seeking. I have read the Instructions in Part 2 and have identified the appropriate eligibility category in Block 16.

Signature　Telephone Number　Date

Signature of Person Preparing Form, If Other Than Above: I declare that this document was prepared by me at the at the request of the applicant and is based on all information of which I have any knowledge.

Print Name　Addres　*Signature*　Date

Initial Receipt	Resubmitted	Relocated		Completed		
		Rec'd	Sent	Approved	Denied	Returned

Form I-765 (Rev. 4/24/01)Y

Tear-Out Checklists

Chapter 5, Applying for a Tourist Visa From Overseas:

    Tourist Visa Checklist

Chapter 6, Applying for a Change to Tourist Status in the U.S.

    U.S. Change of Status Checklist

Chapter 7, Applying for a Student Visa From Overseas

    Checklist for Student Visa Application

    Overseas Family Member's Checklist

Chapter 8, Applying for a Change to Student Status in the U.S.

    Checklist for Applying for Change of Status to Student

    Checklist for Family Members in the U.S.

Chapter 10, In the U.S. As a Tourist

    Checklist for Extension of Visitor Stay

Chapter 11, In the U.S. As a Student

    Checklist for Reinstatement Application

    Checklist for M-1 Student Transfer Application

    Checklist for M-1 Student Extension Application

    Checklist for Visa Renewals

Chapter 12, Can You Work While You Are in School?

    Checklist for Work Permit Based on Economic Hardship

    Checklist for Optional Practical Training Application

    Checklist for International Organization Internship Work Permit Application

    Checklist for Practical Training Work Permit Application

Tourist Visa Checklist

Here are all the items you'll need to present for your tourist visa application:

- ☐ Form OF-156
- ☐ valid passport
- ☐ two photographs
- ☐ application fee; currently $45
- ☐ documents showing the purpose of your trip
- ☐ documents showing your plan to remain in the United States for a limited time period
- ☐ documents showing that you have a residence in your home country and other binding ties that will draw you back
- ☐ documents showing that you will be able to support yourself financially while you are in the United States

U.S. Change of Status Checklist

Here are all the items you'll need to present for your application to change to tourist status within the United States:

- ☐ INS Form I-539
- ☐ original I-94 card
- ☐ documents showing you have not fallen out of status
- ☐ copy of valid passport
- ☐ application fee; currently $120
- ☐ documents showing the purpose of your stay
- ☐ documents showing your plan to remain in the United States for a limited time period
- ☐ documents showing that you have a residence in your home country and other ties that will draw you back
- ☐ documents showing that you will be able to support yourself financially while you are in the United States

Checklist for Student Visa Application

Here is what you will need to apply for your student visa.

- ☐ Form I-20 from your school
- ☐ Form OF-156, Nonimmigrant Visa Application
- ☐ valid passport
- ☐ documents showing that you will return to your home country
- ☐ documents showing your academic credentials
- ☐ documents showing that you can pay your tuition, fees and living expenses
- ☐ fee (currently $45 plus any reciprocity fee)
- ☐ two passport-style photos

Overseas Family Members' Checklist

- ☐ Form OF-156, Nonimmigrant Visa Application.
- ☐ proof of family member's relationship to you (copy of marriage or birth certificate)
- ☐ copy of your Form I-20AB or Form I-20 MN
- ☐ passport (valid for at least six months after the consular appointment)
- ☐ documents showing that your family members will return to your home country
- ☐ copies of your documents showing that you can pay your tuition, fees and the whole family's living expenses
- ☐ fee (currently $45)
- ☐ two passport-style photos

Checklist for Applying for Change of Status to Student

☐ Form I-539, Application to Extend/Change Non-immigrant Status

☐ Form I-20 A-B for F status applicants, and Form I-20 M-N for M status applicants (from your school)

☐ your I-94 card

☐ document showing that you will return to your home country

☐ documents showing your academic credentials

☐ documents showing that you can pay your tuition, fees and living expenses for you and any accompanying spouse or children

☐ documentation of any scholarships, fellowships, assistantships, grants or loans from your school, government or private sources

☐ documents showing that you have not fallen out of lawful immigration status in the United States

☐ fee (currently $120)

Checklist for Family Members in the U.S.

☐ Form I-539 Supplement-1

☐ proof of family member(s) relationship to you, such as copies of marriage certificate and/or birth certificate(s)

☐ family member(s) I-94 cards

☐ documents showing that they have not fallen out of lawful immigration status

☐ separate proof of reasons that they'll return to their home country

Checklist for Extension of Visitor Stay

- ☐ Form I-539
- ☐ fee, currently $120
- ☐ your original I-94 card
- ☐ copy of the page of your passport showing your picture and the expiration date
- ☐ written statement in support of your request
- ☐ other documents that support your extension request

Checklist for Reinstatement Application

Here's what you'll need to apply for reinstatement:

☐ Form I-539

☐ Form I-538 (optional, but it may speed up your application)

☐ new Form I-20, with your DSO's signature

☐ your I-94 card (original, for you and any family members)

☐ your written request for reinstatement

☐ proof of your continued ability to pay your tuition, fees and living expenses (recommended, not required)

☐ fee (currently $120)

Checklist for M-1 Student Transfer Application

- ☐ Form I-538
- ☐ fee (currently $70)
- ☐ your I-20 ID copy
- ☐ your I-94 card
- ☐ new I-20
- ☐ if your transfer is after six months of study, your written statement of explanation and any accompanying evidence

Checklist for M-1 Student Extension Application

☐ Form I-539, signed by DSO
☐ your form I-20 ID
☐ your I-94 card and those of any spouse and children
☐ fee (currently $120)

Checklist for Visa Renewals

- ☐ Form OF-156
- ☐ fee (currently $45 plus any reciprocity fee)
- ☐ passport good for at least six months
- ☐ two passport-style photos
- ☐ Form I-94 (original or copy)
- ☐ Form I-20 endorsed for reentry by your DSO
- ☐ transcripts and school records of your attendance
- ☐ documents showing that you can pay your tuition, fees and living expenses
- ☐ documents showing that you will return to your home country

Checklist for Work Permit Based on Economic Hardship

- ☐ Form I-538
- ☐ photocopy of your Form I-20 ID
- ☐ Form I-765
- ☐ Form I-765 Signature Card
- ☐ copy of the front and back of any previous work permits that you've received
- ☐ two photos, INS style
- ☐ supporting documents to show economic need
- ☐ sworn statement by you summarizing the reasons you need work authorization
- ☐ copy of the identity page and visa page from your passport
- ☐ copy of your I-94 card
- ☐ fee (currently $100)

Checklist for Optional Practical Training Application

☐ copy of Form I-20

☐ copy of Form I-20 ID

☐ Form I-538

☐ Form I-765

☐ Form I-765 Signature Card

☐ original Form I-94

☐ copy of the identity page and visa page from your passport

☐ if you have a job offer, a copy of the offer letter

☐ two photos

☐ fee (currently $100 for Form I-765 plus $70 for Form I-538)

Checklist for International Organization Internship Work Permit Application

- ☐ Written certification from the international organization
- ☐ Form I-20 ID
- ☐ Form I-538
- ☐ Form I-765
- ☐ two photos
- ☐ Form I-765 Signature Card
- ☐ fee (currently $100 for Form I-765 plus $70 for Form I-538)

Checklist for Practical Training Work Permit Application

☐ Form I-20 ID
☐ Form I-538
☐ Form I-765
☐ two photos
☐ Form I-765 Signature Card
☐ fee (currently $100 for Form I-765 plus $70 for
   Form I-538)

Index

W

CATALOG

...more from Nolo

	PRICE	CODE

BUSINESS

Avoid Employee Lawsuits (Quick & Legal Series)	$24.95	AVEL
The CA Nonprofit Corporation Kit (Binder w/CD-ROM)	$59.95	CNP
Consultant & Independent Contractor Agreements (Book w/CD-ROM)	$29.95	CICA
The Corporate Minutes Book (Book w/CD-ROM)	$69.95	CORMI
The Employer's Legal Handbook	$39.95	EMPL
Firing Without Fear (Quick & Legal Series)	$29.95	FEAR
Form Your Own Limited Liability Company (Book w/CD-ROM)	$44.95	LIAB
Hiring Independent Contractors: The Employer's Legal Guide (Book w/CD-ROM)	$34.95	HICI
How to Create a Buy-Sell Agreement & Control the Destiny of your Small Business (Book w/Disk-PC)	$49.95	BSAG
How to Form a California Professional Corporation (Book w/CD-ROM)	$59.95	PROF
How to Form a Nonprofit Corporation (Book w/CD-ROM)—National Edition	$44.95	NNP
How to Form a Nonprofit Corporation in California (Book w/CD-ROM)	$44.95	NON
How to Form Your Own California Corporation (Binder w/CD-ROM)	$39.95	CACI
How to Form Your Own California Corporation (Book w/CD-ROM)	$34.95	CCOR
How to Form Your Own New York Corporation (Book w/Disk—PC)	$39.95	NYCO
How to Form Your Own Texas Corporation (Book w/CD-ROM)	$39.95	TCOR
How to Write a Business Plan	$29.95	SBS
The Independent Paralegal's Handbook	$29.95	PARA
Leasing Space for Your Small Business	$34.95	LESP
Legal Guide for Starting & Running a Small Business	$34.95	RUNS
Legal Forms for Starting & Running a Small Business (Book w/CD-ROM)	$29.95	RUNS2
Marketing Without Advertising	$22.00	MWAD
Music Law (Book w/Disk—PC)	$29.95	ML
Nolo's California Quick Corp (Quick & Legal Series)	$19.95	QINC
Nolo's Guide to Social Security Disability	$29.95	QSS
Nolo's Quick LLC (Quick & Legal Series)	$24.95	LLCQ
The Small Business Start-up Kit (Book w/CD-ROM)	$29.95	SMBU
The Small Business Start-up Kit for California (Book w/CD-ROM)	$29.95	OPEN
The Partnership Book: How to Write a Partnership Agreement (Book w/CD-ROM)	$39.95	PART
Sexual Harassment on the Job	$24.95	HARS
Starting & Running a Successful Newsletter or Magazine	$29.95	MAG
Tax Savvy for Small Business	$34.95	SAVVY
Working for Yourself: Law & Taxes for the Self-Employed	$39.95	WAGE
Your Limited Liability Company: An Operating Manual (Book w/Disk—PC)	$49.95	LOP
Your Rights in the Workplace	$29.95	YRW

CONSUMER

Fed Up with the Legal System: What's Wrong & How to Fix It	$9.95	LEG
How to Win Your Personal Injury Claim	$29.95	PICL
Nolo's Encyclopedia of Everyday Law	$28.95	EVL
Nolo's Pocket Guide to California Law	$15.95	CLAW
Trouble-Free Travel...And What to Do When Things Go Wrong	$14.95	TRAV

ESTATE PLANNING & PROBATE

8 Ways to Avoid Probate (Quick & Legal Series)	$16.95	PRO8
9 Ways to Avoid Estate Taxes (Quick & Legal Series)	$29.95	ESTX
Estate Planning Basics (Quick & Legal Series)	$18.95	ESPN
How to Probate an Estate in California	$49.95	PAE

ORDER 24 HOURS A DAY @ www.nolo.com
Call 800-728-3555 • Mail or fax the order form in this book

	PRICE	CODE
Make Your Own Living Trust (Book w/CD-ROM)	$34.95	LITR
Nolo's Law Form Kit: Wills	$24.95	KWL
Nolo's Simple Will Book (Book w/CD-ROM)	$34.95	SWIL
Plan Your Estate	$39.95	NEST
Quick & Legal Will Book (Quick & Legal Series)	$15.95	QUIC

FAMILY MATTERS

	PRICE	CODE
Child Custody: Building Parenting Agreements That Work	$29.95	CUST
The Complete IEP Guide	$24.95	IEP
Divorce & Money: How to Make the Best Financial Decisions During Divorce	$34.95	DIMO
Do Your Own Divorce in Oregon	$29.95	ODIV
Get a Life: You Don't Need a Million to Retire Well	$24.95	LIFE
The Guardianship Book for California	$34.95	GB
How to Adopt Your Stepchild in California (Book w/CD-ROM)	$34.95	ADOP
A Legal Guide for Lesbian and Gay Couples	$25.95	LG
Living Together: A Legal Guide (Book w/CD-ROM)	$34.95	LTK
Using Divorce Mediation: Save Your Money & Your Sanity	$29.95	UDMD

GOING TO COURT

	PRICE	CODE
Beat Your Ticket: Go To Court and Win! (National Edition)	$19.95	BEYT
The Criminal Law Handbook: Know Your Rights, Survive the System	$29.95	KYR
Everybody's Guide to Small Claims Court (National Edition)	$24.95	NSCC
Everybody's Guide to Small Claims Court in California	$24.95	CSCC
Fight Your Ticket ... and Win! (California Edition)	$24.95	FYT
How to Change Your Name in California	$34.95	NAME
How to Collect When You Win a Lawsuit (California Edition)	$29.95	JUDG
How to Mediate Your Dispute	$18.95	MEDI
How to Seal Your Juvenile & Criminal Records (California Edition)	$34.95	CRIM
Nolo's Deposition Handbook	$29.95	DEP
Represent Yourself in Court: How to Prepare & Try a Winning Case	$34.95	RYC

HOMEOWNERS, LANDLORDS & TENANTS

	PRICE	CODE
California Tenants' Rights	$27.95	CTEN
Contractors' and Homeowners' Guide to Mechanics' Liens (Book w/Disk—PC)—California Edition	$39.95	MIEN
The Deeds Book (California Edition)	$24.95	DEED
Dog Law	$14.95	DOG
Every Landlord's Legal Guide (National Edition, Book w/CD-ROM)	$44.95	ELLI
Every Tenant's Legal Guide	$26.95	EVTEN
For Sale by Owner in California	$29.95	FSBO
How to Buy a House in California	$29.95	BHCA
The Landlord's Law Book, Vol. 1: Rights & Responsibilities (California Edition) (Book w/CD-ROM)	$44.95	LBRT
The California Landlord's Law Book, Vol. 2: Evictions (Book w/CD-ROM)	$44.95	LBEV
Leases & Rental Agreements (Quick & Legal Series)	$24.95	LEAR
Neighbor Law: Fences, Trees, Boundaries & Noise	$24.95	NEI
The New York Landlord's Law Book (Book w/CD-ROM)	$39.95	NYLL
Renters' Rights (National Edition)	$24.95	RENT
Stop Foreclosure Now in California	$29.95	CLOS

HUMOR

	PRICE	CODE
29 Reasons Not to Go to Law School	$12.95	29R
Poetic Justice	$9.95	PJ

IMMIGRATION

	PRICE	CODE
How to Get a Green Card	$29.95	GRN
U.S. Immigration Made Easy	$44.95	IMEZ

	PRICE	CODE

MONEY MATTERS

	PRICE	CODE
101 Law Forms for Personal Use (Book w/Disk—PC)	$29.95	SPOT
Bankruptcy: Is It the Right Solution to Your Debt Problems? (Quick & Legal Series)	$19.95	BRS
Chapter 13 Bankruptcy: Repay Your Debts	$34.95	CH13
Creating Your Own Retirement Plan	$29.95	YROP
Credit Repair (Quick & Legal Series, Book w/CD-ROM)	$19.95	CREP
How to File for Chapter 7 Bankruptcy	$34.95	HFB
IRAs, 401(k)s & Other Retirement Plans: Taking Your Money Out	$29.95	RET
Money Troubles: Legal Strategies to Cope With Your Debts	$29.95	MT
Nolo's Law Form Kit: Personal Bankruptcy	$24.95	KBNK
Stand Up to the IRS	$24.95	SIRS
Surviving an IRS Tax Audit (Quick & Legal Series)	$24.95	SAUD
Take Control of Your Student Loan Debt	$24.95	SLOAN

PATENTS AND COPYRIGHTS

	PRICE	CODE
The Copyright Handbook: How to Protect and Use Written Works (Book w/CD-ROM)	$34.95	COHA
Copyright Your Software	$24.95	CYS
Domain Names	$24.95	DOM
Getting Permission: How to License and Clear Copyrighted Materials Online and Off (Book w/Disk—PC)	$34.95	RIPER
How to Make Patent Drawings Yourself	$29.95	DRAW
The Inventor's Notebook	$24.95	INOT
Nolo's Patents for Beginners (Quick & Legal Series)	$29.95	QPAT
License Your Invention (Book w/Disk—PC)	$39.95	LICE
Patent, Copyright & Trademark	$34.95	PCTM
Patent It Yourself	$49.95	PAT
Patent Searching Made Easy	$29.95	PATSE
The Public Domain	$34.95	PUBL
Web and Software Development: A Legal Guide (Book w/ CD-ROM)	$44.95	SFT
Trademark: Legal Care for Your Business and Product Name	$39.95	TRD

RESEARCH & REFERENCE

	PRICE	CODE
Legal Research: How to Find & Understand the Law	$34.95	LRES

SENIORS

	PRICE	CODE
Beat the Nursing Home Trap: A Consumer's Guide to Assisted Living and Long-Term Care	$21.95	ELD
The Conservatorship Book for California	$44.95	CNSV
Social Security, Medicare & Pensions	$24.95	SOA

SOFTWARE
Call or check our website at www.nolo.com for special discounts on Software!

	PRICE	CODE
LeaseWriter CD—Windows	$129.95	LWD1
LLC Maker—Windows	$89.95	LLP1
Personal RecordKeeper 5.0 CD—Windows	$59.95	RKD5
Quicken Lawyer 2002 Business Deluxe—Windows	$79.95	SBQB2
Quicken Lawyer 2002 Personal Deluxe—Windows	$69.95	WQP2

Special Upgrade Offer
Save 35% on the latest edition of your Nolo book

Because laws and legal procedures change often, we update our books regularly. To help keep you up-to-date, we are extending this special upgrade offer. Cut out and mail the title portion of the cover of your old Nolo book and we'll give you **35% off** the retail price of the NEW EDITION of that book when you purchase directly from Nolo. This offer is to individuals only.

Prices and offer subject to change without notice.

Order Form

Name _____

Address _____

City _____

State, Zip _____

Daytime Phone _____

E-mail _____

Item Code	Quantity	Item	Unit Price	Total Price

Subtotal	
Add your local sales tax (California only)	
Shipping: RUSH $9, Basic $5 (See below)	
"I bought 3, ship it to me FREE!"(Ground shipping only)	
TOTAL	

Method of payment

☐ Check   ☐ VISA   ☐ MasterCard
☐ Discover Card   ☐ American Express

Account Number _____

Expiration Date _____

Signature _____

Shipping and Handling

Rush Delivery—Only $9

We'll ship any order to any street address in the U.S. by UPS 2nd Day Air* for only $9!

* Order by noon Pacific Time and get your order in 2 business days. Orders placed after noon Pacific Time will arrive in 3 business days. P.O. boxes and S.F. Bay Area use basic shipping. Alaska and Hawaii use 2nd Day Air or Priority Mail.

Basic Shipping—$5

Use for P.O. Boxes, Northern California and Ground Service.

Allow 1-2 weeks for delivery. U.S. addresses only.

For faster service, use your credit card and our toll-free numbers

**Call our customer service group
Monday thru Friday 7am to 7pm PST**

Phone	1-800-728-3555
Fax	1-800-645-0895
Mail	Nolo
950 Parker St.
Berkeley, CA 94710

Order 24 hours a day @ www.nolo.com

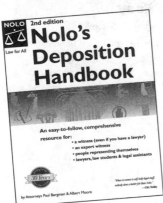

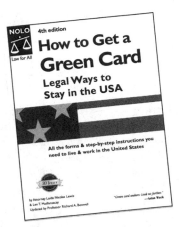
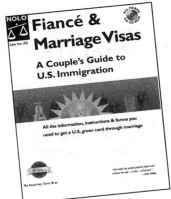

Take 2 Minutes
& Give Us Your 2 cents

Your comments make a big difference in the development and revision of Nolo books and software. Please take a few minutes and register your Nolo product—and your comments—with us. Not only will your input make a difference, you'll receive special offers available only to registered owners of Nolo products on our newest books and software. Register now by:

PHONE
1-800-728-3555

FAX
1-800-645-0895

EMAIL
cs@nolo.com

or **MAIL** us
this registration card

REMEMBER:
Little publishers have big ears. We really listen to you.

fold here

REGISTRATION CARD

NAME _____ DATE _____

ADDRESS _____

_____

CITY _____ STATE _____ ZIP _____

PHONE _____ E-MAIL _____

WHERE DID YOU HEAR ABOUT THIS PRODUCT? _____

WHERE DID YOU PURCHASE THIS PRODUCT? _____

DID YOU CONSULT A LAWYER? (PLEASE CIRCLE ONE)   YES   NO   NOT APPLICABLE

DID YOU FIND THIS BOOK HELPFUL?   (VERY)   5   4   3   2   1   (NOT AT ALL)

COMMENTS _____

_____

_____

WAS IT EASY TO USE?   (VERY EASY)   5   4   3   2   1   (VERY DIFFICULT)

DO YOU OWN A COMPUTER? IF SO, WHICH FORMAT? (PLEASE CIRCLE ONE)   WINDOWS   DOS   MAC

We occasionally make our mailing list available to carefully selected companies whose products may be of interest to you.
☐ If you do not wish to receive mailings from these companies, please check this box.
☐ You can quote me in future Nolo promotional materials. Daytime phone number _____.

| ISTU 1.0 |

NOLO IN THE NEWS

"Nolo helps lay people perform legal tasks without the aid—or fees—of lawyers."

—**USA TODAY**

Nolo books are ..."written in plain language, free of legal mumbo jumbo, and spiced with witty personal observations."

—**ASSOCIATED PRESS**

"...Nolo publications...guide people simply through the how, when, where and why of law."

—**WASHINGTON POST**

"Increasingly, people who are not lawyers are performing tasks usually regarded as legal work... And consumers, using books like Nolo's, do routine legal work themselves."

—**NEW YORK TIMES**

"...All of [Nolo's] books are easy-to-understand, are updated regularly, provide pull-out forms...and are often quite moving in their sense of compassion for the struggles of the lay reader."

—**SAN FRANCISCO CHRONICLE**

fold here

nolo
950 Parker Street
Berkeley, CA 94710-9867

Attn: ISTU 1.0